One of the defining features of Romantic writing, critics have long argued, is its characterization of the self in terms of psychological depth. Many Romantic writers, however, did not conceive of the self in this way, and in *Romantic Identities* Andrea K. Henderson investigates that part of Romantic writing that challenges the "depth" model, or operates outside its domain. Henderson explores various forms of Romantic discourse, explains their economic and social contexts, and examines their differing conceptions of identity. Individual chapters treat the Romantic view of the self in embryo and at birth, the relation of gothic characterization to the ghostliness of exchange value, anti-essentialism in Romantic physiology, the conception of self as genre in writings by Percy and Mary Shelley, and the link between economic circulation and the distrust of psychological interiority in Scott.

CAMBRIDGE STUDIES IN ROMANTICISM 20

ROMANTIC IDENTITIES

CAMBRIDGE STUDIES IN ROMANTICISM

General editors
Professor Marilyn Butler   Professor James Chandler
University of Oxford   University of Chicago
Editorial board
John Barrell, *University of York*   Paul Hamilton, *University of Southampton*
Mary Jacobus, *Cornell University*   Kenneth Johnston, *Indiana University*
Alan Liu, *University of California, Santa Barbara*
Jerome McGann, *University of Virginia*   David Simpson, *University of Colorado*

This series aims to foster the best new work in one of the most challenging fields within English literary studies. From the early 1780s to the early 1830s a formidable array of talented men and women took to literary composition, not just in poetry, which some of them famously transformed, but in many modes of writing. The expansion of publishing created new opportunities for writers, and the political stakes of what they wrote were raised again and again by what Wordsworth called those "great national events" that were "almost daily taking place": the French Revolution, the Napoleonic and American wars, urbanization, industrialization, religious revival, an expanded empire abroad and the reform movement at home. This was an enormous ambition, even when it pretended otherwise. The relations between science, philosophy, religion and literature were reworked in texts such as *Frankenstein* and *Biographia Literaria*; gender relations in *A Vindication of the Rights of Woman and Don Juan*; journalism by Cobbett and Hazlitt; poetic form, content and style by the Lake School and the Cockney School. Outside Shakespeare studies, probably no body of writing has produced such a wealth of response or done so much to shape the responses of modern criticism. This indeed is the period that saw the emergence of those notions of "literature" and of literary history, especially national literary history, on which modern scholarship in English has been founded.

The categories produced by Romanticism have also been challenged by recent historicist arguments. The task of the series is to engage both with a challenging corpus of Romantic writings and with the changing field of criticism they have helped to shape. As with other literary series published by Cambridge, this one will represent the work of both younger and more established scholars, on either side of the Atlantic and elsewhere.

For a complete list of titles published see end of volume

ROMANTIC IDENTITIES

Varieties of Subjectivity, 1774–1830

ANDREA K. HENDERSON

Department of English, University of Michigan

CAMBRIDGE
UNIVERSITY PRESS

Published by the Press Syndicate of the University of Cambridge
The Pitt Building, Trumpington Street, Cambridge CB2 IRP
40 West 20th Street, New York, NY 10011–4211, USA
10 Stamford Road, Oakleigh, Melbourne 3166, Australia

First published 1996

Printed in Great Britain at the University Press, Cambridge

A catalogue record for this book is available from the British Library

Library of Congress cataloguing in publication data
Henderson, Andrea K.
Romantic identities : varieties of subjectivity, 1774–1830
/ Andrea K. Henderson.
p.   cm. – (Cambridge Studies in Romanticism : 20)
Includes bibliographical references and index.
ISBN 0 521 48164 3 (hardback)
1. English literature – 19th century – History and criticism.
2. Romanticism – Great Britain.   3. Identity (Psychology) in
literature.   4. Subjectivity in literature.   5. Self in literature.
6. Byron, George Gordon Byron, Baron, 1788–1824. Prisoner of
Chillon.   7. Shelley, Percy Bysshe, 1792–1822. Cenci.   8. Scott,
Walter, Sir, 1771–1832. Heart of Midlothian.   I. Title.
II. Series.
PR457.H47 1996
820.9'353 – dc20   95 23333 CIP

ISBN 0 521 48164 3 hardback

C E

for my family

Contents

Illustrations

Acknowledgments

Ours is an age that still privileges the canonical Romantic image of the single author, struggling with the ideas within; but it was not the writers I treat of here, speaking of the communal construction of identities and ideas, from whom I first learned that we truly do make one another. This book is the product of the influence of the many people who have inspired, helped, challenged, and supported me during its composition.

I owe thanks, first of all, to the teacher whose very way of thinking was so compelling that I decided upon first contact with her to study Romanticism – a field to which I had previously had little exposure – simply in order to work with her: Marjorie Levinson. The extremely powerful and critical nature of her engagement with literature has and continues to inspire me, while her unflagging generosity, both intellectual and personal, has seen me through many a difficulty. I owe more than I can say here, and probably more than I know, to her example and her friendship.

I owe special thanks too to Stuart Curran; his commentary, drawing on the extraordinary breadth of his knowledge, has been invaluable. Margreta de Grazia, with infinite kindness and patience, not only undertook to read this manuscript – one outside her area of interest – but read it with great care and a remarkable critical eye.

To others at the University of Pennsylvania and beyond I also owe thanks: to Houston Baker (who provided financial support through his PARSS seminar when it was most needed), Phyllis Rackin, and Peter Stallybrass. Adela Pinch and Yopie Prins both read individual chapters with great care and insight. Marlon Ross and George Bornstein provided useful commentary on the shape of the work as a whole. Jay Grossman, Teresa Goddu, Anne Cubilié, Abby Schrader, Mark Schoenfield, Margaret Russet, David Golumbia, Jeff Masten, Lisa Freeman, and Ted Steinberg all read and commented on parts of the manuscript as well as patiently listening to me talk through new ideas and boosting my faith in those ideas at critical moments. For their editorial advice I would like to thank James Chandler, Marilyn Butler, and Josie Dixon.

I owe a special thanks to the University of Michigan Society of Fellows – and to Bob Weisbuch and James Boyd White in particular – not only for financial support and the great gift of time, but also for three wonderful years of true fellowship at its most congenial and diverse. I am grateful to Dror Wahrman for his critical commentary on the manuscript and the many things he has taught me about British history and politics. I am grateful too to Zoë Strother, for helping me see the world anew through the eyes of the art historian. Herman Stevens, with the knowledge of the classicist and the vision of the novelist, has opened my eyes to nuances, previously unseen, in literature and life.

Two of the chapters that follow originally appeared elsewhere in somewhat different form: "Doll-machines" in *Genders* 12 (Winter 1991), and "An embarrassing subject" in *At the Limits of Romanticism*, eds Mary Favret and Nicola Watson (Bloomington: Indiana University Press, 1994). I am grateful to those publishers for allowing me to reprint them here.

Those in my family – especially Glenn, Dorothy, and Teri Henderson – have always provided steadfast support of every kind, and this book is dedicated to them.

Introduction
From coins to hearts: Romantic forms of subjectivity

> When I began to inquire,
> To watch and question those I met, and held
> Familiar talk with them, the lonely roads
> Were schools to me in which I daily read
> With most delight the passions of mankind,
> There saw into the depth of human souls –
> Souls that appear to have no depth at all
> To vulgar eyes.
>
>   – Wordsworth, *The Prelude*[1]

Wordsworth's claim here – that it is the poet's task to reveal that human souls are characterized by depth – is one that is generally considered quintessentially Romantic. Critics have long argued that one of the defining features and enduring legacies of Romantic writing is its characterization of the self in terms of psychological depth. M. H. Abrams, in his landmark study *Natural Supernaturalism*, took as his starting point a conviction that Wordsworth's "vision is that of the awesome depths and height of the human mind,"[2] and saw in Romantic psycho-biography a secularized reworking of theological themes and motifs. Similarly, Harold Bloom, in his important work on the internalization of the quest romance, succinctly remarked that "Wordsworth's Copernican revolution in poetry is marked by the evanescence of any subject but subjectivity, the loss of what a poem is 'about.' "[3]

More recently, Jerome McGann has argued in *The Romantic Ideology* that "poetry like Wordsworth's belongs to what Hans Enzensberger has called 'The Consciousness Industry' – a light industry, if the pun be permitted, which Wordsworth and the other Romantics helped to found, and which they sought to preserve free of cultural contamination."[4] McGann, a founder of revisionist criticism in Romantic studies, takes the recognition of this characteristic of Romanticism a step further: he reminds us that this "consciousness industry" must not be taken for granted, assumed to be part of a natural inexorable movement towards a true understanding of the mind. Instead, McGann explores the ways the Romantic notion of "the depth of human souls," despite its self-representation as universal, reflects the peculiar exigencies of late eighteenth- and early nineteenth-century social life: "Amidst the tottering structures of early nineteenth-century Europe, poetry asserted the integrity of the biosphere and the inner, spiritual self, both of which were believed to transcend the age's troubling doctrinal conflicts and ideological shifts."[5]

In the past ten years or so, numerous studies have appeared that, in one way or another, historicize the Romantic investment in what Clifford Siskin describes as "a self-made mind, full of newly constructed depths."[6] From Marjorie Levinson's account of Wordsworth's conversion of ideological contradiction into psychic opportunity[7] to Siskin's exploration of the disciplinary potential of a self understood to develop and deepen with time,[8] these studies have shown us the way historical and ideological circumstances literally informed this conception of subjectivity. This book pursues the aims of such analyses in that it seeks to historicize Romantic subjectivity; it does so, however, not by linking this model of psychological depth to its historical context but by exploring and contextualizing other, competing models of the self that were produced during the period. The depth model, which criticism has, in effect, canonized as *the* Romantic view of subjectivity, was, during the Romantic period itself, only one available model among many. In recent years, studies of individual Romantic writers have often revealed the existence and importance of conceptions of the self that do not involve a notion of depth, and yet the tendency to link Romanticism with psychological depth remains, and the "egotistical sublime" of *The Prelude*, although challenged in its day, still serves as a touchstone for Romanticism as a whole. This book undertakes to examine a set of non-canonical models of the self – models that could, nevertheless, lay a claim to being peculiarly "Romantic" in that they were clearly shaped by the major social, philosophical, and aesthetic issues of the day. I will show, furthermore, that these models are to be found not only in non-canonical writing but even in the works of the period's canonized authors.

Challenges to the depth model of subjectivity have become particularly popular in recent years and typically derive from the post-structuralist attack on the very idea of self-identity: as Slavoj Žižek puts it, "the fundamental gesture of post-structuralism is to deconstruct every substantial identity...to dissolve the substantial identity into a network of non-substantial, differential relations."[9] From Derrida's insistence on the logical impossibility of complete self-presence, to Lacan's description of the subject as barred, the sign of a lack, to Althusser's claim that subjectivity is the result of ideological interpellation, post-structuralism, loosely defined, has challenged the belief in "the depth of human souls" from several angles. Studies in the literature of specific periods have often pursued this challenge in a more historical vein – in these works subjectivity is often described as a set of politically motivated textual effects that work to define various subject-positions within a social structure. Subjectivity (and its instability) has thus become a point of reference for studies of all sorts. But the proliferation of interest in, and work on, subjectivity suggests that, like the key concepts of other debates of the previous decade, it may well be on its way to exhaustion. One is reminded of the fate of the term "essentialism": the very word implies a debate organized in terms of a binary opposition, and the categories that define that opposition, "essentialism" and "constructionism," have come to seem so anxiously overworked and even restrictive that the issues they encapsulate are now often negotiated using different categorical tools. In the case of "subjectivity," the debate the term implies centers on whether human subjects should be conceived, as in the subject/object dyad, as agents, or whether, like British "subjects of the crown," they should be understood as subject*ed*. The latter view, like the view that most of our epistemological categories are constructed rather than essentially given, is the one generally avowed; ideologies of rich inwardness and individual agency have been the primary target of recent scholarship. The reference to "subjectivity" in my title might, then, seem to suggest that I will apply a post-structuralist hermeneutics of suspicion to the notion of the "deep self" as it appears in a literary movement renowned for celebrating it. While I do hope to show that the canonical Romantic model of "deep" subjectivity is of limited usefulness in helping us understand Romantic conceptions of the subject, this is not my only aim. I think it is also necessary to apply the hermeneutics of suspicion to the binary structure of the subjectivity debate itself. The Romantic era saw the production of a diversity of models for understanding subjectivity, a diversity that often goes unnoticed in our tendency to focus on the depth model, even when we challenge the depth model by revealing its ideological functions.

Romanticism and post-structuralism have together organized our thinking on the issue of subjectivity along a certain axis: subjectivity is either about self-determination or entrapment in ideology, depth or its absence. But there are popular Romantic conceptions of identity that effectively dissolve this opposition. For instance, in chapter 3 I describe an understanding of personal identity, popular among English radicals in the late 1790s, that based hope for human freedom in the belief that human beings, like paper, took their character from external impressions. Moreover, many ideologies of subjectivity produced during the Romantic age are structured according to models in which the presence or absence of depth is not the primary issue; in chapter 4, for example, I describe the way Shelley in *The Cenci* uses two literary genres – poetry and drama – to understand the relation of spiritual to corporeal subjectivity. Romantic models of subjectivity take many forms. It is the goal of this book to give the reader a sense of the multiplicity of these forms.

Each of the book's chapters focuses on a model of identity that enjoyed some prominence in the late eighteenth or early nineteenth centuries and relates its internal structure and logic to its social context. Since the goal of this study is to reveal a range of Romantic ideologies of identity, it is not designed to work in narrative fashion toward the construction of a single alternative model for understanding Romantic identity. Rather, it is meant to foreground the variety of models available during the period and to trace their complex relations to the depth model and to other social constructs. Each chapter, therefore, focuses on the representation of identity in a limited realm and explores its significance within that realm and in terms appropriate to it. The aim of such localism is not to find *the* context that will definitively ground a text or its reading but instead to juxtapose various texts and contexts in order to produce new insights into both. While the primary texts I have selected cannot be termed representative in the strict sense, since they are intended to suggest variety rather than exemplify a single or limited set of paradigms, they have nevertheless been chosen to represent a cross-section of literary genres – the novel, poetry, drama – as well as non-literary genres, from philosophical treatises to political tracts to medical monographs. As we will see, subjectivity was an issue at stake in all these domains, and during the period the dialogue between them was more intimate than our current sense of rigid disciplinary boundaries would lead us to expect. Altogether, these texts span the full chronological range traditionally defined as Romantic, from the first stirrings of the gothic in the late eighteenth century to the work of the second-generation Romantic poets.

The theoretical paradigms brought to bear on these works, while informed primarily by materialist and feminist thought, are various and are designed to suit the primary texts at hand. Thus, while chapter 2, for example, draws on the work of Lukács and Irigaray to link the flat and purely formal quality of gothic characterization to exchange value, chapter 5 draws on the work of Marx, Negri, Bataille, and Deleuze and Guattari to relate the flatness of Scott's ideal characters to his *resistance* to economic circulation. My method of approach, my focus on the peculiarities and contexts of particular texts or discourses, thus recapitulates, on a larger scale, one of the primary lessons of the Romantic texts I treat. The character of Romanticism, like the characters within many Romantic works, has no deep truth. It is a creature of surfaces, of context, and of varying forms; and when it appears most self-consistent, it may be least so.

Thus, I try to avoid the implementation of what would in effect be a hermeneutics of depth. Moreover, I try to avoid it not only at the global level, when discussing Romanticism generally, but also at the local level, in my discussions of particular models of identity. My aim is not simply to translate metaphors of identity into their political subtext, losing sight of what could be called the "surface text" in the process. Instead, I try to show the ways those metaphors exert a power of their own. That is, I do not want to engage in what Michael Taussig calls "a dominant critical practice which could be called the 'allegorizing' mode of reading ideology into events and artifacts, cockfights and carnivals, advertisements and film, private and public spaces, in which the surface phenomenon, as in allegory, stands as a cipher for uncovering horizon after horizon of otherwise obscure systems of meanings."[10] The vehicles for understanding identity can play as large a role as the motives for that understanding in making identity meaningful. In chapter 2, for instance, we see that once anxiety about the diminishing usefulness of genealogy in the determination of identity has encouraged the association of identity with monetary value, identity comes to seem not only mercurial but insubstantial and spectral as well. Thus, the "solution" to the problem of measuring human value – the money form – brings with it a cluster of metaphoric associations that play their own part in creating the ghostly world of gothic character.

While this book's primary goal is to complicate current notions of Romantic subjectivity, it also aims to suggest fresh perspectives on a set of current theoretical issues. It is my belief that many of the stalemated arguments within literary studies are likely to find solutions not in the form of answers, but through the modification of the terms of debate. It is here that historically remote texts prove particularly helpful: they can provide ways not only to challenge the usefulness of a theoretical construct in a particular instance, but also to help us rethink the terms and assumptions of that construct. Thus, in chapter 1, obstetrical and embryological texts of the late eighteenth century are used to suggest challenges to, and ways of historicizing, Kristeva's notion of abjection, and in chapter 3 essentialism and contextualism are reconceived in terms of their significance in early nineteenth-century physiology. In the same way that the chapters are intended to provide specific local examples of Romantic-era notions of identity, the book's theoretical challenges are played out on a specific, local level.

The first chapter is the only one that focuses on the canonical Romantic model of identity, but it outlines its development in a non-literary realm: that of embryology and obstetrics. Opening with a discussion of conceptions of mother and child that pre-date the Romantic era proper, the chapter traces what could literally be called the birth of canonical Romantic subjectivity. I argue that the conceptualization of childbearing labor in mechanistic terms, in the context of the development of early industrial capitalism, threatened to align birth with commodity production. This threat prompted the reconception of the maternal body as a part of nature as it was soon to be defined in high Romantic art: the realm of the spontaneous and incalculable, a realm not governed by hard and fast laws. Some years later, embryological growth, which had previously been understood as the mechanical reproduction of a family line, was reimagined as arising from the embryo's supra-physical inner impulses. The result of these two related trends is a model of the genesis of the self that is peculiarly Romantic in the canonical sense, a model that both emphasizes the child's role in its own development and represents fetal development and birth as activities that transcend the world of mechanical laws and commercial relations. We thus find what we have assumed to be the achievement of a cluster of gifted poets anticipated in the realm of science and medicine.

While chapter 1 aims to defamiliarize canonical Romantic subjectivity by tracing its development in obstetrical and embryological theory, subsequent chapters focus on non-canonical models of subjectivity within the literary domain. The second chapter returns to the problem with which the first one opened: the conceptual alignment of commodities and persons. I argue in chapter 2 that as the traditional genealogy-based model of identity was called into question by the ideals of the French Revolution and the realities of capitalist and industrial development, a commercial model of identity which had long been emerging rapidly gained ground. This model tended to polarize identity into an essential identity akin to use value, on the one hand, and a social identity akin to exchange value on the other. I trace the development of this model first in eighteenth-century moral theory and the sentimental novel, where the association of identity and value, and the division of both into grounded use value and mercurial exchange value, are clearly laid out. I then discuss the ways British monetary crises of the end of the eighteenth century exacerbated the sense of a dangerous division between use and exchange value, and show the repercussions of this division for the understanding of personal identity. I argue that while the canonical Romantic model of identity centers on grounded use value, early gothic novels represent personal identity as violently polarized and are driven by a fascination with the vagaries of exchange-value identity. That is, while on the one hand gothic characters are straightforwardly comprehensible, on the other they are peculiarly mysterious, ghostly, and flat because of their association with exchange value and the money form. I show that the flatness of gothic characterization has kept the gothic from enjoying full canonical status not just because of a critical taste for representations of psychological depth, but also because such depth signals a resistance to the commodification of identity, a resistance in which we are, for the most part, still invested.

Chapter 3 takes up the problem of identity from another angle, that of the challenge to hierarchical systems of classification posed by French Revolutionary and English radical thought. I argue that Revolutionary ideology encouraged the replacement of the hierarchical genealogical system of personal identification by a non-hierarchical, "horizontal" system wherein identity is based on context. This shift tends to make identity a literally superficial matter, as it is in the gothic novel, although for a different reason. In this case, the surface assumes a special significance because it is the site of dynamic physical interactions with the outside world which are constitutive of identity. I first describe this shift in taxonomic method and its significance for conceptions of identity in the discipline in which it was most apparent: biology. I show that Revolutionary pathology and physiology in particular were characterized by what historians of science have termed a shift from essentialism to localism. I then turn to British Romanticism, which is generally responsive to this flattening of hierarchical distinctions and the new interest in environmental influences on identity, but which often qualifies the role of external influence on identity formation by constructing an inner, self-generated identity that is resistant to it. I argue that Byron's "The Prisoner of Chillon" and the accompanying "Sonnet on Chillon" dramatize the shift from an essential to a contextual and finally to an interiorized subject and that, viewed in these terms, the poems' motives and meanings must be reassessed.

Byron associates context-based identity with subjugation to the material world, and, temporarily at least, he can only respond to this problem by adopting a Wordsworthian notion of resistant interiority. Chapter 4 considers in more detail the role of materiality and the body in Romantic poetry. The investment in what Charles Rzepka describes as the "self as mind" generally has the effect of de-emphasizing the role of the body in the establishment of identity.[11] Perhaps no Romantic poet is better known for idealizing persons than Shelley, but I demonstrate in this chapter that this idealization is not unproblematic for him. I argue that in *The Cenci*, one of the most corporeally grounded and pessimistic of Shelley's mature works, he deliberately magnifies the importance of what he terms the external or corporeal being and traces the effects of that magnification on the inner being or "inmost spirit." More specifically, the play explores the relationship of outer and inner being in terms of their resemblance to two representational modes: drama and poetry. *The Cenci*, through its conflation of corporeality and theatricality and its negative representation of the quintessentially theatrical Count Cenci, dramatizes the dangers of grounding identity in the body. At the same time, however, the play shows in its representation of Beatrice's experience that even the inmost being, which is linked to poetry, must draw upon the theatrical, material world in order to do its characteristic imaginative work. When the spirit is completely divorced from the body the self becomes disorganized and unstable. Thus, the play suggests that while external life may be little more than a theatrical mask, the circumscription of the representation of that life can have profoundly pernicious consequences. Ultimately, then, while the corporeal and theatrical aspect of being is demonized and destroyed in the figure of Count Cenci, the imaginative poetic dimension is sacrificed in the figure of Beatrice, whose ability to imagine what she knows about her body is tragically limited. Turning then briefly to another work that conceives of the self in terms of genre – Mary Shelley's *Mathilda* – I show that Mary Shelley suggests a solution of sorts to the poetry/drama antagonism that leads to such tragedy in *The Cenci*: she subsumes both poetry and drama in the prose narrative form, and defines the latter as the genre most expressive of human subjectivity. Nevertheless, she can only imagine full selfhood as a posthumous production, its achieved form only possible when the story of one's life has been fully told. Thus for both Mary and Percy the generic forms that define Romantic subjectivity give rise to contradictions that lead ultimately to its dissolution.

The fifth chapter returns to the novel and the topic of the impact of marketplace relations on conceptions of identity. At the same time, like chapter 4, it focuses on a work that discovers problems in the canonical Romantic model of interior identity. Walter Scott's *The Heart of Mid-Lothian* opens as a novel very much concerned with discovering and exploring the heart of both persons and society as a whole, but it associates both of these "hearts" with economic circulation and the fluidity of the market. Unlike the characters of the gothic novel, whose mysterious public identities are sharply distinguished from their static and obvious private identities, the troublesome characters of Scott's novel are mysterious even with respect to their private identities; in fact, these characters' mystery is specifically represented as an inner quality. Now, interiorized Romantic identity, precisely because of its hiddenness, comes to be associated with the incomprehensibility and unpredictability of the market. It is as if the exchange value that is associated with social identity in the gothic has been driven into the depths that canonical subjectivity had offered as a safe haven from the world of commercial relations. For Scott, the notion of a psychic interiority that changes over time is linked to an increase not just in social mobility but in circulation generally and finds its fullest expression in characters who change with dangerous rapidity and are fundamentally deceptive. Ultimately, then, the novel discovers that the notion of a heart or core in either society or the individual is threatening because such a core becomes, in both cases, the center of movement or circulation, a place of dangerous fluidity. In the final third of the novel, Scott makes an effort to overcome this difficulty by trying gradually to eliminate the depth model, with which the novel opened, and define an ideal world wherein there would be no need to distinguish a core from a periphery or surface because circulation would not be necessary to social life and individual persons would be utterly static and self-identical. In this vision of what I term a "colonial pastoral," characters associated earlier with the marketplace are refigured as wild and dark-skinned, and good characters, in an inversion of the ideals of canonical Romantic subjectivity, become triumphantly flat.

Wordsworth's desire to see "into the depth of human souls" gestures to a doctrine of personal identity that met with considerable success in its own time and that continues to be influential. But in its day that doctrine contended with numerous other conceptions of identity, many of which taught what thinkers like Bachelard have more recently suggested: "being does not see itself…It does not stand out, it is not *bordered* by nothingness: one is never sure of finding it, or of finding it solid, when one approaches a center of being."[12] Those "vulgar eyes" Wordsworth describes, while they may not have seen "depth" in human beings, may well have seen other things – things like the fascinating ghostliness of personal value, or the lovable flatness of the honest and immobile character. The vulgar "I's" discerned by those vulgar eyes may prove quite new "schools…in which [to] read / With most delight the passions of mankind."

CHAPTER I

Doll-machines and butcher-shop meat: models of childbirth in the early stages of industrial capitalism

In 1931, chemical embryologist Joseph Needham suggested that "it can hardly be a coincidence that so many among the great embryologists of the past were men of strongly philosophic minds...It is not really surprising, for of all the strange things in biology surely the most striking of all is...transmutation...This coming-to-be can hardly have failed to lead, in the minds of those most intimately acquainted with it, to thoughts of a metaphysical character."[1] Biological models of growth and birth do indeed have far-reaching philosophical and, I would add, social implications. Scientific and popular conceptions of human embryology and obstetrics bring into focus issues relating to gender,[2] modes of creation and production, the mother–child relationship, and paradigms of nature and the natural – all of which have a bearing on the construction of identity. It is my contention that, in the context of growing industrialization, British eighteenth-century mechanistic accounts of fetal development and childbirth brought childbearing into ever-closer alliance with economic modes of production. By the late eighteenth century the tendency of this alliance to make mothers appear to be machines and babies to be little more than commodities became increasingly intolerable; these mechanically produced commodity-children posed a threat to bourgeois humanist ideals of the sort that were soon to find their fullest expression in high Romantic poetry. In addition, this connection made the mother appear to stand in a relation of ownership to the child, and this was particularly a problem given the weakening of traditional patriarchal power in the period.[3] Avoiding the conflation of childbearing and economic production became an ever-more pressing task during the late eighteenth and early nineteenth centuries. I will describe here a movement from William Smellie's explicitly mechanistic account of birth to William Hunter's non-mechanistic one – a movement from a maternal body of bone to one of flesh. This body of flesh is represented as a part of nature as the term was to be defined by Romantic writers: a place of freedom from fixed laws. I will then trace a somewhat later shift – one with similar social implications – from a preformationist to an epigenetic theory of fetal growth, describing the way the latter provides a model of spontaneous and even spiritualized self-making, a literally embryonic form of the self-made man. These two trends combined to form a model of childbirth that could be characterized as high Romantic, and I close by showing that this new model gave rise to a characteristically Romantic problem: the tendency to represent the relationship between mother and child as antagonistic. The mother–child relation represents a special case in the epistemological framework that operates in terms of subject–object relations, and we will see that the image of the infant as an object in relation to its subject mother gave rise to an opposed image of the mother as an object in relation to her subject infant.

I

A novel of the first half of the century like *Moll Flanders* serves well to set the historical stage for us through its focus on issues of production and reproduction. Everything in Moll's world is subject to commodification, not least of all her children. The most we hear of the first two is this: "my two children were, indeed, taken happily off my hands by my husband's father and mother, and that, by the way, was all they got by Mrs. Betty."[4] The pun on "got" here demonstrates the easy slippage between creation, childbearing, and grasping accumulation. But the commodification of babies is even more subtly and deeply woven into the text than this example suggests. Robert Erickson argues that significant parallels can be drawn between thievery and midwifery in the novel, and that Moll's first pickpocketing scene, in which she steals a watch from a pregnant woman, is described in terms of a delivery. In fact, as he says, "from our point of view, the adjectives for describing babies and watches in the novel are almost interchangeable."[5] But it is, of course, in the "adoption agency" portion of the novel that the commodification of children is most clearly outlined. As Lois Chaber puts it:

The governess' streamlined service industry, like its modern counterparts, approximates the mass production techniques of manufacturing proper. The pregnant women are gathered under one roof, meeting the primary condition for capitalistic organization; birth, like traditional forms of production (the nurse's weaving, for example) is being removed from the home. The process even culminates in the marketing of the babies, though with the ironic twist that the producers pay to get rid of their products. This is truly Marx's "alienation," whereby human value is divorced from the product – the child – and where the capitalistic entrepreneur – the governess – literally profits from the "labor" of others – the unwed mothers.[6]

Chaber argues that Moll "escapes, by whatever means, from the eternal feminine cycle of reproduction into the historical social cycle of production" (213), and seems in general to consider this an empowering move. On the other hand, in her discussion of the governess's lying-in and adopting-out agency, she quotes Juliet Mitchell's lament that childbearing under capitalism becomes no more than a "sad mimicry of production."[7] According to Chaber, "in applying capitalistic production methods to the domestic reproductive sphere, Defoe underscores their dehumanizing effects; on the other hand, he forces us to acknowledge bitterly that the only commerce allowed women like the governess is in women's bodies" (221). I would argue, however, that the novel presents the governess's way of life as just one among many, matter-of-factly and without bitterness. Childbirth appears to be just another form of economic activity, and it is Defoe's relative ease with this that marks this text as an early eighteenth-century product of a mercantile sensibility. Initially, the image of commodity-children produced by laboring women was not generally offensive.[8]

II

If we turn now to the realm of obstetrical theory and practice we will see that it is there that the links between childbirth and other forms of production are most clearly delineated. Eighteenth-century midwifery was, of course, the site of a struggle between traditional (mostly female) midwives and men-midwives who were variously associated with other branches of the (mostly male) medical establishment. As Ornella Moscucci notes, "until the early eighteenth century childbirth and the lying-in period were a kind of ritual collectively staged and controlled by women, from which men were usually excluded," but "between about 1730 and 1770, men-midwives managed to undermine public confidence in the midwife's capacities."[9] This "professionalization" of midwifery contributed to the association of childbirth with other, scientifically supervised forms of production, and it is significant that men-midwives initially distinguished themselves by their use of instruments to assist in the delivery or extraction of the fetus. Gradually, the professional man-midwife with his instruments came to dominate the practice of midwifery.

In the texts of William Smellie, one of the foremost man-midwives of mid-eighteenth-century Britain, we get a direct view of the mechanistic trend within male midwifery itself – a trend that tightened the metaphoric relation of childbirth and economic production. Smellie opens his *Set of Anatomical Tables* of 1754 with the comment that he has "reduced" the art of midwifery "into a more simple and mechanical method."[10] Not only are the midwife's procedures laid out in mechanical terms, but the body of the mother is itself understood as a productive machine of sorts. Significantly, however, the overall effect of Smellie's model is precisely to efface the image of maternal labor. The woman is not represented, as Emily Martin hypothesizes, as a worker at the machine of her uterus;[11] rather, the midwife is represented as a worker at the machine of the maternal body. Smellie may have accorded with his contemporaries in the belief that the womb (as opposed, for instance, to the child) did the work of expulsion,[12] but neither the uterus nor the woman as a whole tends to figure as a laborer in Smellie's account. First of all, the reader of Smellie's manuals is unlikely to ascribe agency to the mother precisely because she never appears in them as a whole being. The figures in the *Set of Anatomical Tables*, unlike many earlier depictions of pregnant women, never present entire women; the bodies from which the engravings were made appear as fragments not only in the plates but in the glosses as well. Secondly, in *A Collection of Cases and Observations*, where we do hear of whole women, they are consistently described as having a passive relation to the delivery: "in the course of the same year, I was bespoke to attend a woman, who had been *subject to* tedious labours."[13] When active labor is mentioned, it is the labor of the midwife: "I have assisted in a number of such cases, where, by a cautious management, the parts were gradually opened, and the woman safely delivered" (258). Maternal fatigue is contrasted not with maternal industry but with passivity: "she had a refreshing sleep of two or three hours; the pains, which were weak before, grew strong and more frequent, and the woman was safely brought to bed" (259). At times, even maternal weakness is effaced: "the forceps and fillet were contrived with a view to save the child...when *nature* was exhausted" (v, my emphasis).

Fittingly, it is not the muscular uterus but the static and solid structure of the pelvis that preoccupies Smellie. The first series of plates

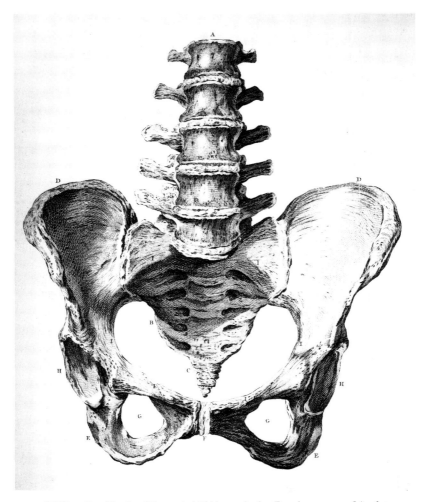

1   William Smellie, *Set of Anatomical Tables*, 2nd edn. (London: n.p., 1761), plate 1.
First published 1754.

in his *Set of Anatomical Tables* consists of engravings of pelvises – rigid, mechanical objects that are discussed primarily in terms of the negative, obstructive role they tend to play in the delivery process (see fig. 1). The plates of pelvises that open the book are counterposed by the very structure of the book to the closing plates of forceps and other tools – extensions of the male hand that themselves enclose the infant in order to free it from enclosure in the pelvis. These pelvises, these fleshless bones, tend to assume an abstract, curiously commodified quality: "Dr. *Lawrence* once shewed me the *Pelvis* of a woman, who died soon after delivery, in which all the three bones were separated almost an inch from one another. I likewise saw the same phenomenon in a *Pelvis* belonging to Dr. *Hunter*."[14] Denuded of their original "owners," the pelvises now serve as the purified possessions and even professional badges of their doctor owners – an ownership relation that, as it happens, is underscored by contemporary typographical practice. Interest in the pelvic bones was common among man-midwives generally; in an illustration in Baudelocque's manual, measuring instruments enclose and penetrate – and are almost indistinguishable from – the bones they measure (see fig. 2). The trend was to present childbirth as a mechanical process, having affinities with mechanical production, but with the role of the woman herself in the productive process effectively masked. She appears not as a laborer but *only* as a machine – and an oddly inactive and poorly constructed one at that.

Sterne, in *Tristram Shandy*, satirizes the type represented by Smellie and, more specifically, Dr. John Burton, in his Dr. Slop, "scientific operator,"[15] a man who, in Robert Erickson's words, functions as an "emblem of lumpish mortality" (229).[16] Burton argued that "the Art of delivering a Woman of her Child and Secundines is entirely a mechanical Operation, whether it be done by turning the child in the Womb, to extract it by the Feet, or by Assistance of Instruments, so the mechanical Laws or Rules are to be our general Guide."[17] As Erickson remarks, since it is ultimately Slop and not the female midwife who delivers Tristram, his birth (and life) are revealed to be a "*manufactured, highly contingent affair*" (229). But it is that contingency, that bit of the unknown, that finally always allows Tristram (and Sterne) to elude simple materialism.

As the century progressed, the connection between childbearing and production was to become more generally disturbing, and arguments against materialism and mechanism arose within midwifery itself. In 1760 Elizabeth Nihell published a treatise on midwifery that is as much a diatribe against the mechanistic treatment of the human body and the omnipotence of sordid commercial interests as it is a plea for the continued use of female midwives. Nihell's rhetoric is "anti-instrumentarian" in the broadest sense; she opens her treatise by saying something she thinks should not need saying, but that is at best only the unstated concern of most eighteenth-century authors of midwifery manuals:

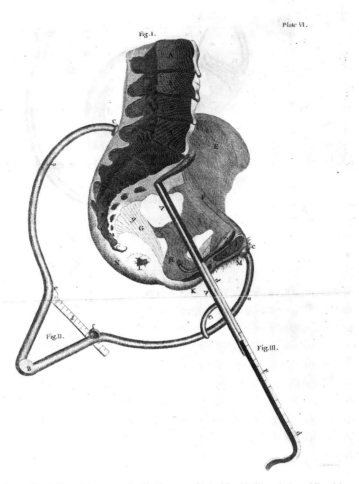

2 Jean-Louis Baudelocque, *An Abridgement of Mr. Heath's Translation of Baudelocque's Midwifery*, by William Dewees (Philadelphia: Thomas Dobson, 1811), plate 6. First published 1781.

The preservation of so valuable a part of the human Species as pregnant women, as well as that of their dear and tender charge, their children, so powerfully recommended by the voice of Nature and Reason, to all possible human providence for their safe birth, forms an object so sensibly intitled to the private and national care, and even to that of universal society, that all enforcement of its importance would be an injury to the human understanding, or at least to the human heart. It would look too like imagining that it could be wanted.[18]

Human hearts and hands serve as the touchstones of Nihell's rhetoric; for pregnant women, it is "those of their own sex, from whom, at their greatest need, they used to receive the most effectual service, and who alone are capable of discharging their duty by them, with that sympathy for their pains, that tender affectionate concern, which may so naturally be expected from those who have been, are, or may be subject to the same infirmities" (4). Hand and heart are distinguished from tools and selfish interest by the feeling of which they are capable:

> The keen instrumentarians bring an argument they imagine capable of banishing or exterminating all the midwives. The men, they say, enjoy alone the glorious privilege of using instruments, in order, as they pretend, to assist nature. But let them, I intreat of them, answer, whether if the question could be decided by votes, where is the kingdom, where is the nation, where is the town, where, in short, is the person that would prefer iron and steel to a hand of flesh, tender, soft, duly supple, dextrous, and trusting to its own feelings for what it is about? (36)

Not only does Nihell repeatedly argue for the superiority of hands to tools in assisting the mother, but she complains that the "instrumentarians" make the mother herself into a productive machine:

> As to the reproach which Mr. Smellie makes to us of being interested, I can, for myself, prove that I have delivered gratuitously, and in pure charity, above nine hundred women. I doubt much, whether our critic can say as much, unless he reckons it for a charity, that which he exercised on his automaton or machine, which served him for a model of instruction to his pupils. This was a wooden statue, representing a woman with child, whose belly was of leather, in which a bladder full, perhaps, of small beer, represented the uterus. This bladder was stopped with a cork, to which was fastened a string of packthread to tap it, occasionally, and demonstrate in a palpable manner the flowing of the red-colored waters. In short, in the middle of the bladder was a wax-doll, to which were given various positions.
>
>   By this admirably ingenious piece of machinery, were formed and started up an innumerable and formidable swarm of men-midwives, spread over the town and country. By his own confession, he has made in less than ten years nine hundred pupils, without taking into the account the number of midwives whom he has trained up, and formed in so miraculous a manner. See the preface of this author. He speaks of his *machine* in the first page. (50–51, Nihell's emphasis)

Smellie is represented here as an industrial-type producer, diabolically using his machine of the maternal body to make midwives by the hundreds, according to a centralized, standardized, and utterly de-humanizing plan. Smellie's mechanistic views are, to Nihell, danger-ously inappropriate to the study of the human body; she asks if his pupils could possibly discern "the proportion and analogy between a mere wooden machine, and a body, sensible, delicate, animated, and well organized?" (51). The image of the "doll-machine" or "wooden-woman" (52) is invoked again and again in the treatise as a figure of the commercialization and mechanization that are for Nihell the salient features of man-midwifery. Not surprisingly, Nihell attributes Smellie's work and that of man-midwives generally to a "mercenary interest" (63) rather than a sympathetic, humane one: "these gentlemen expect no small fees, and will not attend without them" (70).

A good humanist, Nihell digresses at length to decry the high death rate among children on parish support – "there are...[those] who can call such children a *burthen*!" (199) – and speaks of these children as human sacrifices to "that black Demon of INTEREST" (195). Never-theless, Nihell herself, when speaking of the health of mother and child, frames the issue in terms of their value: "Yet how serious, how important is it for women, if they *tender* their own lives, and that of the *precious burthen* of which they are the *depository*..." (119, my emphasis). Nihell is perfectly comfortable arguing that "in all ages, in all civilized countries, the wife is considered as the peculiar property of a husband, insomuch, that all laws human and divine consecrate, if I may use the expression, to him alone, exclusive of all other men, the access to the reserved parts of the wife's body" (222–223). This apparent contra-diction can be explained by the fact that Nihell unselfconsciously distinguishes between forms of value; women and children are repositories of value of an absolute and static sort, a use value unrelated to both exchange value and production. Not surprisingly, Nihell does not describe childbirth as a form of production, mechan-ical or otherwise, but, like her later male contemporaries, ascribes agency in delivery to a mythical nature figure: "Her deliverance lingers; Nature, from some vice of conformation...appears faint, remiss, insufficient, in short, in her expulsive efforts; in the mean time, the pains of the patient grow more and more intense" (160). Nihell's is an older, more traditional notion of value; she does not oppose the description of people in terms of economic value *per se*, but in terms of *marketplace* value, a form of value that was becoming ever-more unstable and that was increasingly linked to large-scale, depersonalized production.[19]

Nihell's complaints, along with her advocacy of female midwives, did not prevent the use of man-midwives from becoming increasingly common. But a subtle change within male midwifery itself served to modify some of the trends that had disturbed her. In 1774 Smellie's pupil, William Hunter, published an obstetrical atlas that was to become one of the most highly regarded of the period, one that offered a solution of sorts to the troublesome image of maternal production. This solution relied on the effective combination of two related trends: toward a more humanized representation of the fetus, and toward an animalistic, rather than a mechanistic, conception of the mother. Perhaps the most obvious visual difference between Smellie's engravings and Hunter's is that the former focus on solid bones, whereas the latter focus on pliable, soft tissue.[20] It is interesting to compare, for instance, plate IX of Smellie's *Set of Anatomical Tables* with plate XII of Hunter's *Gravid Uterus*, both of which are images of full-term fetuses in the womb (figs. 3 and 4). Smellie's fetus is enclosed in the pelvic girdle while Hunter's is surrounded by amorphous tissue. Similarly, whereas Smellie offers us several diagrams of simple pelvic bones, Hunter presents numerous engravings of sheer uterine muscle. Hunter's muscles, however, do not suggest power or activity any more than do Smellie's pelvises. Plate VIII, for instance, of the womb with its "contents" removed, suggests little more than a fleshy blanket (see fig. 5).

This focus on soft tissue in representations of the mother can be related to another peculiarity of Hunter's illustrations. Ludmilla Jordanova notes that in some of the engravings the mother's legs have been cut off and the artist has faithfully depicted them in cross-section – with the result that, as she puts it, the legs resemble "chunks of meat" (see fig. 6).[21] That the artist had used a line to indicate a sheet covering the legs in other plates drawn from the same subject, and that a cross-section of the leg serves no didactic purpose in this manual and is not alluded to in the text, signal the gratuitous nature of this labor-intensive rendering. The maternal body here is a body of flesh, of animal flesh. What we are seeing in the move from Smellie to Hunter is a redefinition of the natural as the fleshy rather than the mechanical. While both men claim to follow "nature," nature is for Hunter an order so amorphous and even wild that it almost seems to stand in opposition to hard and fast mechanical laws. Hunter's is an early form of the nature of Romanticism, a nature characterized by freedom

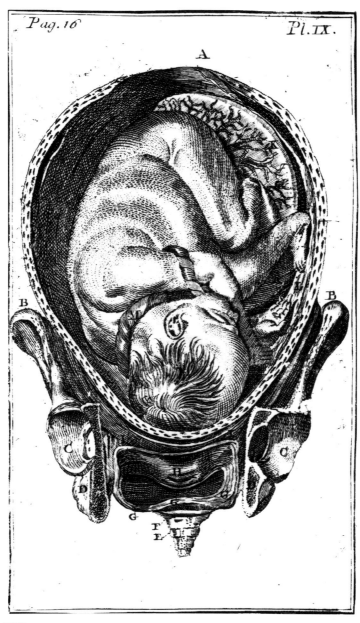

3   William Smellie, *Set of Anatomical Tables*, 2nd edn. (London: n.p., 1761), plate 9.
First published 1754.

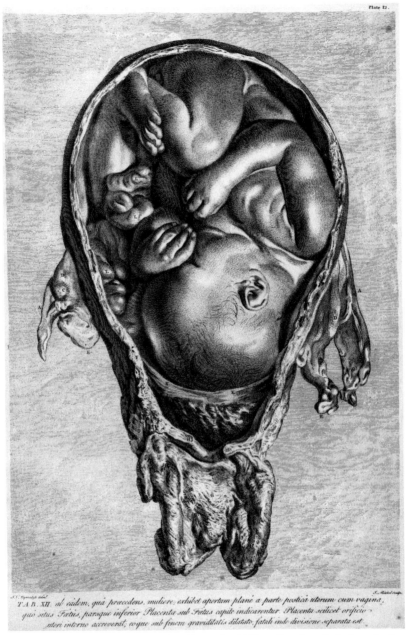

Plate 12.

T A B. XII. ab eadem, quâ præcedens. muliere, exhibet apertum planè a parte postica uterum cum vagina; quo situs Fœtus, parsque inferior Placenta sub Fœtus capite indicarentur. Placenta scilicet orificio uteri interno accreverat; eoque sub finem graviditatis dilatato, fatali inde divisione separata est.

4   William Hunter, *The Anatomy of the Human Gravid Uterus* (London: Sydenham Society rpt., 1851), plate 12. First published 1774.

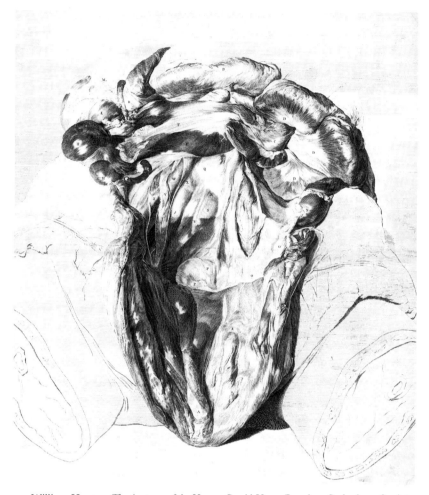

5   William Hunter, *The Anatomy of the Human Gravid Uterus* (London: Sydenham Society rpt., 1851) plate 8. First published 1774.

rather than regularity, a difference that surfaces here as the difference between flesh and bone.[22]

One result of this effort to salvage the natural and the maternal from the realm of mechanism and production is that they acquire, through their very incalculability, a power that emasculates Hunter as scientist. We can turn to the "father of embryology," William Harvey, for the traditional metaphor for the scientist's relation to nature: "Nature is

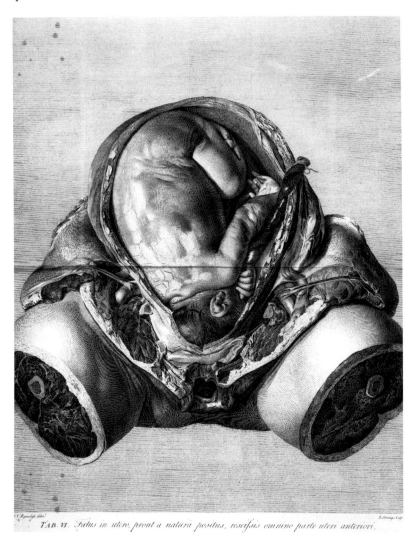

TAB. VI. *Fœtus in utero, prout a natura positus, resectis omnino parte uteri anteriori.*

6   William Hunter, *The Anatomy of the Human Gravid Uterus* (London: Sydenham Society rpt., 1851), plate 6. First published 1774.

herself to be addressed; the paths she shows us are to be boldly
trodden; for thus, and whilst we consult our proper senses, from
inferior advancing to superior levels, shall we penetrate at length into
the heart of her mystery."[23] Hunter discusses nature rather differently:

Since I begin to think for myself, Nature, where I am best disposed to mark her, beams so strong upon me, that I am lost in wonder and count it sacrilege to measure her meanest feature by my largest conception. Ay, ay, the time will come when our pert philosophers will blush to find that they have talked with as little real knowledge, and as peremptorily, of the animal powers, as the country miller who balances the powers of Europe.[24]

When he should be most able to "mark" nature, Hunter suddenly finds himself passively "beamed upon" by a force to which his resources are hopelessly unequal, hopelessly small. His feminization relative to nature finds its analog in philosophers, presumably men of reasonably high station, who are revealed as pert, blushing, and powerless. This odd relation to nature, wherein the male scientist is feminized relative to a feminine figure, is evidenced in other ostensibly minor and ungendered editorial decisions. Whereas Smellie claims to "have done something towards reducing that Art [of midwifery], into a more simple and mechanical method," to have avoided the representation of "extreme Minutiae" in the plates, and to have had them done in a "strong and distinct manner" rather than consulting "delicacy and elegance,"[25] Hunter takes care to point out in his preface that "in this work the greater part is tolerably well finished; some very highly and delicately."[26] Naomi Schor has argued that the "normative aesthetics of neo-classicism" linked femininity and detail through its association of women with the mundane, the superficial, and the ornamental – those things opposed to the ideal, the essential, and the universal.[27] In this case, the opposition in Smellie's text of the terms "strength" and "delicacy" sufficiently hints at the gender implications of a detailed manner of engraving. Hunter and his work, rather than penetrate nature in "manly" fashion, are feminized in the face of it.

Hunter's faith in the power of nature, translated into the realm of obstetrical practice, gave rise to a kind of doctorly passivity; he was to argue throughout his career that even in cases of face presentations "the great rule is to do nothing."[28] He complained that too many midwives acted precipitately because they did not realize "what great things nature is capable of effecting."[29] Hunter's manual never shows or even mentions the obstetrical tools that tended to be the special stock-in-trade of specifically male midwives; he consistently argued that nature must be allowed to work at its own pace *through* the mother (compare figs. 4 and 7). As Harvey Graham remarks in *Eternal Eve*, a history of obstetrics and gynaecology that reads as a celebration of

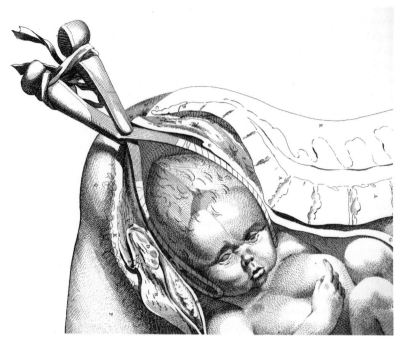

7   William Smellie, *Set of Anatomical Tables*, 2nd edn. (London: n.p., 1761), plate 16.
First published 1754.

male intervention, "unfortunately, [Hunter] carried his belief in the efficacy of nature a little far" (319).

It should be noted that the difference between Smellie's approach and Hunter's can be understood not simply in terms of changing times and attitudes – that is, chronologically – but also in terms of class. Whereas Smellie conducted his practice primarily among the lower and middle classes, Hunter tended to move among the aristocracy.[30] It is not surprising, then, that Hunter was more resistant to a commercial conceptualization of childbirth. But Hunter was not alone in his rejection of the forceps; Moscucci argues in *The Science of Woman* that "a conscious and massive swing away from instrumental intervention occurred about 1770" (48).[31] For Hunter and those like him, childbirth management was to resemble typical manual labor as little as possible: tools were not to be used and one was to avoid intervention of any kind. In Hunter's work even the midwife's labor is demechanized and minimized. Childbirth takes on, finally, a miraculous quality that allows it to transcend the world of ordinary human activity, that realm of cold instruments and sordid intentions that Nihell so despised but had made the special domain of men. Hunter portrays childbearing as an activity that takes place outside the laws of production and necessity and then ascribes the surplus power that comes of that transcendence to a feminized nature figure rather than to women themselves or even man-midwives. Hunter's maternal body, the passive site of a nature that is wild both in the sense of being free and beastly, could be seen as a prototype for the later understanding of the female body. The simul-taneous spiritualization and corporealization of the bourgeois woman during the next century reflects the pressure on the capitalist class to distance itself from its modes of production (which it does by making its ideal woman "aristocratically" spiritual, angelic) while restricting the power granted to women (through the common focus on the body in representations of women and members of the working class).[32]

But the modification of the representation of the mother's body comprises only half of Hunter's strategy; he also modifies the represen-tation of the baby. Unlike Smellie, who speaks almost exclusively of fetuses, even at nine months' development, Hunter generally speaks of "children." In the plates showing six to nine months' development the unborn being is always referred to as a "child." The creature of plate xxiii, being of six months' development, is referred to as a fetus, but then that of plate xxv, of five months' development, is referred to as both: "the womb fully opened, and the foetus taken out; shew the exact dimensions and proportions of the child." Then again, the text accompanying plate xxxi, which shows four months' development, refers to a fetus, but that for plate xxxii, showing three months' development, refers to a child. Fittingly, these "children" are beauti-fully rendered, and in spite of Hunter's claim that the engravings are completely naturalistic, these unborn infants tend to lack the distorted heads and limbs that we generally associate with babies even after birth. As Jordanova puts it, Hunter's "full-term foetus strives to be realistic – it has long elegant fingers and magnificent hair. It is almost too perfect" (402).

If we return now to the issue of the mother's hamhock-like legs in Hunter's text, we see that the violence that they suggest has many meanings. This violence reflects in part an effort to contain female power, the power of mysterious, even wild, flesh. Angela Carter's comment on the Marquis de Sade's characters applies here: "Sade is a great puritan and will disinfect of sensuality anything he can lay his hands on; therefore he writes about sexual relations in terms of butchery and meat."[33] But the threat here lies not simply in female power in itself but also specifically in female power over the fetus. The "perfect" baby is enclosed in a mother of ambiguous status. As Jordanova notes, "Hunter's plates, in contrast [to earlier depictions], convey an almost oppressive intimacy between mother and child" (406) (compare figs. 4 and 6 with fig. 8). But whereas Jordanova emphasizes the children's fullness – she says they "possess and confidently inhabit their mothers' bodies" (409) – I would accent the oppressiveness of the mother. These babies are being born to mothers whose childbearing labor is just barely being salvaged from the mechanical world of production and ownership. At the same time, the very character of the strategy for demechanization that is at work here – animalization – lends the maternal body a wild and grotesque quality that itself threatens the integrity and status of the child.

A French text of the end of the century, Sade's *La philosophie dans le boudoir*, encapsulates and exaggerates some of the social issues that are at stake in accounts of mother–child relations in this age of political and economic revolutions. One of Eugénie's instructors, Madame de Saint-Ange, argues that there "is no prerogative more secure than that of mothers over their children," and Dolmancé supports her by noting that the

imbeciles who believed in God, persuaded that our existence is had of none but him and that immediately an embryo begins to mature, a little soul, emanation of God, comes straightway to animate it…had to regard as a capital crime this small creature's undoing…'Twas God's work; 'twas God's own: dispatch it without crime? No. Since, however…we have evolved the principle of generation, and now that this material mechanism offers nothing more astonishing to the eye than the development of a germ of wheat, we have been called back to Nature and away from human error…We are absolute proprietors of what emanates from us.[34]

For Sade, since generation is a straightforward process of material production, it is subject to the general laws governing production: when the child was God's work, it was God's own, but now that it is understood as the product of a material process, it must be considered the mother's work and therefore hers to do with what she will. That Sade effaces the laborious aspect of childbearing by comparing it to growing fingernails and defecating, considering all three as forms of "emanation," hints at the anxiety his own paradigm of maternal production elicits in him. According to his relentless

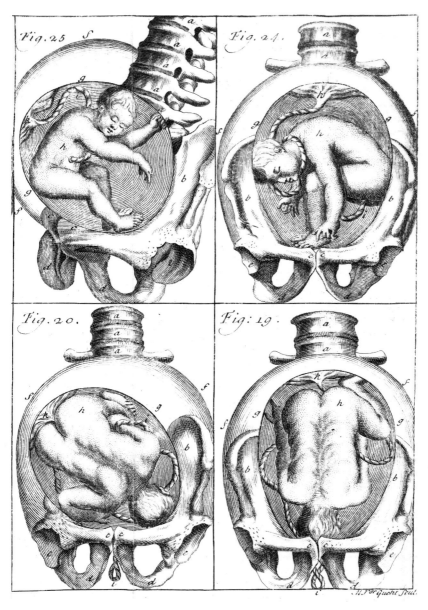

8   Hendrik Van Deventer, *The Art of Midwifery Improv'd* (London: Printed for E. Curll,
F. Pemberton, and W. Taylor, 1716), figs. 25, 24, 20, and 19.

marketplace logic, maternal production leads to maternal ownership
and control. When not making an argument for abortion, Sade, like
so many other writers of the period, finds this maternal control
troubling – he ends the novel with the book's only scene of overt
violence, and it is not only against a mother but involves sealing her
genitalia.

   This aggressive denial of the continuity of intrauterine life and
independent existence finds a subtle analog in Hunter's work. Hunter's
obstetrical atlas, unlike Smellie's, includes no engravings or discussion
of the liminal moment of parturition. The *Gravid Uterus* opens with
engravings of a full-term fetus and works its way back to conception, a
compilation decision that establishes a developmental pattern but one
that moves backwards, away from the moment of birth itself. The book
thus diverts attention from parturition and makes conception the
climactic event – conception being, mysterious as it was, perhaps less
troublingly mysterious than the moment when the baby is both part of
its mother and a separate being.

   The anxiety suggested here lends credibility to a psychoanalytic
concept like Kristeva's "abjection" (that which "preserves what existed
in the archaism of pre-objectal relationship, in the immemorial *violence*
with which a body becomes separated from another body in order to
be"[35]) in a way that the concerns of Smellie's texts simply do not.
Abjection describes a mother–child antagonism that may be more
definitively felt in an historical social context such as Sade and
Hunter's; the need to "sew up the mother" in order to constitute
oneself as a subject is not necessarily a timeless need but is, at least in
part, a specific response to a particular conjunction of economic and
social forces. Kristeva's own peculiarly gothic language itself hints at
the historically specific character of abjection, and it is perfectly fitting
that abjection should prove such a suitable paradigm for understanding
writings of this period: incest, undefined identities, and unaccountable
mothers become increasingly common in the literature of the late
eighteenth and early nineteenth centuries, from Walpole's *Mysterious
Mother* to Shelley's *Frankenstein*, and, as we will see in the final chapter,
are even an issue in a novel like Scott's *The Heart of Mid-Lothian*.
Psychoanalytic critic Barbara Schapiro, in her book devoted to the
topic of mothers in Romanticism, offers an examination of "the
preoedipal dynamics in Romantic poetry" and argues that the fact
"that the wounded narcissist should be such a characteristic Romantic
figure at least suggests that the Romantics were open to the deeper

layers of the psyche and in touch with those earliest, formative stages of personality development in which external reality and one's own identity are first being realized."[36] Schapiro offers no explanation for this concern with the "preoedipal" but can understand it only as a matter of being "open to" and "in touch with" universal facts of psychic existence. I would argue that the Romantics were sensitive to certain aspects of psychic and domestic life because they became, during this period, focal points of social power.

IV

As the quotation from Sade suggested, the changing relation of the fetus or child to its mother is also played out at the level of theories of conception and intrauterine growth. Many aspects of the difference that can be traced between Smellie's work and that of his pupil are roughly analogous to a shift that occurred slightly later within the discipline of embryology – a shift that was, for the British, largely a German import. Theoreticians of generation in the eighteenth century were divided into three general camps: ovist preformationist, animalculist preformationist, and epigenesist. Preformationists understood growth as an increase in size of an already complex creature – one whose limbs, organs, and so forth were understood to be initially invisible only because of the limitations of the human eye. The ovists, the dominant of the two preformationist groups, imagined the egg to be the bearer of this miniature being. Within this group, some subscribed to the theory of *emboîtement*; as Haller explained it: "it follows that the ovary of an ancestress will contain not only her daughter but also her granddaughter, her greatgranddaughter and her greatgreatgranddaughter, and if it is once proved that an ovary can contain many generations, there is no absurdity in saying that it contains them all."[37] Animalculist preformationism, a theory that the preformed being resides in the sperm, enjoyed a vogue from around 1683 to 1740.[38] Epigenesis, or the theory that the embryo develops and becomes more complex in its organization, that it changes morphologically rather than just in size, was available as theory throughout the century but did not really catch on until the end of it. As Shirley Roe writes: "in the late eighteenth and early nineteenth centuries, the most important contributions to embryology came from Germany, where Blumenbach...and others pursued developmental researches from an epigenetic point of view."[39]

It is significant that epigenesis, a modern form of which had first been proposed by William Harvey in the late seventeenth century, did take so long to catch on, and that its final triumph was not the result of any single discovery. As Roe notes, "none of these investigators ever really disproved preformation in any significant experimental way; most simply rejected it out of hand" (150). Jane Oppenheimer argues that preformationism "collapse[d] under its own weight. But it also fell, as it rose, on the basis of more serious philosophical principles."[40] Oppenheimer suggests that Wolff's definitive work on epigenesis was long uninfluential not because it was unknown but because his was a "biology of change" (135) that could only find a truly receptive audience around the turn of the century, in the age of revolutions. But the choice of epigenesis over preformationism had an even more profound social significance than this observation suggests. While a preformationist, Haller wrote that

in our century a proscribed notion has been *revivified* and some great men have pretended that there are little animals which are engendered by an equivocal generation, *without father and mother*, and that all the viscera and all the parts of these animals do not exist together, but that the *nobler parts* are formed first by epigenesis and that then the others are formed little by little afterwards.[41]

This description alone suggests several implications of adherence to an epigenetic theory of growth. Often associated with theories of spontaneous generation, epigenesis is here linked to "equivocal generation" and genealogical ambiguity. What is noble in the epigenesist creature is not part of its patrilineal (or even matrilineal) inheritance but a sort of upstart development out of nothing. Haller's use of the word "revivified" here is apt; he hints that epigenesis as theory was itself enjoying an unaccountable and ghostly reanimation.[42] But around the turn of the century epigenesis was to triumph definitively over its rivals. It offered, after all, the perfect high Romantic model of human development: a child is less indebted to its parents and its genealogy than to itself for its growth, and to whatever extent the child is not credited with that growth, it is understood as the work of a (non-mechanical) nature. As Needham describes it, "Wolff. . .borrowed from Leibniz the idea of a monad developing into an organism by means of its own inherent force, and to this he joined the Stahlian notion of a supra-physical generative force in nature."[43] Shirley Roe remarks that nineteenth-century epigenesists took for granted that "the creation of both the individual and the species are under the guidance of immanent, nonmechanical laws of nature" (153). This turn away from mechanism – preformationism "was the only mechanistic explanation of development that was consistent with the dominant religious world view"[44] – accomplished within embryology a change similar to the one accomplished by Hunter. Nature appears as a realm of freedom, of spontaneous growth not bound by hard and fast laws. The fetus is the perfect capitalist subject – it makes itself, and so is neither simply the inheritor of paternal power nor the commodity-like product of its mother's labor. The Nature–Philosophy school with which Wolff was associated was thus Romantic not only in its methods, with its dislike of mechanical theories and its interest in social institutions,[45] but also in the human subject it described. Von Baer, who was also associated with the school, published an embryological work in 1828 that concludes with the high Romantic argument that "the history of the development of the individual is the history of its increasing individuality in all respects."[46] It is not surprising that Kant should remark in the *Critique of Judgement* that "even supposing we failed to see the enormous advantage on the side of the advocate of *epigenesis* in the matter of empirical evidences in support of his theory, still reason would antecedently be strongly prepossessed in favour of his line of explanation."[47] Early nineteenth-century epigenesis sketches us a picture of a fetus characterized by canonical Romantic subjectivity.

Fittingly, although he never specified his opinions on embryology, readers of Hunter's works consider it likely that he tended toward an epigenetic model.[48] His fetus has to make itself to avoid slipping into the world of commodity-like objects, and in particular to avoid being the mere product of its mother's body; as we have seen, this fetus necessarily stands in a strained relation to its mother. Credit for fetal development must be shared by the fetus itself and a nature that is both powerful and safely removed from man's mechanical contrivances.

v

Interestingly, Nihell suggests that the intimacy of the mother–child relationship does not, from a woman's perspective, pose a threat: the female midwife "can discern the container from the contents, what belongs to the mother from what belongs to the child, as well as what is foreign to both" (33). Proper object relations are threatened only by the men who "have introduced themselves by force and violence, as one may say, sword in hand, with those murderous instruments" (57), "and who behind all the tender alluring words, of superior skill and safety in the employing of them, conceal the ideas with which they are full, of cutting, hacking, plucking out piece-meal, or tearing limb from limb" (4). Nihell repeatedly represents male intervention as a rape of a pregnant woman that violates the integrity of both mother and child. If mother–child intimacy takes on an abject quality, it is simply the *result* of the introduction of paternal law – a law, finally, not of happy distinctions, but of "tearing limb from limb." Nihell's metaphors suggest that if human flesh starts to look like animal meat in late eighteenth-century texts like Hunter's, it is because men, instrumentarian by nature, have brought their hacking and chopping tendencies to a traditionally female domain: she speaks of "that multitude of disciples of Dr. Smellie, trained up at the feet of his artificial doll, or in short of those self-constituted men-midwives made out of broken barbers, tailors, or even pork-butchers (I know myself one of this last trade, who, after passing half his life in stuffing sausages, is turned an intrepid physician and man-midwife)" (71).

It is important to note, however, that women of the period did not all share a single view of childbirth. Two poems to unborn children written by women in the closing decade of the century reflect the diversity of representations of the mother–child relation within women's writing alone. In Isabella Kelly's "To an Unborn Infant" the baby rests happy and unoppressed in its mother's womb: "Thy mother's frame shall safely guard thee…Shield thee from the least alarms."[49] The description of the fetus as an "Emblem of the rose unblown" not only associates it with gradual, blooming growth, but also reminds one of the popular and traditional eighteenth-century depiction of the opened-out womb as resembling a flower bearing a baby (see fig. 9). There is no hint here that parturition represents a liminal moment of catastrophic change. The child, imagined, it seems, as a girl, smoothly takes up her mother's name and story, and inherits her mother's charms (and martyrdom):

> Live, sweet babe, to bless thy father,
>   When thy mother slumbers low;
> Slowly lisp her name that loved him,
>   Through a world of varied woe.
>
> Learn, my child, the mournful story
>   Of thy suffering mother's life;
> Let thy father not forget her
>   In a future, happier wife.

The Form of a Child in the Womb, difrob'd of its Tunicles, proper and common.

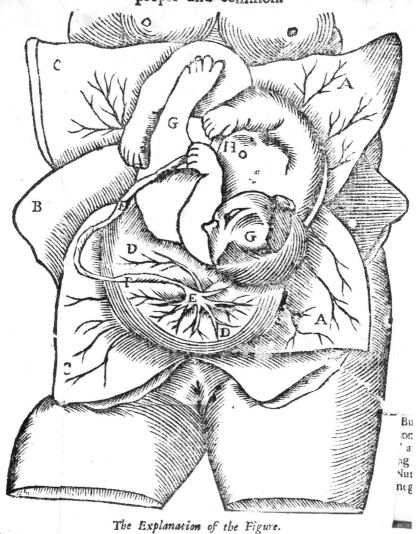

The Explanation of the Figure.

9 Plate from Aristotle, pseud., *Aristotle's Master-Piece Compleated* (Glasgow: 1784 edn.). (This popular text was reprinted throughout the century.)

> Babe of fondest expectation,
>   Watch his wishes in his face;
> What pleased in me mayst thou inherit,
>   And supply my vacant place.

This "feeble" baby by no means makes herself but passively becomes a replacement of her mother: "the hour approaches / That presents the gift of life." The mother here is neither machine nor meat, and her relation to her child is far from antagonistic. This poem presents a view of mother–child relations Elizabeth Nihell would probably have sympathized with.

Anna Barbauld's "To a Little Invisible Being Who Is Expected Soon to Become Visible" has quite a different character. A poem that appears to dramatize the transitional moment between preformationist and epigenetic accounts of embryological growth, it represents the baby as having rights to an inheritance it nevertheless has to roughly demand from a potentially hostile world. This baby, "curiously" made (the emphasis on its curious frame and initial invisibility reminds one of the preformationist argument that the embryo, like an insect, had limbs so delicate and minute that they were simply invisible in the early stages of development), already contains a full complement of power:

> What powers lie folded in thy curious frame, –
> Senses from objects locked, and mind from thought!
> How little canst thou guess thy lofty claim
> To grasp at all the worlds the Almighty wrought! [50]

But the child is urged not simply to await its due, but actively to seek it: "Launch on the living world, and spring to light!" The child's relation to its mother is especially vexed; although the child's growth and appearance is once represented as the blooming of a flower – "Haste, infant bud of being, haste to blow!" – in every other case the emphasis is on its necessary struggle against maternal constraint: "Haste, little captive, burst thy prison doors!"; "And nature's sharpest pangs her wishes crown, / That free thee living from thy living tomb." Not surprisingly, given the child's almost adversarial relation to its mother's body, the transitional movement from inside to outside is represented as somewhat ominous; the speaker hopes the baby will be "Auspicious borne through life's mysterious gate." Unlike the mutually supportive mother and child of Kelly's poem, these two seem to be locked in a zero-sum game; the child must escape the mother to make use of its power, but the mother seems to want to keep it close in order to claim its power for herself. The speaker's intense interest in the child's powers – the first lines of the first two stanzas both refer to them – and the fact that they are described as lying folded in the child's frame, give the opening of the sixth stanza a peculiar resonance: "She longs to *fold* to her maternal breast / Part of herself, yet to herself unknown" (my emphasis). Here, toward the end of the poem, the baby's powers are appropriated for the baby-maker mother. But the tension established between mother and child continues to dominate the poem, which ends on a commercial note: "Anxious I'd bid my beads each passing hour, / Till thy wished smile thy mother's pangs o'erpay." This is a world of maternal love and care that cannot be kept distinct from the world of inheritance, ownership, and power. It is not surprising then that it is a world of subtle mother–child antagonism and ominous parturition.

Hunter's focus on fleshy nature and the epigenesist's model of an internally motivated embryo served as diversionary tactics: birth was prevented from appearing to be a form of production controlled by women (the mother and her female assistants) because it was figured instead as the work of a mysterious nature and a willful fetus. But behind the diversion still loomed a system of economic relations that perpetually threatened to make a child merely a commodity in a world of commodities. The child suffers, as Kristeva puts it, "a possession previous to [its] advent," and one could claim, using Kristeva's own language, that this problem arises because in the framework of early industrial capitalism the mother becomes "not at all an other with whom [it] identif[ies] and incorporate[s], but an Other who precedes and possesses [it], and through such possession causes [it] to be."[51] In the late eighteenth and early nineteenth centuries a child must, of necessity, resist a strong connection to its mother in order to establish itself as a self-made subject, "one that is capable of the limitless self-improvement valorizing and valorized by an 'open' society and a 'free' economy."[52] The child that does not resist possession by the mother finds itself unable to become a complete subject precisely because it is positioned as an object, as a possessed being, in both the economic and the gothic sense. Like the abject characters of the gothic novels of the period, such a child becomes nothing more than, in Kristeva's words, "an empty castle, haunted by unappealing ghosts – 'powerless' outside, 'impossible' inside" (49).

CHAPTER 2

"An embarrassing subject"
Use value and exchange value in early gothic characterization

As we saw in the previous chapter, even a spiritualizing, individualist account of the genesis of the self could not completely prevent the association of persons and commodities, an association that tends to give rise to a kind of gothic abjection. As Charles Rzepka points out, "Romantic visionary solipsism" tended to produce, as its repressed double, a gothic sense of the insubstantiality of selves: "as Gray and Hume show, the more we search for the self within, the more it shrinks to a ghost haunting the fringes of experience."[1] The eerie *doppelgänger* of the world described by Romanticism, the gothic world "becomes horrifying as [other people] lose psychological depth. Life in general appears 'theatrical,' a 'death-in-life,' and embodied selves become mere actors or caricatures, or in more severe cases, insensate things altogether, like automata or walking corpses."[2]

In this chapter I argue that the growth of the perceived division between a "true inner self" and a "superficial social self" – the division constitutive of the canonical Romantic model of subjectivity as well as its obverse, gothic subjectivity – can be intimately related to late eighteenth-century economic developments. As Lukács notes, it is not without reason that during the age of Romantic bourgeois revolutions "the hiatus between appearance and essence (which in Kant coincides with that between necessity and freedom) is not bridged...Even worse than that: the duality is introduced into the subject. Even the subject is split into phenomenon and noumenon..."[3] It is my contention that at the moment the traditional genealogy-based model of identity was called into question by the ideals of the French Revolution and the realities of capitalist and industrial development, a market-based model of identity that had long been emerging rapidly gained ground. This model tends to polarize identity into an essential identity akin to use value, on the one hand, and a relational identity akin to exchange value on the other. Romantic interiority focuses on that first pole: it presents a subject that simultaneously appears to have an intrinsic and relatively stable character and to be the product of its own labor. The early gothic novel, however, tends to focus on the opposite pole – making character a matter of surface, display, and "consumption" by others. The gothic novel associates this relational character both with traditional signs of identity and with the vagaries of exchange value, focusing on the danger the old *and* the new systems of identity represented for an increasingly capitalist society. This representation of identity accounts for many of the gothic novel's peculiar thematic and formal features as well as its lower canonical status and association with the feminine. We will see that much of the mystery and violence of the gothic, and much of its distastefulness for us, arises from its vision of a world of what could be called "commodities among themselves."[4] After using eighteenth-century moral theory and the sentimental novel to provide a groundwork for understanding the prevalent models for the evaluation of identity in the period, I will describe the way the gothic novel carries certain trends to their logical – and spine-tingling – conclusions.

I

As early as the seventeenth century, one finds evidence of tension between two modes of personal valuation – one based on social rank and blood lines, reflecting an older and more static order, and the other based on individual merit and associated with capitalist-class imperatives and the growing strength of the market economy. Jean-Christophe Agnew traces this tension in *Worlds Apart* and argues that the expansion of the marketplace during the seventeenth century, both extensively and intensively, caused fundamental changes in the perception of human value and identity. Agnew convincingly shows that developments such as "the maneuvers of class and faction in the wake of the Revolution settlement...the new relation of the state to speculative capital, and...the emergence of a distinctly urban, consumer culture...encouraged some thinkers, at least, to reconsider the notion – first broached by Hobbes of a commodity self: a mercurial exchange value or 'bubble' floating on the tides of what attention others were disposed to invest."[5] I would argue that the continuing extension of market relations, the rapid early development of industrialization, the weakening of larger patriarchal family ties, and the attack on aristocratic privilege precipitated another major shift in the conception of identity in the late eighteenth century.

One must of course be careful in associating these broad social and economic changes with the interests and actions of any single class, and in the past fifteen years historians have refined the category of the "middle class" into ever more specific and numerous subgroups.[6] Nevertheless, as William Reddy demonstrates in *Money and Liberty*, it is undeniable that British elites were learning "between about 1780 and 1820, to invest money in a thoroughly capitalist manner: 'capitalist' in the strict sense of seeking to maximize return through the transformation of production methods" (12). And while "manufacturing and landowning classes were not so distinct as was once supposed" (10), it is clear that the new capitalist class that could be said to draw its members from both needed, in order to establish its hegemony, to develop its own methods for characterizing and evaluating persons. J. G. A. Pocock argues that "the century that followed the Financial Revolution witnessed the rise in Western thought. . .of an ideology and a perception of history which depicted political society and social personality as founded upon commerce: upon the exchange of forms of mobile property and upon modes of consciousness suited to a world of moving objects."[7] Moreover, as I will show, people increasingly did more than present themselves as "marketable" objects and anticipate commercial deceit in others; as the traditional system of identification and valuation of individuals lost its prestige, people came to understand personal identity, in both its public and its private aspects, in terms of the dominant evaluative scheme of the developing capitalist and credit economy, a scheme based on market forces. As we will see, this model for classification was characterized by an internal division between use value and market, or speculative, value.

Hume's 1751 *An Inquiry Concerning the Principles of Morals* provides a useful starting point for the exploration of changing terms of identity in the eighteenth century, analyzing as it does the processes according to which not only moral value but also social identity and status are conferred on individuals. Hume's catalog of behaviors describes the personal characteristics that define both a public and a private identity at the same time that it evaluates those characteristics. This text nicely illustrates the result of the capitalist-class desire that personal identity be based on merit rather than blood lines: identity came to be constructed in terms of an aggregate of characteristics, each of which was understood in commodity terms. Fittingly enough then, the identity described by that aggregate was also understood in those terms.

Hume's principal argument is that moral worth and personal identity are determined on the basis of characteristics whose value resides ultimately in their utility. It comes as no great surprise that the first traits mentioned in the section "Of Qualities Useful to Ourselves" are good mercantile traits: "*discretion,* by which we carry on a safe intercourse with others...[and] weigh each circumstance of the business which we undertake";[8] "what need is there to display the praises of *industry* and to extol its advantages, in the acquisition of power and riches, or in raising what we call a *fortune* in the world?" (62); "all prospect of success in life, or even of tolerable subsistence, must fail where a reasonable *frugality* is wanting" (62). But *An Inquiry*'s mercantile perspective becomes even more apparent on those occasions when the fundamental role of utility, Hume's primary concern, is challenged:

> can it possibly be doubted that this talent itself of poets to move the passions, this *pathetic* and *sublime* of sentiment is a very considerable merit, and, being enhanced by its extreme rarity, may exalt the person possessed of it above every character of the age in which he lives?...No views of utility...enter into this sentiment of approbation, yet it is of a kind similar to that other sentiment which arises from views of a public or private utility. The same social sympathy...gives rise to both...(82–83)

Hume somewhat awkwardly tries to account for the value of poetic sensibility, suggesting that although that value does not originate in considerations of utility, it nevertheless does appear to have a social character. Thus, it seems to arise according to a process that is at least analogous to the one he has focused on. But the hint that rarity is at the root of this value suggests that the importance of exchange to Hume's system of valuation runs even deeper than may at first appear. Hume's naturalizing account of value – his contention that it arises from some combination of reasoned consideration of utility and basic human sociability – is exposed as an idealization of commercial valuation whenever the issue of traditionally upper-class abilities or characteristics arises. At times it becomes quite obvious that market value and not just an abstract notion of utility structures this system, as when he notes that "eloquence, genius of all kinds...have a merit distinct from their usefulness. Rarity, likewise, which so much enhances the price of everything, must set an additional value on these noble talents of the human mind" (85). This book, with its analysis of "that complication of mental qualities which form what, in common life, we call 'personal merit'" (7), does not merely favor mercantile virtues but uses a market scheme for the determination of human value. Men, like commodities, are valued not just for their usefulness but also for qualities whose value is largely conditional and extrinsic:

If refined sense and exalted sense be not so *useful* as common sense, their rarity, their novelty, and the nobleness of their objects make some compensation and render them the admiration of mankind, as gold, though less serviceable than iron, acquires from its scarcity a value which is much superior. (65)

The impulse to describe the ostensibly natural and rational character of status determination under capitalism gives way here to a need to account for the lingering importance of the traditional marks of nobility (such as refined sensibility and good taste) – signs of status that the monied class has chosen to claim for itself. These noble characteristics, since they cannot be accounted for in terms of utility, are imported into Hume's evaluative system under the banner of exchange value rather than use value – but with the result that the ideal of utility is undermined. As we saw above, for instance, common sense, although more useful than refined sense, is actually less valuable. That this can be true gives the lie to the argument for the foundational role of utility that Hume has so patiently constructed.[9]

Adam Smith, in his *Theory of Moral Sentiments* of 1759, takes the assumptions of his "ingenious and agreeable" fellow philosopher one step further, observing that the "happy contrivance of any production of art, should often be more valued, than the very end for which it was intended."[10] Smith frankly acknowledges the tendency for exchange, expenditure, and consumption *per se* to become more important than the considerations of utility to which they are ostensibly subservient. He argues, for instance, that the value of noble accoutrements resides in their utility, but he recognizes that in their daily life people tend to be concerned with the immediate result of expenditure rather than its ultimate aim:

Would you awaken the industry of the man who seems almost dead to ambition, it will often be to no purpose to describe to him the happiness of the rich and the great; to tell him that they are generally sheltered from the sun and the rain, that they are seldom hungry, that they are seldom cold, and that they are rarely exposed to weariness, or to want of any kind...you must describe to him the conveniency and arrangement of the different apartments in their palaces; you must explain to him the propriety of their equipages, and point out to him the number, the order, and the different offices of all their attendants. (186)

The avid desire of this hypothetical interlocutor for an *inventory* of the exorbitant privileges of upper-class life signals the fact that aristocratic status has been re-encoded with a mercantile social value. Nevertheless, this value clearly exceeds the requirements of utility. Smith finds in this excess an explicit link to political economy in that even the non-utilitarian behavior of the rich leads them "by an invisible hand to make nearly the same distribution of the necessaries of life, which would have been made, had the earth been divided into equal portions..." (184–185). But although he argues that utility is ultimately served in spite of human folly, it is the folly that Smith makes most visible:

What pleases these lovers of toys is not so much the utility, as the aptness of the machines which are fitted to promote it. All their pockets are stuffed with little conveniences. They contrive new pockets, unknown in the clothes of other people, in order to carry a greater number. They walk about loaded with a multitude of baubles, in weight and sometimes in value not inferior to an ordinary Jew's-box, some of which may sometimes be of little use, but all of which might at all times be very well spared, and of which the whole utility is certainly not worth the fatigue of bearing the burden. (180)

Smith goes on to demonstrate the power of that quintessential embodiment of exchange value: money. As we discovered with Hume, even in the realm of personal evaluation Smith asserts that relative value finally triumphs over bourgeois ideals of intrinsic value grounded in utility:

We are no more concerned for the destruction or loss of a single man, because this man is a member or part of society, and because we should be concerned for the destruction of society, than we are concerned for the loss of a single guinea, because this guinea is a part of a thousand guineas, and because we should be concerned for the loss of the whole sum. (89)

The loss of a man, like the loss of a guinea, is no great threat to the health of a society concerned primarily with amassing large sums – a society where men, like coins, possess a limited and relative value. Smith's analogy exposes the impulse behind, and the implications of, Hume's scheme.

In spite of its focus on utility, then, Hume's *Inquiry* describes personal identities in commodity terms, as determined on the basis of an exchange value that often diverges from use value. Ironically enough, it is the moments when the *traditional* signs of nobility become an issue that exchange value explicitly enters the scene and threatens the ideal of a personal identity grounded in considerations of private and social utility. It is not insignificant that, in Hume's chapter on "Political Society," this threat prompts a series of reflections on what could be called gothic horrors: infidelity, incest, secrecy, spying, immoral gallantry, and murder.

II

The sentimental novel of the latter part of the eighteenth century registers considerable anxiety over the problem of personal value and identity. This anxiety is expressed and managed through a distanced and often comic treatment of the issue. A case in point, Henry Mackenzie's *The Man of Feeling* (1771), takes the associations we saw in Hume and Smith a pessimistic step further. Mackenzie includes both exchange value and traditional signs of nobility in the category of empty forms and opposes them to true content, which, by implication, amounts to real virtue and use value:

> "Honour and Politeness! this is the *coin* of the world, and passes current with the fools of it. You have substituted the *shadow* Honour, instead of the substance Virtue; and have banished the reality of friendship for the fictitious semblance which you have termed Politeness: politeness, which consists in a certain ceremonious jargon, more ridiculous to the ear of reason than the voice of a *puppet*. You have invented sounds, which you worship, though they tyrannize over your peace; and are surrounded with *empty forms. . .*"[11]

Honor and money and even certain words are all associated with empty form in this critique of the world the capitalist class has created. Signs of upper-class status have been imported into the marketplace and have acquired, like money, what Lukács would argue is the typical quality of objects and ideas under capitalism: sheer formality.[12] It is interesting to recall in this context that in that more playful and more famous sentimental novel, Sterne's *A Sentimental Journey*, Yorick describes Englishmen as coins who, by virtue of their limited circulation, at least retain a legible superscription, unlike their politely smooth French brothers.[13] (It is perfectly fitting that in 1770 a novel should be written in which the protagonist is literally a circulating bank-note: Thomas Bridges's *Adventures of a Bank-Note.*) In *The Man of Feeling*, deceptive surfaces are a constant theme and are linked to the money form; as Harley is reminded, "all's not gold that glisters" (30). Dress, even when appropriate to its wearer, can be misleading, as when Harley mistakes a recruiting officer for a neighbor's servant because of his hat (77). The misanthropist, whose complaint is quoted above, recognizes that these forms have been worshipped, fetishized, in spite of the fact that they tyrannize over their own producers. His reference to a puppet hints that people themselves have become empty, hollow forms, expressions of a power not their own. As the narrator says later in the book: "we take our ideas from sounds which folly has invented; Fashion, Bon ton...are the names of certain idols, to which we sacrifice the genuine pleasures of the soul: in this world of semblance, we are contented with personating happiness; to feel it is an art beyond us" (70). This complaint is, of course, a humanist one that is itself thoroughly "bourgeois," a reminder of the ideals the capitalist class used to strengthen its own position: utility, authenticity, the natural. All of these were ideals that Hume was, for the most part, able to consider as being at the center of social life.[14] But the world of the man of feeling of the 1770s is a world of "shadowy" forms emptied of content; of hollow, powerless people who have, in essence, sacrificed their souls; a world of coins – the prototype of the gothic world.

III

By the end of the eighteenth century, anxieties concerning the deepening division between use value and exchange value, and the problems that division produced in the realm of personal identification and evaluation, had become even more acute. Speculative capital especially, with its extreme immateriality, foregrounded the distinction between tangible and intangible values. Since, as Pocock argues, "property was acknowledged as the social basis of personality, the emergence of classes whose property consisted not of land or goods or even bullion, but of paper promises to repay in an undefined future, was seen as entailing the emergence of new types of personality, unprecedentedly dangerous and unstable" (235). But the rift between forms of value was in itself creating problems in the determination of identity. At the end of the century, moreover, the French Revolution challenged the naturalness of the genealogical system of distinctions while simultaneously foregrounding the contingency of commodity and monetary value. Burke, in his *Reflections on the Revolution in France*, shows that he is fully aware of the disruption this represented: "Are all orders, ranks, and distinctions to be confounded, that out of universal anarchy, joined to national bankruptcy, three or four thousand democracies should...be organized into one?"[15] The problem is not, of course, that

France is actually devoid of wealth, but that it has established a paper currency without a solid and consistent backing. The difference the French Revolutionary *assignats* introduced between real and apparent value is, to Burke's eyes, the forerunner to bankruptcy. And it is not by chance that he associates the breakdown of hereditary and other distinctions with this toying with value, for he recognizes that the "alchemistical legislators" of France "reduce men to loose counters merely for the sake of simple telling, and not to figures whose power is to arise from their place in the table" (201). If people are treated like money-style ciphers in a society where money itself has a highly variable value, then there is no hope for social stability: "Who would insure a tender and delicate sense of honour to beat almost with the first pulses of the heart, when no man could know what would be the test of honour in a nation, continually varying the standard of its coin?" (109). The standards of honor and morality that Hume and Smith worked so hard to root in utility are here quite frankly exposed in their connection with exchange; even personal value becomes contingent when the coin standard fluctuates.

In 1790, when the *Reflections* first appeared, these issues were very much on the minds of the British but had no immediate analog on the British economic scene. The British monetary system was not without its problems, but these were relatively minor: the shortage of silver coin had been a constant cause of complaint throughout the eighteenth century,[16] and in the latter half of the century there was considerable discussion of the role of banks and the use of paper credit. Hume remarked that the investigation of the relation of prices to exporting "had made me entertain a doubt concerning the benefit of *banks* and *paper-credit*, which are so generally esteemed advantageous to every nation..."[17] Smith, too, showed some reservations regarding paper money: "The commerce and industry of the country, however, it must be acknowledged, though they may be somewhat augmented, cannot be altogether so secure, when they are thus, as it were, suspended upon the Daedalian wings of paper money, as when they travel about on the solid ground of gold and silver."[18] The outbreak of war with France in 1793, however, was followed within a month by what Frank Fetter calls "one of the worst financial and commercial crises that England had experienced up to that time."[19] In response, the Bank of England issued Exchequer Bills "not in excess of 50 per cent of the value of 'goods' or 'such personal securities of a given number of persons as shall be satisfactory to the Commissioners.'"[20] In 1796 in Ireland and in 1797 in England fears of an invasion drove people in town and country to demand specie (gold or silver) for their notes: "following a rumor of invasion farmers brought their livestock and produce into town and on receiving payment went to the banks and converted their notes into specie."[21] The result was the Restriction, the suspension of specie payments. Given Burke's fears, it is ironic that England's own specie standard was challenged not only by costs arising from the war with France, but also as the result of the collapse of the *assignats* beginning in 1795. This collapse "led to an increase in the use of a metallic currency in France, and substantial amounts of gold and silver probably found their way from the vaults of the Bank [of England] into the monetary system of England's enemy."[22]

The problem of stable value, as reflected both in commodity prices and the monetary system itself, was thus acutely felt in the period of the burgeoning of the gothic novel. The division between intrinsic and socially determined value that was already a problem for Hume, Smith, and Mackenzie makes itself even more powerfully felt in the early gothic novel. The reader of early gothic fiction – those novels by Walpole, Lewis, and Radcliffe written before the turn of the century[23] – notices first of all that gothic characterization is strongly bifurcated. On the one hand, characters are offered to the reader as entirely coherent and distinct personalities and we are asked to value and respond to them according to these personalities. These personalities, moreover, appear to be exact expressions of, and are fundamentally tied to, private and intrinsic merit. But on the other hand, the novel represents characters as mysterious in relation to one another and presents them in a series of shifting interrelations.

There can be no doubt, for instance, that Radcliffe's *The Italian* represents Ellena Rosalba as a "good" young woman: virtuous, chaste, sincere. As readers we feel fairly assured that Ellena's personality will undergo no abrupt changes, and, in fact, one of the complaints traditionally levelled against the gothic novel is that characters like Ellena not only do not change abruptly but do not change at all. One reason gothic characterization fails to produce a depth-effect is that it suggests so few contradictions or complications at the level of personality or private character – the level at which certain canonical Romantic texts offer fruitful contradictions and dialectical energies.[24]

At the same time, however, *The Italian* constantly keeps us wondering about Ellena's identity *vis-à-vis* other characters: is Schedoni really her father? Does she merit Vivaldi's hand in marriage? Who is her mother

and what is she like? While limiting our knowledge of practical and
familial relations between characters, the novel hints at relational
identity through a tissue of parallels and repetitions – a network so
complicated and various that it could hardly be considered directly
informative. To offer just one example, Ellena's first sight of Olivia
parallels Vivaldi's first sight of Ellena. Both spectators are fascinated by
the modesty, grace, and piety of a veiled woman attending a service:

> It was in the church of San Lorenzo at Naples, in the year 1758, that Vincentio
> di Vivaldi first saw Ellena Rosalba. The sweetness and fine expression of her
> voice attracted his attention to her figure, which had a distinguished air of
> delicacy and grace; but her face was concealed in her veil.

> Among the voices of the choir, was one whose expression immediately fixed
> her attention; it seemed to speak a loftier sentiment of devotion than the
> others, and to be modulated by the melancholy of an heart, that had long
> since taken leave of this world...Her face was concealed by a black veil.[25]

Gothic repetitions stage compulsive rehearsals of similarity and difference as if the obvious personalities of these characters were not truly
sufficient to the construction of identity. In sum then, the novel
produces identities through two separate processes: the display of
personal qualities through speech or action and the differential display
of character (what we see, for instance, in the structural paralleling of
two characters) – with the emphasis on the latter. For the modern
reader of these texts, hints regarding relational identity tend either to
go unnoticed or simply to irritate. Expecting a certain kind of character
development, that is, with expectations shaped by the canonical view of
Romantic subjectivity, we notice only that the intrinsic character
presented in these novels tends to be static and dull, and that it does
not correspond to the fluid relational character that sets the plot in
motion.

This bifurcation of character harks back to Hume and Mackenzie
and signals a division analogous to that between utility and market
value. On the one hand, characters have both an undeniable and
reasonably stable identity to which their fellows and the reader should,
according to the ethics of the novel, respond. But on the other hand,
they have a strictly relational identity that is frighteningly fluid and a
source of fascination for the characters and the novel's readers. The
market quality of this relational identity is most explicit in scenes like
that in *The Mysteries of Udolpho* when Morano tells Emily that Montoni
tried to sell her to him,[26] or that in *The Castle of Otranto* when Matilda

complains to Bianca that she should not "make a property of" Theodore.[27] Again and again, a character's "real" value stands opposed to his social value: when Valancourt tells Emily he is ruined financially, she determines that she must not involve herself with him, and yet "she was compelled to admire his sincerity,"[28] and finds it difficult to give up loving him. Similarly, Ellena Rosalba, in *The Italian*, helps to support herself and her aunt by embroidering silks, and we are told that this industry "did honor to her character" (9). Ellena keeps her vocation a secret, however, since public knowledge of it would actually decrease her social status. The issue of Ellena's status represents the typical driving tension of the Radcliffean novel: in spite of her obvious personal merits, does Ellena really deserve to fetch such a high price on the marriage market? As a general rule, neither we nor those in the novel have doubts about a character's "personality" – the problem is not, for example, that Vivaldi mistakes Schedoni for a good guy – the confusion and the threat reside in relational identity: what does it say about Ellena if Schedoni is her father?

Altogether then, gothic characterization suggests a model of identity strikingly similar to those we saw implied in the work of Hume and Mackenzie. The old genealogical model of personal identification and evaluation has by now lost a considerable amount of prestige and is increasingly being replaced by the model used to classify commodities. This model's two fundamental categories, utility and exchangeability, and their tendency to become mutually exclusive (recall Hume and Smith), are thus imported into the realm of personal evaluation. On the one hand we have identity as it "should" be: a matter of personality and intrinsic individual virtue. On the other hand we have a relational, changeable identity associated with the superficiality, contingency, and indeterminacy of market values. Moreover, just as the traditional values that find their way into Hume's system do so under the banner of exchange value, so here the outmoded criterion of birth is linked to exchange value – as in *The Man of Feeling*, it falls into the category of "empty forms." Indeterminacy of identity, then, is associated both with the old, genealogy-based notion of identity and with new, increasingly fluid market relations. By means of this connection, capitalist-class culture was able to use the two forms of value that were most threatening to its self-representation as natural, useful, and inevitable against one another: genealogy appears as arbitrary, a mere social fiction like exchange value, while the fluctuations of social value, crystallized in exchange value, come somehow to seem, like genealogy,

a phenomenon of the past, rather than one of the most marked features
of an expanding capitalist society. Again, it is in the lyric poetry of the
period that the privileged category of "utility" (an apparently "real,"
materially grounded value, but one that is, as Baudrillard demonstrates, itself an ideal[29]) most clearly comes to the fore. In the gothic
too what ostensibly matters most is personality – that aspect of identity
associated with use value. But what is far more interesting is relational
identity – "exchange-value" identity and the residual traces of genealogy – because in social life that is what is really at stake. Early gothic
characterization derives its peculiar energy and appeal from its love/
hate relationship with relational identity.

Relational identity, the simultaneously forward- and backward-
looking side of gothic characterization, focuses the anxieties that
generate the gothic genre and lend it some of its best-known features.
As in Hume and Mackenzie, *traditional* class indices, such as dress and
name, signal a value extrinsic to an idealized system of value based on
the useful and natural and so seem like empty (although still powerful)
forms. Clothes often function as disguises, and while in the sentimental
novel such disguise generally takes the form of mimicking the garb of a
higher class, in the gothic it tends not only to serve ambition but also to
mask individual peculiarities of all kinds – the evil man dressed as a
monk among many monks being one of the most common and sinister
of such images. This difference reflects a subtle difference in the two
genres: in the world of the sentimental novel, it is the fault of the man
who does not dress his part that clothes do not work as signs of status,
whereas the gothic finds coded dressing threatening in itself, blaming,
as it were, the clothes and not just the man. Dress seems by its very
nature to flatten out rather than clarify the differences between
persons. In *The Italian*, for instance, Schedoni and Bianchi do not
realize that they are living in the same town because "her veil, and the
monk's cowl, might easily have concealed them from each other if they
had met" (382–383). Even when the manipulation of costume is done
by or for a protagonist, we almost wish the opportunity for it were not
there; Ellena dressed as a nun makes readers nervous, and their fears
are realized when her habit is used as a pretense for taking Vivaldi to
the Inquisition. Characters whose only interest is in matters of form
and appearance are immediately suspicious: in *The Romance of the Forest*,
the first sign that the Lady Abbess is not to be trusted is that she is
"exact in the observance of every detail of form."[30] Traditional signs of
one's role and rank are automatically suspect.

More importantly, the relational identities constituted by signs such as dress and manners, signs that are already metaphoric ghosts in Mackenzie ("you have substituted the shadow Honour instead of the substance Virtue,")[31] become literally ghostly in the gothic. To give just a few examples of this spectralization from *The Italian*: "she seemed like a spectre newly risen from the grave, rather than a living being" (67); "he resembled a spectre rather than a human being" (110); "shadowy countenances and uncertain forms seemed to flit through the dusk" (311). Terry Castle has brilliantly argued that "the other" is spectralized in *The Mysteries of Udolpho* and that the underside of Romantic individualism – the growing palpability of subjective reality – is the increasing sense that others are merely specters, phantasms of the observer's mind.[32] Castle offers three sets of evidence for such a reading of the novel: cases of the appearance of someone after thinking of him; a sense that the other is always present, especially when absent; and finally, as Castle puts it, the fact that "every other looks like every other other" (238). In this final category Castle includes those uncanny repetitions I have already mentioned. But the deindividuation Castle describes is not always, or even usually, presented in the novel as a subjective effect, and her constant reference to an "other" does not quite make sense in the absence of a governing subject-position. Although Castle's point is convincing overall, I would argue that the dreamlike effects she describes in her third category reflect not just a subjective spectralization of others but a general confusion (from any perspective) regarding relational identity. The condemnation of external signs of status and the fear that real virtues have been replaced by ghostly forms is vividly and literally rehearsed here; people themselves have taken on an indeterminate, spectral quality.

On the one hand, this ghostliness reflects the nostalgic character, the eerie "pastness" of genealogical identity. At the same time, however, since relational identity is associated not just with traditional status markers but also with market value and speculation, it is not surprising that in their relations to one another characters have the qualities of commodities as they were soon to be described by Marx: they are immaterial, fetishized, transparent, metaphysical, and they only acquire value in relation to others.[33] The analogy Irigaray draws between the role of the commodity as defined by Marx and "the status of woman in so-called patriarchal societies"[34] suggests a second analogy between commodities/women and characters in gothic novels.

One could substitute "gothic characters" for "women" in the following quotation: "*As commodities, women are thus two things at once: utilitarian objects and bearers of value.*"[35] Those processes by which relational character is determined result in a "spectralization of the other" because they are not grounded in intrinsic value: "in order to have a *relative value*, a commodity has to be confronted with another commodity that serves as its equivalent. Its value is never found to lie within itself. And the fact that it is worth more or less is not its own doing but comes from that to which it may be equivalent. Its value is *transcendent* to itself, *super-natural, ek-static.*"[36] This supernatural and relational aspect of identity is, indeed, not a character's own doing. Not surprisingly, the exchange-value side of character lends itself to a metaphoric description powerfully reminiscent of that used in Mackenzie's account of social life; these are people of shadows and forms who tend to "bubble" each other (an eighteenth-century metaphor for deception) and whose very voices – traditional signs of self-presence – are nothing more than puppet-voices, signs of hollowness. The association of the marketplace, theatricality, and shadows is nicely encapsulated in the fair scene in *The Italian*:

> They...passed...into a market place...on one spot...the *improvisatore*, by the pathos of his story, and the persuasive sensibility of his strains, was holding the attention of his auditors, as in the bands of magic. Farther on was a stage raised for a display of fireworks, and near this a theatre, where a mimic opera, the 'shadow of a shade,' was exhibiting, whence the roar of laughter...mingled with the heterogeneous voices of the venders... (273)

The ultimate sign of the importation of marketplace evaluation into the realm of personal identification is the focus on surfaces to the point that characters resemble the reified form of the exchange value of the commodity: money. Extreme flatness of character, images of identically dressed groups of people, and the sense of identity as mere sign all suggest this. As William Patrick Day notes, "in *Otranto*, Theodore, the nominal hero, proves an ineffective cipher,"[37] a fate common to early gothic heroes and heroines. In their social relations people become as interchangeable as coins, usually with unpleasant consequences. In *The Italian*, the association of people and coins is humorously made palpable through a pun on Vivaldi's servant's name:

"Paulo made him merry, perhaps?" asked Vivaldi.
...
"But the coaxing ways you talked of," repeated Vivaldi, "what were they? – a ducat, or so?"
"A ducat!" exclaimed the man, "no! not a *paolo*!"
"Are you *sure* of that?" cried Vivaldi, shrewdly.
"Aye, sure enough, Signor. This fellow is not worth a ducat in the world!"
"But his master is, friend," observed Vivaldi, in a very low voice, while he put some money into his hand. (366–367)

Paulo may not be worth a ducat, but he may after all be worth a *paolo*, especially in relation to his master. Traditional master–servant roles and the modern emphasis on money intersect in a scene of indeterminate relational identity.

Problems in the determination of value, with people as with goods, are related to a problem in the determination of origin: "*In order to become equivalent, a commodity changes bodies.* A super-natural, metaphysical origin is substituted for its material origin. Thus its body becomes a transparent body, *pure phenomenality of value.*"[38] In the world of the gothic, where people's material origins (their parents, and especially their mothers) are so often unknown, not only their origin but their very existence takes on a supernatural quality. The mysterious Schedoni is quite typical – "an Italian, as his name imported, but whose family was unknown" – and only differs from the good characters of *The Italian* in that "he *wished* to throw an impenetrable veil over his origin" (34, my emphasis). Not surprisingly, the novel's final resolution of the gap between relational and intrinsic identity involves a revelation of material origins: who was born to whom and where. Such revelations serve to reconnect persons with the site of their original "production," and this is as close as the gothic novel comes to focusing on production rather than social consumption, given that, unlike the *Bildungsroman* and much Romantic poetry, it does not show individuals producing or determining themselves.

At the same time that it thrills its readers with its focus on the mystery and fascination of a world where people tend towards sheer transcendental form, the gothic constantly teases them by moving to reground its characters in the natural, an impulse that often takes the form of reintroducing the body, and usually a body subjected to violence. Elaine Scarry argues that the image of opened or dead bodies often serves to ground a belief system that has been challenged: "the sheer material factualness of the human body will be borrowed to lend that cultural construct the aura of 'realness' and 'certainty.'"[39] The logic of this tactic is, of course, particularly compelling in a context where the hegemonic class understands the body as the site of sincerity and the natural.[40] The binary oppositions that Irigaray outlines speak powerfully to the issue of the status of the body in gothic characterization: "that economy subjects women [gothic characters] to a schism that is necessary to symbolic operations: red blood/semblance; body/value-invested envelope; matter/medium of exchange; (re)productive nature/fabricated femininity" (188). The gothic novel titillates the reader with images of the first set of terms: red blood, body, matter, reproductive nature. The suggestion of corporeality frequently appears at the moments of greatest semantic indeterminacy: beside books "written in unknown characters" lie instruments of torture (*Italian*, 102). Often, however, especially in Radcliffe's novels, the effort to turn the narrative to something palpable fails or is simply cut short – the rape of the heroine never actually occurs, the corpse turns out to be a wax effigy. Rather than find the body she expects, Ellena at one point "discovered what *seemed* a dreadful *hieroglyphic*, a mattrass of straw, in which she *thought* she beheld the death-bed of the miserable recluse; nay more, that the impression it still retained, was that which her *form* had left there" (*Italian*, 140, my emphasis) – just another elusive sign, a form from which the body has been evacuated. Neither personalities nor bodies, neither the useful nor the natural, will stabilize the gothic world of relations gone wild.

Irigaray's comment on the perversion of the commodity serves as an interesting gloss on the issue of the role of the reader in this world of perverse relations:

Man endows the commodities he produces with a narcissism that blurs the seriousness of utility, of use. Desire, as soon as there is exchange, "perverts" need. But that perversion will be attributed to commodities and to their alleged relations. Whereas they can have no relationships except from the perspective of speculating third parties.[41]

Unfortunately for the characters of the gothic, while the third thing that serves to direct the relations between commodities does exist, even if unacknowledged (human agents), the third thing that would direct the relations of people-as-commodities does not exist, at least not within the world of the novel. In that world, there is no privileged "speculating third party"; the common impulse to voyeurism and the fascination with spectacle and speculation generally only lead to a dangerous enthrallment, as Day points out (24). Readers of the novel, on the other hand, are granted a special pleasure: they are presented with mysterious relations about which they can make certain judgments because they know the mystery will be resolved along conventional lines. The novel thus both plays out a problem (identity-as-exchange value), thereby interesting readers, *and* it offers readers a privileged vantage from which to view the problem, so that the issue of agency finally seems, if vexed, at least manageable.

IV

Of course, my gesture toward Irigaray foregrounds the question of the relation of women to the gothic mode of characterization. It is clear, first of all, that the association of women and the gothic is an overdetermined one, and one that reflects more than the simple fact that many women wrote and read gothic novels. The gothic is, truly, the world of "commodities among themselves," differing from Irigaray's vision in that *all* people represent such commodities, and this association of character with commodity generates a parallel association with the feminine. It is perfectly fitting that these texts often focus on women, and especially young, unmarried ones: "*The virginal woman...is pure exchange value.* She is nothing but the possibility, the place, the sign of relations among men. In and of herself, she does not exist: she is a simple envelope veiling what is really at stake in social exchange."[42]

In the gothic, of course, veiling appears literally and frequently and is often a sign of the traffic in women; Ellena, for instance, must choose in *The Italian* between taking the veil (becoming a nun) and wearing the marriage veil. That it so happens that Ellena is forced to make this choice to satisfy a mother superior and her lover's mother shows, however, that in the gothic it is not simply masculine power that women serve to support and veil. No character, male or female, effectively directs the action in the gothic. It is significant that, as Eve Sedgwick notes, in the gothic novel "always for women, and very often for men, life begins with a blank. The mother, if known, has disappeared temporarily, and an aunt may substitute. The women's names suggest the blank, the white, the innocent, and the pristine: Blanche (who lives in Chateau-le-Blanc), Virginia, Agnes, Ellena Ros*alba*, Emily St. *Aube*rt, even Signora Bianchi" (261). Although female characters in the gothic may constitute a blank page, the male characters are in no position to use them as the site of symbolic or practical operations that would construct men as deeply meaningful subjects.[43] If the practical sign of the effective use of women for the support of the social and symbolic order is the successful exchange of women,[44] it comes as little surprise that the threat of incest should be such a popular gothic theme.

Gothic characters are linked with the feminine not just in their association with exchange, but also in their superficiality and "theatricality." Naomi Schor has shown that the "normative aesthetics of neo-classicism" linked the feminine and the superficial, an association supported in part by the assumption that women have a special interest in personal ornamentation and display – an interest, that is, in their consumption by others.[45] This association is predicated, Schor suggests, on the argument that women have to compensate for an essential lack and a lack of essence.[46] For Radcliffe calculated self-representation is indeed preeminently the virgin's task: Ellena "was...embarrassed to observe, in the manners of young people residing in a convent, an absence of that decorum, which includes beneath its modest shade every grace that ought to adorn the female character, like the veil which gives dignity to their air and softness to their features" (*Italian*, 94). But in the gothic all characterization takes on the qualities of mere show, from the wild gesticulations of the characters in *The Castle of Otranto* to the pretense of religiosity that makes the goal throughout *The Italian* the unmasking of father Schedoni (103).

We see then that Irigaray's universalizing paradigm for gender relations is played out in a rather unusual way at this moment in cultural history: the early gothic novel dramatizes a period in the development of capitalist relations in which all persons, whether men or women, could be characterized by a bifurcation of identity, with the accent on its ghostly and relational aspect. This is not to say that a masculinist or patriarchal social order is not still in place, both within the gothic and in the culture that produced it, but the fact that in the gothic the "phallic function" is so easily and frequently dislodged from the biologically male is one sign that economic relations have, at least to an extent, unsettled traditional gender ideologies.

The longstanding critical dismissal of the gothic, then, arose not simply because it is inherently inartistic *or* because it was often written and read by women. The peculiar "femininity" of the gothic arises in part as the result of the intersection of gender and economic paradigms; the gothic expresses a concern with relations, extrinsic signs, and indeterminate value – qualities associated with the feminine but also associated with an aspect of market relations (exchange value unconnected to utility) that the capitalist class has continually to repress. Traditional complaints about the gothic, although usually presented as strictly aesthetic complaints, often reflect impatience with its emphasis on relational value and betray an unconscious recognition of its palpably "bourgeois" character. One fears that the book is as superficial as its characters appear to be, and suspects that a put-on, a show, is being foisted not just on the characters but also on oneself. The gothic emphasis on form makes the novel itself appear to represent nothing more than an arbitrary and hollow exchange value, and older criticism of the gothic constantly reiterates the disjunction between its considerable commercial success (high exchange value) and its "real" worth (low use value). The gothic, it is said, offers us only "trappings," "décor," "stage-sets," and "machinery." These terms bring to mind associations that threaten the self-conception of the capitalist class and they imply some recognition on the critic's part that the gothic lays out the maneuvers and characteristics of that class a bit too clearly. Trappings and décor remind us of the association of both women and the upwardly mobile with ornamentation in excess. Stage-sets bring to mind the pervasive sense of the theatricality of social relations that Agnew argues is characteristic of life in a capitalist economy. This theatricality is elevated to a structural feature, a quality of the setting, in the gothic. And machinery suggests the "problem" of industrialization, of dehumanized and inorganic modes of production that create breaches that literature since the Romantic period has been expected to heal. The gothic novel's formal features display too openly the way the capitalist class as a whole is an upstart class whose hegemony is not, in fact, grounded in utility, sincerity, and nature.

Although Radcliffe's novels, for instance, are resolved by the discovery of a correspondence between relational and intrinsic value – Ellena is not only virtuous herself but so were her parents, and they were of a reasonably high class as well – such discovery generally tends to be "mechanically" tossed in and anti-climactic. One thinks here of Lukács's analysis of the tendency of bourgeois thought towards an empty formalism; in such a system, it is the task of art to restore a sense of wholeness and depth,[47] but Radcliffean gothic simply disturbs us with its hollow forms. Many canonical Romantic works respond to the bifurcation of identity by dismissing relational identity and forging images of depth, images that are figures for intrinsic identity. This inwardness thus represents a literally more profound resistance to commodification. But for that very reason, the gothic lends itself to a more thorough analysis of certain social pressures than much of the lyric poetry that dominates our sense of the literary period – a poetry that, for all its concern with social problems and reform, often obscures the issue of relational power with its emphasis on personality. Even the "trappings" of the gothic can be put to rhetorical and analytical use, particularly in discussions relating to the period, from Norbert Elias's description of late eighteenth-century courtly manners as a "ghostly *perpetuum mobile*"[48] to Marx's description of the "enchanted, perverted, topsy-turvy world, in which Monsieur le Capital and Madame la Terre do their ghost-walking as social characters and at the same time directly as mere things."[49] We post-Romantics have ourselves adopted the depth model as a sort of protection against the effects of capitalism, and this gives rise to our blindness to the special insights of the gothic. The early gothic novel is not a *Bildungsroman* gone awry; it traces problems in the perception or "consumption" of other people rather than the work involved in personal growth.

Robert Kiely's comment on the novels of the Romantic period – "they are not all bad; indeed, some are very good. But in nearly every case one has a sense of unresolved struggle, of intelligence and energy at odds" – is on the mark in more ways than he may have intended.[50] Kiely opens his study of the gothic by noting that "the English romantic novel is, in some ways, an embarrassing subject" (1). But if the Romantic novel is an embarrassing subject, it is so at least in part because it presents an embarrassing "subject" – a subject who is little more than a "mercurial exchange value or 'bubble,'"[51] a hollow puppet, a woman, a commodity, a coin.

CHAPTER 3

From "race" to "place" in "The Prisoner of Chillon"

Flatness of character can, as we saw in the previous chapter, signal the ascendance of commercial categories for conceptualizing identity and value. But this flatness can take on other meanings and implications when it appears in a different context: that of the challenge posed by the French Revolution – and the English radical thought it stimulated – to hierarchical systems of classification. In this chapter I argue that one can trace, in a variety of discourses of the Romantic era, a model of identity that facilitated the transformation of the genealogy- and rank-based system of identity to the individualist system – while being different from both. This model is the result of a shift from the vertical axis of the hierarchical genealogical system to the horizontal axis of a system wherein identity is based on context. Like the commercial system of classification at work in the gothic novel, this conception of identity accentuates the superficiality of being. But whereas superficiality in the gothic signals the determination of identity in terms of an external evaluative grid, the superficiality of context-based identity signals the determination of identity in terms of external physical influences. And while Romantic inwardness functions as a type of resistance to the ghostly and formal nature of gothic character, we will see that it can also be used to qualify the potentially thoroughly levelling effects of context-based identity.

When the topic of the relation of identity to context is raised, Romanticists typically think first of a writer like Godwin and then of issues such as Hartleyan associationism, materialism, and Lockean views of the mind. The tendency, in short, is to turn to psychology, and a psychology that appears, moreover, to be tied to a belief in individualism and the importance of self-consciousness. In this chapter we will begin by taking a brief look at Godwin's *Enquiry Concerning Political Justice*, in which anti-essentialism and contextualism are linked to individualism; but rather than privilege the association of identity with individualism, we will then turn back to Revolutionary France, and to a realm where the shift from hierarchical to contextual notions of identity is perhaps most visible: biology, where taxonomic schemes had long been of central importance. It is with these physiological texts in mind that we will examine Byron's "The Prisoner of Chillon" – not because the poem reflects a knowledge of the physiology *per se*, but because the physiology brings to the fore aspects of the shift from hierarchy to context that are latent even in Godwin's writing but that we might easily overlook. Issues of essentialism and localism, interaction with the environment, and the passive nature of identity-formation play a central role in these physiological works, and, just as important for our purposes, they are separable from issues of individualist psychology. Against the background of these physiological texts we will see that in "The Prisoner of Chillon" and the sonnet on Chillon three distinct notions of identity – genealogical, contextual, and individualist – are forcefully dramatized and differentiated.

I

In their accounts of individual development and social life, French Revolutionary thinkers like Condorcet emphasized the shaping effect of society on human character as a first step toward demonstrating the possibility and necessity of social change. The French were of course not alone in arguing against essentialist accounts of character and in favor of contextualist ones. At the end of the eighteenth century English radicals challenged the naturalness of hereditary distinctions of rank by offering powerful reformulations of the Lockean thesis that the character of the mind was less a matter of innate tendency than acquired habit. This idea functions as a fundamental premise in one of the most influential political treatises of the age: Godwin's *Enquiry Concerning Political Justice*. In the first book of *Political Justice*, where Godwin scrupulously outlines the first principles of his philosophy, he argues that "the actions and dispositions of mankind are the offspring of circumstances and events, and not of any original determination that they bring into the world."[1] Godwin is insistent upon the non-existence of innate character attributes: "the actions and dispositions of men are not the offspring of any original bias that they bring into the world in favour of one sentiment or character rather than another, but flow entirely from the operation of circumstances and events acting upon a faculty of receiving sensible impressions" (98). Godwin argues that identity has less to do with the externalization of interior and innate tendencies than with passive responses and interactions, and he reiterates this belief forcefully and unambiguously, especially in his first edition of *Political Justice*.[2] He considers even the physical characteristics with which one is born as insignificant: "In fine, it is impression that makes the man, and, compared with the empire of impression, the mere differences of animal structure are inexpressibly unimportant and powerless" (107).

For Godwin, not only is identity formed by external influences, but "internal" and "external" never become powerfully opposed categories. A disjunction between internal and external character is almost impossible to achieve, even when desired – for, as Godwin continually affirms, "everything in the universe is linked and united together" (108). In fact, sincerity is critically important in his philosophy because not only one's experiences but also one's actions immediately determine one's *being* – "the link which binds together the inward and the outward man is indissoluble" (315). At the same time that he de-essentializes persons by binding them to the world that surrounds them, he also de-essentializes them by treating them as no more than an aggregate of properties. He habitually treats traditionally "in-dividual" units as a collection, including the "individual" itself: he refers to the concept of virtue, for instance, as an aggregate of ideas and judgments (100), and describes personal identity as no more than a linked collection of thoughts, themselves springing from external circumstances.

As we saw with Hume, then, virtue and character are treated as aggregates of qualities. Hume's concern was to sum up, as in an inventory, the value of such qualities, and finally to ascribe their total worth to their possessor. For Godwin, however, such qualities always remain manifestations of external influence, and while they do define their possessor's value (as in the famous anecdote of Fénelon and his valet), the possessor is so entirely their object, so without a will of his own, that he could be said to be (in almost gothic fashion) *possessed by them*. And just as character is deterministically acquired from without, it is displayed on the surface; as Godwin puts it: "What is born into the world is an unfinished sketch, without character or decisive feature impressed upon it. In the sequel there is a correspondence between the physiognomy and the intellectual and moral qualities of the mind" (105). Character, as flat as paper, awaits a stroke or impression from without, and in Godwin's optimistic view of the utopian potential of

acquired identity, there is no gothic disjunction between a superficial
and an "essential" self.

These acquired and disparate qualities, moreover, aren't even stable
over time, as Godwin points out: "ideas are to the mind nearly what
atoms are to the body. The whole mass is in a perpetual flux; nothing is
stable and permanent; after the lapse of a given period not a single
particle probably remains the same. Who knows not that in the course
of a human life the character of the individual frequently undergoes
two or three revolutions of its fundamental stamina?" (104). As the
language here suggests, Godwin's anti-essentialism is intimately tied to
his belief in fundamental and quietly revolutionary change.

Godwin's conception of what we would call genetics also reflects his
resistance to the idea of innate or hereditary character, and makes the
social implications of his principles quite explicit. He argues against
those who believe instincts "to be original, a separate endowment
annexed to our being" (101); no language of hereditary endowments is
to be trusted. The anti-aristocratic import of his thinking on these
matters is at times quite obvious: "A generous blood, a gallant and
fearless spirit is by no means propagated from father to son" (107). In a
rhetoric reminiscent of Anna Barbauld's poem to an unborn baby,
Godwin asks "How long has the jargon imposed upon the world which
would persuade us that in instructing a man you do not add to, but
unfold his stores?" (109, my emphasis). In fact, Godwin speaks quite
forthrightly against a preformationist conception of development:
"Who is there in the present state of scientifical improvement that will
believe that this vast chain of perceptions and notions is something that
we bring into the world with us, a mystical magazine, shut up in the
human embryo, whose treasures are to be gradually unfolded as
circumstances shall require?" (100–101). But unlike the true epigenesist,
Godwin does not attribute character to mysterious "supra-physical"
inner impulses; it is external impressions that form character. Those
traits with which a baby is born Godwin attributes to the effect of pre-
natal external impressions on the mother, although he adds that these
early characteristics are relatively insignificant in the formation of
identity (108).[3]

In *Political Justice*, then, we see how a context-based model of identity
can be used to displace a more essentialist and hierarchical one. But
Godwin's emphasis on the importance of context over heredity is
finally subordinated to the end of convincing the reader of the
importance of reflection, self-consciousness, and individualism. The

premise that the characters of men and women are the result of external influence serves to neutralize and level out the hierarchical model of innate, genealogy-based rank. But as *Political Justice* proceeds an emphasis on private mental activity serves as the basis for a new hierarchy, a meritocracy founded on one's powers of independent and even oppositional reflection. The passive/contextual model of personal development thus ultimately serves to clear a space for a model of character as formed by active individualist thought: "the most desirable state of mankind is that which maintains general security, with the smallest incroachment upon individual independence" (76). The latter model having formed the basis for the canonical Romantic notion of character, it is easy to overlook or underestimate the importance of the former. In order then to bring it vividly before our eyes, we turn next to French Revolutionary texts that emphasize not only contextual over hierarchical classification, but also the material world of the body over the mental domain of self-consciousness and individualism.

II

As Godwin's recourse to biological language to describe the fluctuating nature of mind shows, psychology was not the only domain to feel the influence of anti-essentialist arguments. Indeed, it is in the biological sciences – where, during the eighteenth century, so much energy had been devoted to the task of hierarchical classification – that broad shifts in methods of classification are perhaps most visible. Innovations in human pathology and physiology in particular exemplify not only changes in methods of classification but also the impact of those changes on the understanding of personal identity.

The political Revolution in France, considered by many to have ushered in the world of modern European politics,[4] was in many respects paralleled by a medical revolution that is similarly considered to have marked the beginnings of modern medicine. In his *History of Medicine*, Fielding Garrison associates the nineteenth century with "The beginnings of the organized advancement of science"[5] and opens his discussion of it by attributing the changes it brought to "the great industrial or social-democratic movement of civilized mankind, which, following close upon the political revolutions in America and France, intensified the feeling for intellectual and moral liberty."[6] In fact, this "feeling for liberty" could be argued to have taken very specific forms: writings of the leaders of the clinical schools of the period show in their treatment of people and even data a notion of identification analogous to that of Godwin. The liberation of thought, like the liberation of persons, involved the breakdown of static hierarchical systems of classification in favor of more contingent contextual ones. As Erwin Ackernecht simplistically but tellingly remarks: "Medicine has lost interest in systematics [systematic classification] to the same extent that she has acquired actual knowledge."[7] The doubly-revolutionary character of the medicine of the period is visible even in the writings of scientists and practitioners who did not explicitly associate their work with the Revolutionary project.

The identification of symptoms and diseases within the science of pathology could serve as a case in point. The nosological method that dominated eighteenth-century medicine was a taxonomic one based on resemblances. As Foucault describes it, "It is a space in which analogies define essences. The pictures resemble things, but they also resemble one another. The *distance* that separates one disease from another can be measured only by the *degree* of their *resemblance*."[8] The classification of diseases follows the same guidelines as the classification of species generally:

The supreme Being is not subjected to less certain laws in producing diseases or in maturing morbific humours, than in growing plants and animals...He who observes attentively the order, the time, the hour at which the attack of quart fever begins, the phenomena of shivering, of heat, in a word all the symptoms proper to it, will have as many reasons to believe that this disease is a species as he has to believe that a plant constitutes a species because it grows, flowers, and dies always in the same way.[9]

This system of classification is static and structurally complete, any "new" disease simply finding its proper place within the existing framework. The doctor, as Foucault puts it, "communicate[s] with the ontological order – which organizes from the inside, prior to all manifestation – the world of disease" (7). Foucault continues:

"Never treat a disease without first being sure of its species," said Gilibert [1]. From the *Nosologie* of Sauvages (1761) to the *Nosographie* of Pinel (1798), the classificatory rule dominates medical theory and practice...Before it is removed from the density of the body, disease is given an organization, hierarchized into families, genera, and species...Just as the genealogical tree, at a lower level than the comparison that it involves and all its imaginary themes, presupposes a space in which kinship is formalizable, the nosological picture involves a figure of the diseases that is...no[t] its visible trajectory in the human body. (4)

But French clinical medicine of the Revolutionary period began to define disease in terms of its *"seat* in an organism" rather than its "place in a *family"* (10, my emphasis), thereby enacting a shift analogous to the one Godwin aims at in the social realm. A genealogical system was abandoned and the context or location of morbid symptoms became primary in the determination of the identity of a disease. The essences of diseases, like their ultimate causes, ceased to be major concerns; pathologists now assumed that disease could only be known in its local manifestations.

One of the most influential pathologists of the end of the century, whose writings were quickly translated and made available in Britain, is the "creator of descriptive anatomy,"[10] Marie-François-Xavier Bichat. Bichat is perhaps best known for his *Anatomie générale*, a work that defined the seat of disease as the twenty-one types of membrane that, according to him, make up the body; he argued that lesions take on different meanings in the context of different tissues. As L. S. Jacyna remarks, Bichat offered a "topographical" account of tissues: "His was essentially a *spatial* arrangement of animal tissues, which showed little regard for how these structures emerged through time."[11]

But context became significant in the determination of health and disease not only at the micro-level of identifying diseases but also at the macro-level of relating a person's health to his or her environment. As part of the Revolutionary project it was determined that "a medical topography of each department should be drawn up, 'with detailed observations concerning the region, housing, people, principal interests, dress, atmospheric constitution, produce of the ground,'"[12] and so on. On a variety of levels, then, context was understood to be constitutive of one's being rather than an accidental circumstance surrounding it.[13]

These interests represent the epitome of trends initiated in the eighteenth century,[14] many of which also influenced writers like Godwin. French sensationalists of the turn of the century traced their ideas back to Condillac, who, in turn, owed much to Locke. Condillac had subordinated Lockean reflection to sensation, thereby eliminating any need for a pool of innate ideas.[15] The French ideologues who worked in this tradition sought to establish a "science of man" that would incorporate psychology with physiology and the study of society.[16] Works like physiologist/reformer Jean-Georges Cabanis's *Rapports du physique et du moral de l'homme* of 1805 are considered founding texts of psychosomatic medicine.[17] Moreover, as Elizabeth Haigh puts it: "Cabanis' notions of sensationalism and psychology had important social implications. As long as one assumes that all human beings receive the same impressions from the external world through sensory organs which behave in a consistent way, one may believe in the possibility of achieving human equality."[18]

Bichat, whom we discussed earlier, is often classed as an ideologue and was much influenced by the work of Cabanis. A man of many talents, he not only did pioneering work in pathology but was a prominent physiologist as well. In his manuscript *Discourse on the Study of Physiology*, under the heading "Moral Sciences," Bichat writes:

> At first glance it seems that physiology, which is entirely occupied with matter, cannot be connected with the intellectual sciences. However I observe that there is as much of a relationship with them as there is with the physical sciences, and even more...Life must be divided into two: *exterior life* and *interior life*. It is only the order of the exterior life – namely sensation and perception – which is connected with metaphysics...Since Locke and Condillac found the source of our ideas in the senses, it has become essential to understand these senses; it is necessary, in the theory of the brain, to understand the intimate senses: imagination, memory – all these questions are shared equally by the metaphysician and the physiologist. Advantages of the *physiologist-metaphysician*: he not only understands the senses, but he also knows that their faculty of receiving impressions varies and he understands the laws of sensibility [*sic*] ...[19]

We see here not only the important role physiology was to play in the study of metaphysics, psychology, society, and morality, but also the special emphasis on the significance of the "exterior life," a point to which we will return later.

Bichat's *Physiological Researches on Life and Death* (*Recherches physiologiques sur la vie et la mort*, 1800) nicely illustrates the replacement of essentialist and hierarchical models for understanding identities by more contingent localist ones, and shows the ways that this change influenced not only the identification of diseases but also the identification of whole organisms, including persons. For Bichat, the essence of life itself is of no moment since it is not susceptible to scientific determination: "This principle is that of life; unknown in its nature, it can be only appreciated by its phenomena: an habitual alternation of action and reaction between exterior bodies, and the living body."[20] Life, like other concepts, is only visible in the form of a relationship, as in Bichat's notorious dictum that "Life consists in the sum of the functions, by which death is resisted" (10). This emphasis on relationship, and the willingness to define traditionally unified concepts or objects in terms of an aggregate (such as we saw with Godwin), is manifested in Bichat's work on every level. We see the latter tendency at work not only in his displacement of medical interest from entire organs on to the tissues that comprised them, but also in his description of animal life generally. Bichat describes the externally oriented part of the animal as comprised of two lives, a right and a left: "the animal life is as it were double. . .its phenomena performed as they are at the same time on the two sides of the body. . .there is a life to the right, a life to the left" (22). In addition, while plants have only an organic or interior life, animals are comprised of an organic life which is "clothed" with organs designed for interaction with the world:

[the vegetable or organic life] will be seen existing only within itself, having with what surrounds it the relations only of nutrition. . .The other [animal life] will be observed combining with this interior life, which in the highest degree it enjoys, an exterior life by which it acquires a very numerous series of relations with all surrounding bodies, a life, which couples it to the existence of every other being. . .Thus it might be said, that the vegetable is only the sketch, or rather the ground-work of the animal; that for the formation of the latter, it has only been requisite to clothe ["revêtir"] the former with an apparatus of external organs, by which it might be connected with external objects. (12–13)

Not only is the animal life taken to be merely the result of an addition to vegetable life, but its higher status is understood to arise from its capacity to relate to external objects. In fact, Bichat's model of life could be argued to invert what we take to be standard Romantic assumptions as well as current ones: where we might tend to consider animal life as marked by rich interiority, Bichat locates the special qualities of the animal solely in its capacity for rich exteriority – as he puts it, it "lives externally" ("il existe hors de lui").[21] He describes the animal organs, moreover, as a *clothing* over the organic life, thereby associating animal life with superficiality.

Animal and especially human life thus comes to be defined in terms of a relation to the environment rather than an internal essence. And it is perhaps not surprising that Bichat uses an optimistic and Revolutionary language to describe the interrelations that constitute life. The relationships of the various "lives" that comprise the animal life itself, for instance, are characterized by equality and harmony. The most noticeable feature of the animal life is its symmetry: "The organs of the animal life are symmetrical, those of the organic life irregular in their conformation. . .in man [this symmetry] is exactly traced, as well as in all the genera which are nearest to him in perfection" (18). For Bichat, the animal life is therefore one of harmonious relationships: "Harmony is to the functions of the organs, what symmetry is to their conformation; it supposes a perfect *equality* of force and action, between their similar parts...harmony is the character of the animal, discordance that of the organic functions" (25, my emphasis).

Similarly, involvement with the external world is described almost entirely in terms of happy correspondence: "In general there exists between the two orders [the action of an external body and the reaction of the animal] a rigorous proportion" (15). For Bichat the brain serves as a relay center that initiates the proper form of reaction: "In the animal life, the first order is established from the exterior of the body, towards the brain; the second from the brain towards the organs of locomotion and the voice" (15). It is worth noting that in *Political Justice* Godwin describes the workings of the mind in very similar terms: "These vibrations, having begun upon the surface of the body, are conveyed to the brain; and, in a manner that is equally the result of construction, produce a second set of vibrations beginning in the brain, and conveyed to the different organs or members of the body" (361). The brain thus becomes not the origin of action but simply one agent in a sequence of actions determined by the outside world. As Bichat writes:

> The external senses are the natural excitants of the brain. The functions of the brain *succeed to theirs*, and this organ would but languish, were it not to *find in them the principle of its activity*. From sensation follow *perception, memory and imagination; from these the judgment*. Now it is easy to prove, that these different functions, commonly known by the name of the internal senses, are governed in their actions by the same laws, which influence the external senses; and that like them, they approach the nearer to perfection in proportion to the degree of *harmony* existing in the symmetrical parts, in which they have their *seat*. (30, my emphasis)

The brain, which, like the heart, is the center of personhood for canonical Romantic subjectivity, functions here not as a solid center but simply as the site of circulation and exchange: "The sanguiferous system...is a middle system, the centre of the organic life, as the brain is the centre of the animal life" (16). As in his discussion of the equality and harmony of parts, one discerns in Bichat's language and physiological models Revolutionary images and assumptions. The middle systems, like the middle ranks or classes, are associated with exchange, but are for that reason considered all the more important.

Just as Godwin argues that mind and body are in "perpetual flux," so for Bichat the centrality of exchange makes identity itself literally and perpetually revolutionary:

A double movement is also exercised in the organic life; the one composes, the other decomposes the animal. Such is the mode of existence in the living body, that what it was at one time it ceases to be at another...The molecules of its nutrition by turns absorbed and rejected, from the animal pass to the plant, from the plant to inorganic matter, return to the animal, and so proceed in an endless revolution. (15–16)[22]

In similar fashion, Bichat refers to the soul as the center of revolutions in affect, revolutions that nevertheless turn out to be the involuntary result of external forces:

the centre of these revolutions of pleasure, of pain, and of indifference, is by no means seated in the organs, which receive or transmit the sensation, but in the soul. The affections of the eye, of the tongue, and the ear, are at all times the same from the same objects, but to these affections at different times, we attach a variety of sentiments...the action of the mind in each several sentiment of pain or pleasure, which has been the effect of a sensation, consists in a comparison between this sensation, and that by which it has been preceded, a comparison, which is not the result of reflection, but the involuntary effect of the first impression of the object. (49)

Bichat later self-consciously comments that "Indeed were I to regard the laws of our material organization only, I might almost say, that constancy is but one of the happy dreams of the poet, and that the sex to which we at present bend, would possess but a very weak hold upon our attentions were their charms too uniform...But here let us forbear to insist upon the principles of physiology, where they tend to the destruction of those of morality" (50). Life is response to environmental change, and so thrives on it. But the potentially destabilizing consequences of that fact for social life are noticeable even to Bichat himself.

In a provocative article on the relational structures of Bichat's physiology John Pickstone draws analogies between Bichat's work, most of which was done under the Directory (1795–1799), and the bourgeois bureaucracy that characterized the government of those years. For Pickstone, Bichat's understanding of the interaction of different parts of the body relies neither on a highly centralized model of vitality and function (such as might suggest the centralization of the Terror years) nor on a model of extreme local autonomy (such as had characterized the early phase of Revolutionary social organization but which no longer seemed viable).[23] As Pickstone argues, "what we may call the professional-bureaucratic ideal was of critical importance in Directory France as an alternative to absolutism, democracy and liberalism."[24] Bichat provides an image of life as the sum of constitutive interactions. Like Godwin, he challenges essentialism through an emphasis on context, but he does so without promoting liberalism or individualism (it is telling that Saint-Simon, who would have consider- ed "*individualisme*" a pejorative term, "leaned...heavily on Bichat's work").[25] Here, then, we see that an emphasis on interaction and context can challenge static hierarchical forms of classification without necessarily being allied to liberal and individualist notions of identity.[26]

III

One of the most influential medical men of the Napoleonic era (one of Napoleon's army surgeons, in fact), F. J. V. Broussais carries the logic of Bichat's assumptions one step further. As he says in his *Treatise on Physiology Applied to Pathology*, "Of all the authors on physiology, Bichat, in our opinion, is the only one who viewed this science in the most correct light."[27] He finds Bichat's only real fault to be that he does not speak *enough* of the relation of the animal to the organic life: "From this arose the unconquerable difficulties encountered by the ingenious Bichat, in his attempts to draw a satisfactory line of demarcation, between the functions of relation, which he denominates *animal life*, and those of nutrition, which he calls *organic life*" (36).[28] In his *Principles of Physiological Medicine*, Broussais describes his own physiology-based pathology as "*a method of observation*" rather than an "*a priori*" system,[29] and, as is so typical of members of the French clinical school, he disavows traditional nosological systems in favor of a localistic method of identification: "These two propositions also exclude...systems of classification founded upon groups of symptoms without reference to the diseased organs. It is evident, that essential diseases, whose seat is not indicated...cannot enter into the doctrine" (27). As Ackernecht puts it, "through Broussais essentialism was buried, and localism was made the law...The artificial creation of disease units, so dear to the systematists, was condemned as 'ontology'" (148–150).

Broussais's method is, like Bichat's, radical not only in its consistent anti-essentialism but also in its emphasis on relational identity:

The mere attention to the study of the organs in relation with their modifiers, will always constitute, for physiologists, a fruitful and inexhaustible source of new truths; from this then we intend to draw...Functions have been made too independent of those modifying agents by which they are maintained; owing to which...medical physiology has not been created.[30]

The very union of pathology and physiology that Broussais hopes to realize relies on a notion of the dynamic relation between health and disease on the one hand and the organism and its environment on the other. For Broussais, medical practitioners can no longer afford to describe health and disease as essentially different states. Any state of being must be understood in terms of those external forces that influence it.

Broussais's treatment of the relation of the individual animal to the external world in his *A Treatise on Physiology* is reminiscent of Bichat's work. Discussion of the skin, for instance, emphasizes not its function as a protective barrier between a person and the outside world but its permeability: "the fixed animal matter is perforated on its external surfaces, and on such of its internal surfaces as are in relation with external bodies, by innumerable openings through which these bodies penetrate" (13). The section on vital powers and vital laws makes it clear that vitality itself depends on relations with external objects: "The tissues are endowed with only one apparent property, which manifests itself by the condensation of the animal matter, at the moment this latter is placed in relation with an external body...Physiologists have called it *contractility*" (17). The book turns early on to the "History of the functions of relation," arguing that "the phenomena of relation are far from being limited to the tissues, in which their domain has been placed by authors..." (35) and that "All the acts of vitality are united and linked together in the economy" (35–36). The emphasis on relations is continual, insistent, and primary. Broussais states that "I shall, therefore, commence the history of our functions by noticing the relations which connect us with external bodies; I shall trace those bodies as they approach and penetrate within us; and study the influences they exercise on our organs" (36). Similarly, he argues that there is "an uninterrupted chain of relations existing between us and external bodies" (41), and refers to the brain as the "centre of relation" (37).

But while in many respects Broussais's work carries Bichat's work out to its logical conclusions, it also introduces into clinical medicine a new and relatively conservative element. Broussais's comments on his method mark him as a scientist of the Napoleonic era: "Assuredly it will not corrupt the mind of any one: it will neither make of those who will contemplate it, systematists nor enthusiasts; it will only render them more circumspect...."[31] Considered "a prominent liberal,"[32] his physiology is nevertheless designed to promote rationality safely without encouraging the kind of zeal for the rational that for so many thinkers characterized the early stages of the Revolution. Broussais's is a method informed by modified versions of Revolutionary principles. Facts themselves, for instance, are treated, although not quite like citizens, not like monarchical subjects either: "The physiological method is entirely founded on this eclectism [of facts] – it every where seeks facts to subject them to strict examination and to determine what inductions can be drawn from them; and it does not execute this task in an insidious manner; it proceeds without mystery, without prejudice, without concealment, so that all those who love the marvellous and what is illusory will immediately abandon it."[33] No *lettres de cachet* will be brought against these facts, and the observer's eclectism guarantees that all manner of facts will be taken into account and, at least initially, accorded equal weight.

Moreover, although he shares Bichat's interest in relational identity, Broussais introduces a new notion to his predecessor's scheme that is significant for our purposes and reminiscent of the depth model of subjectivity: he speaks of a self that can stand aloof from relations. He argues that man is set apart from other creatures not only by his "peculiar form" and "multiplied relations" but also "by the power of reflection, or the faculty of perceiving his own relations, of observing himself whilst he observes every thing else, and of being impelled to this by a pleasure which appears to be independent of the gratification, at least immediate, of his physical wants...."[34] Like Bichat, Broussais argues that man is designed for harmonious interrelations, but he tends more than Bichat to make man the center and focus of that harmony rather than simply a lucky participant in it: "...it is absolutely necessary that he should be endowed with organs destined to correspond with [external bodies]; hence the cause of these relations, as well as the means of exercising them, are found within himself" (36–37). In this emphasis on what man brings to his environment Broussais comes closer to the canonized Romantic conception of man; he comes closer still when he describes his notion of selfhood. As he argues in proposition 33 in his *Principles of Physiological Medicine*, "The centre of relation by the influence of the viscera, excites with or without the concurrence of the will, with or without the consciousness of *self*, (*moi*,) movements in the locomotive apparatus" (18). The self or will is discontinuous with the brain that serves as the center of relation, and thus not only stands independent of the relations that Broussais has largely focused on but in fact is defined and made visible by that independence.

The difference between Broussais's conception of childish activity and Bichat's conception of it nicely symptomatizes Broussais's considerably stronger sense of the existence of a distinct selfhood. For Bichat, in *Physiological Researches*, the energy of childhood is a sign of excessive responsiveness and thus of life:

There is a superabundance of life in the child: In the child, the reaction of the system is superior to the action, which is made upon it from without. In the adult, action and reaction are on a balance; the turgescence of life is gone. In the old man, the reaction of the inward principle is lessened, the action from without remaining unaltered; it is then that life languishes, and insensibly advances towards its natural term, which ensues when all proportion ceases. (11)

Inwardness, a concept that does not often appear in Bichat's writing at all, here signifies little more than a capacity for response. For Broussais on the other hand, the energy of the child is a sign not of an excess of life, but of a defect of the principle of self: "The child continues always to allow no interval to exist between the perception of his want and the execution of those acts proper to gratify it, until consciousness (*moi*) is developed and sufficiently exercised in him. . ."[35] The principle of self is here defined precisely as the difference or space between action and reaction, desire and fulfillment.

Interestingly enough, though, Broussais describes the non-coincidence of desire and the object of its fulfillment as not only unpleasant, but distinctly unsettling:

The *wants*. . .are perceived, in man, by the centre of relation; but if the external bodies by which they are to be gratified are not in a state of correspondence with the external surface, and if the centre of perception is not as yet apprized of them, there results from these wants nothing but a vague sensation of uneasiness, difficult to define, but which compels us to agitate ourselves without any evident motive. . .We may moreover place on the same line, the uneasiness, the sighs, and emotions of young pubescents who have been brought up in entire ignorance of, and separated from, the objects capable of gratifying their first desires.[36]

Non-satisfaction, when not chosen, gives rise not to an adult sense of self but to an adolescent sense of unease. Something of Bichat's optimism and confidence has been lost in this move toward a model of identity wherein the self is no longer defined by its harmonious and constitutive relation to the outside world. It is now precisely the disjunction between desire and fulfillment, a negative relation to the outside world, that constitutes the subject. We have now moved toward a sense of the self which has much in common with canonized Romantic subjectivity.

IV

One can, then, discern in these various turn-of-the-century discourses three distinct ways of understanding personal identification. Godwin, Bichat, and Broussais all argue against essentialist and hierarchical modes of identification and classification. In Broussais's case and certainly in Godwin's, they also move toward a notion of a self-generated identity that in many respects has to construct itself in opposition to its surroundings. It is on the shift from the first to the second of these models that studies in the history of subjectivity have so often focused: the movement from a society of genealogical ranks or orders to an individualist liberal society. But between these ideologies stands a model of contextual identification that facilitates the logical and historical transition from a traditional to a modern notion of identity.

The radical emphasis on equality and the displacement of essentialist taxonomic systems by contextual systems of identification both have analogs in British literary Romanticism. The subjects and poet-figures of British Romantic poetry are often described as being the product of their environment and especially of the influence of nature in its particular local forms – the nature of the Lake District, for example. *The Prelude*, of course, provides ample evidence of Wordsworth's connection of personality and place. And in that natural setting "The mind of man is fashioned and built up / Even as a strain of music"[37] rather than being preformed, the product of his blood. Wordsworth presents this development as the work of powers operating through nature rather than as the result of the ministrations of even one's nuclear family. Personhood thus literally grounds itself in something other than rank or family, and is the result of interaction with a world that, in this case, claims to be untouched by the social world. If this claim proves less than fully convincing, if, for instance, the landscape Wordsworth returns to in "Tintern Abbey" to recall his former self, is, in fact, marked by social relations,[38] the fiction that the self can be the product of relations to a place rather than to persons stands all the more compelling for the difficulty in producing it.

In *The Prelude*, however, as in much Romantic poetry, it is often difficult to distinguish the influence of context from that of an interior faculty for resistance, what Broussais refers to as *"moi."* But one Romantic text in particular takes the issue of personal identity as one of its central themes and very clearly lays out all three of the models of identity we have discussed: Byron's "The Prisoner of Chillon" with the appended "Sonnet on Chillon."

Critical treatments of "The Prisoner of Chillon" have tended to center on two related concerns: whether or not the poem was intended to heroize the prisoner and whether its main interests are political or psychological. These questions have typically divided critics into two camps: those who consider the poem a politically motivated tribute, and those who, in response to the first group, argue that the poem is not political because it functions not as a tribute but as an account of psychological degeneration. Given that representations of psychology and identity are themselves part of a political and social world, however, it would seem reasonable to argue that the poem might be about both. Only recently has it been suggested that the poem's concerns could be psychological and political at once, as in William Ulmer's note on the poem's Dantean politics.[39] But Ulmer's piece is in keeping with the poem's earlier critical history in that it assumes that in so far as the poem is political, its interests must be republican. The assumption that the poem's politics are republican, an assumption originally inspired by Byron's note to the poem and the tone of the sonnet, both of which were later additions, still governs the terms in which political readings of the poem are made. But if one reads this poem as "a Fable," as Byron calls it, about identity, one discovers that it offers a subtly anti-republican message in that it represents the Revolutionary shift from rank- to context-based identity as tragic.

Although inspired by the experience of an historical figure, Byron's tale is, to a large extent, pure fabulation, since much of Bonivard's history was unknown to him until after the poem was written. It is not insignificant that Byron never specifies the prisoner's name in the poem. Whatever Byron might have known about Bonivard's persecution for his Catholicism, his treatment of that persecution differs from the historical data that would have been available to him both in terms of details and their implications.[40] The opening lines of the poem – "My hair is grey, but not with years, / Nor grew it white / In a single

night, / As men's have grown from sudden fears"[41] – immediately
suggest the way the prisoner's condition might align him not with
martyrs for liberty but with members of the aristocracy who suffered
loss, deprivation, and imprisonment during the French Revolution.
Byron himself wrote in a note to these lines: "Ludovico Sforza, and
others. – The same is asserted of Marie Antoinette's, the wife of Louis
XVI, though not in quite so short a period. Grief is said to have the
same effect: to such, and not to fear, this change in *hers* was to be
attributed."[42] It is clear from the outset that not only is the prisoner's
cause not republicanism but also that it is very much a family cause –
"this was for my father's faith" (11), "And for the same his lineal race /
In darkness found a dwelling-place" (15–16). Since this father's faith is
never specified, the persecution the prisoner suffers is linked more
powerfully with his "lineal race" than anything else; the emphasis is on
his brothers' "Dying as their father died" (23).

Byron's decision to alter the Bonivard story by having the prisoner
confined with two of his brothers further transforms what might have
been a tale of individual suffering into a tale about the destruction of a
family or race. As William Ulmer notes, the change also heightens the
poem's resemblance to the Ugolino episode from Dante's *Inferno*, and
in both cases "the moral horror...rests on the plight of a main
character forced to witness the slow deaths of beloved family
members" (26–27). One of the prisoner's first complaints is that his
brothers are no longer able to live a life appropriate to their family/
rank. The younger brother's two salient features – his looks and his
sensitivity – are dear not only for themselves but also for their
connection to the family. These features specifically memorialize the
mother of the prisoners:

> ...the favorite and the flower,
> Most cherish'd since his natal hour,
> His mother's image in fair face,
> The infant love of all his race,
> His martyred father's dearest thought...   (164–168)

It is made clear that this brother is so much loved not just because
his delicate qualities are appealing but specifically because they were
his mother's: the prisoner refers to him as "The youngest, whom my
father loved, / Because our mother's brow was given / To him"
(73–75). This brother's gentleness, moreover, is implicitly coded as
gentility:

> With tears for nought but others' ills,
> And then they flowed like mountain rills,
> Unless he could assuage the woe
> Which he abhorr'd to view below.   (88–91)

This sensibility marks him as a gentleman, one whose function is to assuage the suffering he views "below." The prisoner is distressed not only to see his brother suffer, but also to see his virtues taken out of a setting where they could thrive and serve their proper function: "And truly might it [the prisoner's soul] be distrest / To see such bird in such a nest" (77–78).

The second brother represents the noble character in its other principal aspect:

> The other was as pure of mind,
> But formed to combat with his kind;
> Strong in his frame, and of a mood
> Which 'gainst the world in war had stood,
> And perish'd in the foremost rank
>   With joy:–but not in chains to pine...   (92–97)

This brother, who is also "a hunter of the hills" (103), was meant to battle with his own kind, and would happily perish if it could be in the foremost rank – in both senses of the phrase. It is worth noting that, for all we hear of the closeness of the three brothers, the only mention of real interaction between them is this:

> And each [would] turn comforter to each,
> With some new hope, or *legend old*,
> Or *song heroically bold*;
> But even these at length grew cold.
>   (59–62, my emphasis)

The brothers turn to memories of a feudal tradition to sustain themselves but find that those memories have become insufficient to the task. The point is not simply that these men and the world have lost by their imprisonment; this is a specifically aristocratic tragedy.

Interestingly, and as these cold legends suggest, the poem has something of a nostalgic tone even before the prisoner's brothers die. The prisoner remarks that he "forced [his spirit] on to cheer / Those relics of a home so dear" (101–102). The use of the word "relics" here suggests not only that the brothers serve as family memorials, but also that, even while living, they represent a family in decline. Ultimately, the prisoner objectifies himself as the final relic of this race. Initially referring to himself together with his family in the first person, he gradually comes to speak of himself as an object as he recounts the family's decline:

> We were seven – who now are one,
>
> . . .
>
> Three were in a dungeon cast,
> Of whom this wreck is left the last.   (17–26)

Section II opens with an even more significant memorial: the seven pillars that so obviously echo the seven men. Robert Gleckner points out that memorialization is at work here, although the issues of family and aristocracy do not enter into his discussion. Given that for him the poem represents "a paradigm of the eternal human condition,"[43] this memorialization speaks only to a general sense of human suffering: "Thus the race of man, begun in battle and ended in death and imprisonment, is memorialized in the 'seven pillars of Gothic mould,' the 'seven columns, massy and grey' (lines 27, 29), the seven rings in the seven pillars, and the seven chains in the seven rings – iron clanking against stone."[44] But this family represents not simply the race of man but a race of noble men; and it is worth noting exactly what is serving as a memorial here:

> There are seven pillars of gothic mold,
> In Chillon's dungeons deep and old,
> There are seven columns, massy and grey. . .   (27–29)

One is reminded of an image from *Childe Harold's Pilgrimage III*:

> By a lone wall a lonelier column rears
> A grey and grief-worn aspect of old days,
> 'Tis the last remnant of the wreck of years,
> And looks as with the wild-bewildered gaze
> Of one to stone converted by amaze,
> Yet still with consciousness. . .[45]

In the prisoner's case, the accent is on the fact that the family is being memorialized by solid, massive, gothic structures, suggestive simultaneously of feudal strength and obsolescence. That it should be thus memorialized suggests an ambivalence already introduced by the fact that the sons almost seem to be suffering for their father's sake and to no positive end. As Ulmer points out, "at one point Byron even implicates Bonivard's father in his son's suffering (lines 11–12)" (26). To be part of this noble family seems necessarily to entail suffering; there is a painful irony in being literally tied to these symbols of ancient power.

The rank-specific meanings of the pillars become clearer still when one considers one of the several poems that functioned as influences on this one. Gleckner remarks in a footnote to his discussion of the seven pillars that "Byron early singled out Wordsworth's 'Seven Sisters' as possessing 'all the beauties, and few of the defects, of the writer.' " [46] In fact, this poem has more than the number seven in common with "The Prisoner of Chillon." In Wordsworth's poem the seven children of a lord, a knight who gives more thought to war than to his family, kill themselves to avoid becoming prey to rovers who take advantage of their "Father-knights'" carelessness.[47] The poem's subtitle, and the refrain of every stanza – The solitude of Binnorie – specifically associates solitude with the loss of family. The knight's determination to perform his noble duties makes him heedless of his own noble line. One could argue that in both poems the impulse to act the part of the nobleman distracts one from the attack (whether by "Persecution" or "Rovers") on the institution of the noble family itself. The father figures who doubly authorize a "lineal race"[48] provide their children only an inheritance of loss. The replacement of seven brothers by seven pillars is thus doubly tragic; it serves as a monument to the loss of the race and as a sign of its calcification. Byron blames the destruction of the nobility on "Persecution" by others while simultaneously accusing the nobility of self-destruction.

Byron's internally contradictory conception of the cause of the decline of the aristocracy is similarly registered in his interest in another of the sources or backgrounds to the poem: the Ugolino episode of Dante's *Inferno*. E. H. Coleridge, McGann, Ulmer, and others have remarked the connection between these two pieces. Shelley commented that "Byron had deeply studied this death of Ugolino, and perhaps but for it, would never have written the Prisoner of Chillon."[49] Certainly the episode offers another example of sons suffering for their father's beliefs and actions. But the hint that Ugolino may have eaten his own sons suggests further the image of a family feeding on itself, simultaneously striving to sustain itself and destroying itself. The passing of this race seems both tragic and inevitable.

But of course, the poem's primary concern is the prisoner's relation to this change. We notice that not only do his surroundings seem to replicate his family but also that, more and more, his family replicates his surroundings. We hear for instance that "Our voices took a dreary tone, / An echo of the dungeon-stone" (63–64). The prisoner reports that when the winter's spray hit "And then the very rock hath rock'd, / And I have felt it shake, unshock'd" (122–123). This couplet, one of very few to be set off by an indentation, calls considerable attention to itself by its internal repetitions alone. These lines have a chiastic character even though their parallel terms are not, strictly speaking, interchangeable. The repetitions "rock"-"rocked" and "shake"-"unshocked" are sufficient to bind the lines together and lend a sense of interchangeability to the parts. The result of the punning use of the word "rock," in combination with this linkage of phrases, is to suggest that the prisoner becomes more rock than the rock itself; the "rock hath rock'd," but the prisoner felt it "shake, *un*shock'd." Again, a man is taking on the character of his surroundings.

The narrative action of the poem begins with the deaths of the prisoner's brothers. When the youngest finally dies, the emphasis is less on the loss of a person than on the loss of a family:

> The last – the sole – the dearest link
> Between me and the eternal brink,
> Which bound me to my failing race,
> Was broken in this fatal place.   (215–218)

Above all else, this brother was a link, a tie not only to a family but also to an identity. That the language of bondage should be used here is telling; there is an analogy between being tied to a race and being tied to a place, and here the latter bond replaces the former.[50] The prisoner's identity, once it can no longer be linked to his race, finally becomes nothing more than a passive reflection of this fatal place. In the next section, the prisoner's transformation to rock is solidified: "Among the stones I stood a stone" (236). He rapidly becomes so much a part of his surroundings that he loses consciousness of himself as a person altogether, to the point that he no longer recognizes his surroundings as such: "vacancy absorbing space, / And fixedness – without a place" (243–244). The family, even its one living member, seems to be passing into the landscape, and with it the capacity to confer identity. Place substitutes for race.

Lest it appear that one's loss of connection with family or rank is the necessary dramatic result of imprisonment, it is useful to look at another of the probable source-poems of the piece, Lovelace's "To Althea. From Prison." The poem's premise is precisely that no prison can truly threaten one's sense of self and one's loyalties:

> Stone walls do not a prison make,
>   Nor iron bars a cage:
> Minds innocent and quiet take

> That for an hermitage.
> If I have freedom in my love,
> And in my soul am free,
> Angels alone, that soar above,
> Enjoy such liberty.[51]

Given that it was Lovelace and not Byron who actually suffered imprisonment, and that the prison Byron saw at Chillon was actually a large room in which Bonivard walked freely, we cannot assume that Byron is simply offering us a more "honest," because more pessimistic, appraisal of the effect of imprisonment on elite members of society. Lovelace's imprisonment may make his throat "shriller" (line 18) when he sings in praise of his king, but he demonstrates by example that the cavalier's identity remains intact under any pressure, and the relative absence of a sense of the prison itself in this poem shows that there is no danger that Lovelace is about to become continuous with it. Critics have often focused on images like Joseph Wright of Derby's *The Captive*, a depiction of a pathetic man in tatters, when discussing the cultural milieu of "The Prisoner of Chillon" (see fig. 10). But this focus should not distract us from remembering the other popular image of imprisonment in the period, the type represented by a piece like Richard Newton's *Desmoulins in Prison*, a portrait of a handsomely dressed aristocrat tearfully composing a letter (see fig. 11). In the Revolutionary period artists produced numerous images of confined aristocrats that highlighted the disjunction between noble character and base surroundings (in a manner reminiscent of the first part of Byron's poem), but that also gave the impression that no length of imprisonment could truly degrade that character to the level of its surroundings.

Byron's description of the prisoner, without his family, becoming so fully of a piece with his environment, suggests the relationally determined human being described by Godwin, Bichat, and Broussais. If people are continuously responsive to their environment, then it comes as little surprise that habit should carry the prisoner only so far before he changes fundamentally. But this section of the poem, in which the prisoner comes to be defined entirely by his context, contains suggestions that the period of contextual identification may be only temporary; it is hinted that this is a liminal moment: "For all was blank, and bleak, and grey, / It was not night – it was not day" (239–240). What follows, in fact, makes this section appear to dramatize a transitional moment from rank and family-based identity to canonical Romantic self-consciousness and individualism. Section x proposes to

10   *The Captive*, Joseph Wright of Derby, engraved by T. Ryder, 1786.

DESMOULINS and LUCILE.

11 *Desmoulins in Prison*, Richard Newton, etching by W. Holland, 1795.

fulfill the expectation vaguely raised by some lines in section VIII: when the prisoner loses his last brother, and is the only one of three to remain, his own subjectivity comes quickly to the fore:

> *I* only stirr'd in this black spot,
> *I* only lived – *I* only drew
> The accursed breath of dungeon-dew. . .
>
> 　　　　　　(212–214, emphasis Byron's)

Although rather empty at this point, these "I"'s, which seem almost to occupy the spaces of the three original brothers, enjoy a sudden prominence that seems to hold Wordsworthian promise, a promise the reader expects to be satisfied when section x opens thus: "A light broke in upon my brain, – / It was the carol of a bird. . ." (251–252). In spite of the fact that the prisoner's recall to consciousness causes the walls and floor to "Close slowly round" (262) him as before, the bird nevertheless appears to offer an opportunity to achieve self-consciousness through reflection on one's identification with an external object: "It seem'd like me to want a mate, / But was not half so desolate" (273–274). The prisoner interprets the bird entirely in terms of his own concerns; it had a "song that said a thousand things, / And seem'd to say them all for me!" (269–270). But unlike those objects of the Wordsworthian landscape that teach the poet about himself and his past, objects that provide a lasting way for him to understand himself, this bird precipitates only minimal self-reflection. Rather than continue to ponder himself in the bird, the prisoner rather quickly imagines the bird to be, not a symbol of himself, but of his brother, and he permits himself to fancy that it might even be his brother's soul. Immediately thereafter, the bird flies off and the prisoner is left with nothing:

> I sometimes deemed that it might be
> My brother's soul come down to me;
> But then at last away it flew. . .　　　　(287–289)

The prisoner lacks the capacity for inwardness that is essential to the mature Wordsworthian project; as McGann argues, "when this 'visitant from Paradise' (284) flies away [Bonnivard] is unable to sustain himself from his own inner resources, is unable to become a part of nature's teeming life because he has none of his own to bring to her."[52] The scene finally seems only to recapitulate the prisoner's loss of his family, and the section comes to an end. At this point, it comes as little surprise that the prisoner no longer hopes for release; without family, his life is not only painful but meaningless. As he puts it:

> And the whole earth would henceforth be
> A wider prison unto me:
> No child – no sire – no kin had I. . .   (322–324)

Even freedom would not allow the prisoner to realize himself, to be himself, in any real way, and the reason he gives for this focuses entirely on the fact that he can no longer be part of a family line.

The succeeding section represents a last opportunity for Wordsworthian identity-formation in the prisoner's climb to look out the window. This turn to a "Lakist idea" as Philip Martin calls it, is thwarted in the "sudden diversion at line 356, which represents [Byron's] inability to use Bonnivard's imprisonment as a Romantic metaphor."[53] But it is important to note that before this "diversion" the family situation has once again taken shape in the landscape, although it bears no meaning for the prisoner at all:

> And then there was a little isle,
> Which in my very face did smile,
>   The only one in view;
> A small green isle, it seem'd no more,
> Scarce broader than my dungeon floor,
> But in it there were three tall trees. . .   (341–346)

The comparison of the island to the dungeon and the fact that it contains, despite its size, three tall trees, immediately signals a memorialization of the kind we have already seen. It is also notable that this use of an island recalls Wordsworth's poem, "The Seven Sisters," mentioned earlier. The "seven lovely Campbells" (59) commit suicide by plunging into a lake, in a stream from which appear seven islands that the fishermen say are the burial mounds of the women. This happy discovery of meaning in the natural world is typically Wordsworthian, but Byron's prisoner doesn't "read" his island in any lively way. The result is that the shift of meaning from race to place not only has no consolations, but signals, in fact, the ominous triumph of an indifferent material world. With family gone, the prisoner becomes very much part of his surroundings, but without the capacity for self-reflection, he is simply passively embruted by that context.

The poem's final section is perhaps the most discouraging of all precisely because in it the prisoner has reconciled himself so thoroughly to his surroundings. His comment that "These heavy walls to me had grown / A hermitage – and all my own!" (377–378) recalls Lovelace's poem, but with a painful irony, given that the prisoner has not become contemplative so much as he has come to feel thoroughly at home in his prison: "And half I felt as they [the guards] were come / To tear me from a second home" (379–380). The poem's closing lines offer a final, pathetic explanation of what has happened to the prisoner:

> My very chains and I grew friends,
> So much a long communion tends
> To make us what we are: – even I
> Regain'd my freedom with a sigh.   (391–394)

Martin refers to the first of these lines as a Godwinian motto, and argues that Byron simply imported it because he was trying to write in the Lakist mode (89). But this "Godwinian motto" hardly appears to be a throwaway line, added to close a poem that has not succeeded in being truly Lakist; in many respects it is the point of the whole piece. If a noble identity is no more than a matter of habit, a way of living within a given setting, the nobleman taken out of his context becomes someone quite different. The prisoner finally finds his only comfort in reorganizing his sense of power and rank so that it can operate within the confines of his place:

> We were all inmates of one place,
> And I, the monarch of each race,
> Had power to kill. . .   (385–387)

Mice and spiders now substitute for men.

In sum, "The Prisoner of Chillon" dramatizes the replacement of genealogy-based identity by context-based identity. The destruction of the prisoner's family has an inevitable quality, and seems to be not only necessary but in some respects elicited by the family itself. The prisoner's efforts to cling to his race and the idea of race are pathetic, and sometimes, as in the final lines, even somewhat repellent. But for him to glean his identity from his surroundings seems even worse. For Byron, who is invested in both aristocratic and republican ideals, the loss of aristocratic identity seems necessary, but also threatening. It would seem, in fact, to leave one in a position where identity becomes contingent upon the vagaries of local circumstance. As James Hill argues, "against the kind of purposive relationship between mind and environment that Wordsworth posits for his psychology, Byron introduces a random factor both uncontrollable and crippling in its effect."[54]

Byron's final response to this problem is to take up the Wordsworthian mode. Since identity, from the aristocratic point of view, is a given and not a made thing, the elimination of innate distinctions of rank leaves one with no way to distinguish oneself at all. From the perspective of a capitalist and mercantile class, however, the break-down of such distinctions simply provides a freer field for the exercise of personal abilities. For Wordsworth, the idea that one must turn to oneself to produce a social identity came relatively easily and was paralleled by the notion that one solidifies one's identity through self-contemplation. If one's sense of identity was largely the product of one's surroundings, one nevertheless worked hard to respond to those surroundings in a way that allowed one to fashion that identity. Context offered nothing more than raw materials; one had to make oneself. This was a model of identity that Byron generally did not embrace. As Kim Ian Michasiw notes, "It may be that [Byron's] pride in being an aristocrat, in his social origin, made him aware of the bourgeois taint to dogmas of the autonomous poetic identity. The self-made poet, like the self-made man, appears a climber to a Lord."[55] In addition, Byron's own abrupt rise in status with the publication of the first cantos of *Childe Harold's Pilgrimage* may well have made him uncomfortably aware of the precarious and arbitrary quality of self-made identity. Nevertheless, faced with the problem of passive context-based identity, Byron at least temporarily adopts a Wordsworthian model of the self, a model that provides one a way to distinguish oneself.

Byron turns to this model wholeheartedly and belatedly in the sonnet appended to the original poem. Several critics have noted that it is really only here that a republican message, or at least a message about the sons of liberty, is offered:

> ETERNAL spirit of the chainless mind!
> Brightest in dungeons, Liberty! thou art,
> For there thy habitation is the heart –
> The heart which love of thee alone can bind...   (1–4)

This sounds remarkably like Lovelace's poem, wherein the cell becomes a hermitage to the man with a pure mind. But this sonnet further suggests that to be imprisoned or bound actually encourages a feeling of liberty, that liberty flourishes in adverse circumstances, where it has to be produced from within. It is here, then, that Byron makes a virtue of necessity and redeems a world where one's identity is beset by environmental influences. If, rather than enjoying a role that is under-stood as essential and stable, one has an identity that is produced in response to the outside world, then only by accenting inward labor, resistance to the outside, can one find the freedom to produce an identity that at least has noble features.

It is perfectly fitting that Byron should choose to delineate this model of identity in a sonnet, given that the sonnet form is often considered quintessentially restrictive and often private. Although Byron's sonnet is not obviously a poem of private contemplation, it is strongly reminiscent of Wordsworth's "Nuns fret not at their convent's narrow room," a poem that does present self-reflection and rumination on these very issues. As Stuart Curran remarks, "the sense of isolation, of [what Coleridge called] 'some lonely feeling,' however refined the emotion or privileged the experience, underlies all the great sonnets of Wordsworth's maturity."[56] As we shall see, however, Byron's poem, with its emphasis on interiority, represents a purer form of canonical Romantic subjectivity than Wordsworth's sonnet. "Nuns fret not" is, of course, about confinement, both within a place and by the sonnet form:

> Nuns fret not at their convent's narrow room;
> And hermits are contented with their cells;
> And students with their pensive citadels;
> Maids at the wheel, the weaver at his loom,
> Sit blithe and happy. . .[57]

Almost imperceptibly, the focus shifts from persons actually confined to persons confined by their labor – spatial limitation is of a piece with one's vocation. Confinement, like a vocation, aids in self-determination by providing parameters for being. It becomes clear that the freedom to choose one's own role which was a part of the Revolutionary project appears at this moment to Wordsworth, as it did to thinkers like Burke, to offer too much freedom:

> In truth the prison, unto which we doom
> Ourselves, no prison is: and hence for me,
> In sundry moods, 'twas pastime to be bound
> Within the Sonnet's scanty plot of ground;
> Pleased if some Souls (for such there needs must be)
> Who have felt the weight of too much liberty,
> Should find brief solace there, as I have found.   (8–14)

Local attachments have become local confinements for the nuns, hermits, and weavers who appreciate being locked into place. Freedom to choose one's vocation (which here amounts to choosing one's location), and thereby to choose one's identity, is both a blessing and a curse. Post-Revolutionary man can *choose* his prison, but he must "doom" himself unto one or another, or feel liberty itself as a kind of weight.

The relative conservatism of Wordsworth's poem highlights the conservative aspects of Byron's sonnet, even though the conservative moves of the two are almost diametrically opposed. The turn inward of the "Sonnet on Chillon," like the celebration of confinement in "Nuns fret not," becomes a way of modifying a contemporary scheme designed to promote liberty and equality. In Wordsworth's poem, context-based identity is calcified and rigidified so as to minimize liberty, while in Byron's it is wholeheartedly resisted so as to minimize equality. Byron's "republican" sonnet, while it tells one story about liberty and tyranny, is, in the context of the larger poem, concerned primarily to offer a way out of a republican identity scheme, a scheme designed to render old notions of identity invisible. Byron's sonnet discovers in canonical Romantic interiority, a notion Byron generally does not find congenial, a model for resisting determination by context and recovering something akin to static nobility: the self-made hero. Bonnivard's name will now be borne aloft along with "Freedom's fame" (8) even if his body is confined to a prison. This hero cannot be threatened by social or physical circumstance, and can in fact use those circumstances to produce internal consistency and heroism.

v

Although "The Prisoner of Chillon" dramatizes the shift from race to place in the determination of identity with particular clarity, the issue of context-based identity also arises in some of Byron's other poems of this period. *Childe Harold's Pilgrimage*, Canto III, is a case in point. In his discussion of cantos III and IV of *Childe Harold*, James Hill remarks that "however we account for it, Byron is using a procedural strategy very much like Wordsworth's to present an environmental psychology that is the obverse of Wordsworth's in its insistence on the negative effects of environment on the development of personality, and on the virtual helplessness of the individual consciousness to shape or control its own development" (125). Byron explicitly associates this helplessness *vis-à-vis* the environment with the flattening out of hierarchical distinctions. Stanza 72 encapsulates the problem as Byron sees it:

> I live not in myself, but I become
> Portion of that around me; and to me,
> High mountains are a feeling, but the hum
> Of human cities torture: I can see
> Nothing to loathe in nature, save to be
> A link reluctant in a fleshly chain,
> Class'd among creatures, when the soul can flee,
> And with the sky, the peak, the heaving plain
> Of ocean, or the stars, mingle, and not in vain. (680–688)

The first two lines restate the prisoner of Chillon's situation. The narrator's being is both implicated in, and partly defined by, his changeable surroundings; not only does he become a part of them but a part of them becomes him. This connection with the environment is linked to the narrator's lack of inwardness: "I live not *in* myself." The subsequent lines gesture towards context-based identity as it might appear in Wordsworth's work: "to me, / High mountains are a feeling, but the hum / Of human cities torture."

But the colon following "torture" marks the point where the narrator will turn against the notion of identity as based on context and his own adoption of that notion. The negativity of the statement "I can see / nothing to loathe..." reminds us of Freud's argument in "Negation" that denial is always an admission of sorts,[58] an argument that is particularly compelling in this case given the surplus emotional charge of the word "loathe." Thus, what is ostensibly the one thing the narrator dislikes about nature – being a link in a fleshly chain – would actually seem to pose for him a major obstacle to the Wordsworthian celebration of the nature of which he becomes a portion. The mention of creatures linked together in a chain calls to mind the notion of the Great Chain of Being, an older hierarchical conception of the connection of all living beings in a chain running from "inert matter and stones...through...Man and through the Realms of Angels to God."[59] But the chain is refigured here in a way that utterly transforms its significance: the poem describes not a vertical chain of creatures of different status but a horizontal tie binding all creatures. To be a link in the original Great Chain of Being was to have a place in a taxonomic system that included God, not to be linked with all earthly creatures in a single class. The narrator is clearly lamenting more than just the limitations of the flesh here; for him, to become a part of one's surroundings is to be linked in fraternity with all creatures, to have no way of setting oneself apart. In his *Essay on Man* Pope had hinted at the social significance of any challenge to the hierarchical structure of the Great Chain of Being:

> Vast chain of Being, which from God began,
> Natures aethereal, human, angel, man,
> Beast, bird, fish, insect! what no eye can see,
> No glass can reach! from Infinite to thee,
> From thee to Nothing. – On superior pow'rs
> Were we to press, inferior might on ours:
> Or in the full creation leave a void,
> Where, one step broken, the great scale's destroy'd:
> From Nature's chain whatever link you strike,
> Tenth or ten thousandth, breaks the chain alike.[60]

The restriction on upward mobility within the Chain has a socio-economic resonance: "On superior pow'rs / Were we to press, inferior might on ours." Attempting to ascend the Great Chain of Being threatens the structure of the universe in the same way that social climbing threatens the structure of society. This first epistle of the *Essay on Man* ends with the famous injunction to remember that "One truth is clear, 'whatever is, is RIGHT' " (line 294). By the end of the century, however, Pope's fears were borne out; as W. D. Ian Rolfe remarks, "although allegiance to the Chain continued throughout the eighteenth century, new progressivist thinking inspired scientists to 'temporalise' the Chain and view it as a ladder that organisms might climb rather than a rigid ranking of immutable entities" (302).[61]

The flattening of the Great Chain of Being in Byron's poem is reminiscent of the French Revolutionary levelling of the pyramidical social structure that situated the monarch at its apex. A hierarchical chain of connections now exists only as a memory in a world being transformed by a spirit of *égalité* and a growing emphasis on horizontal affiliations.[62] Becoming "portion of that around oneself" is associated with being, like the prisoner, bound in equality to one's surroundings – and both are opposed to forming a link in a hierarchical chain. The narrator makes it clear that this flattening applies to more than just species divisions in the animal kingdom: just three stanzas earlier the narrator had been lamenting the difficulty of distinguishing oneself among *men*:

> To fly from, need not be to hate, mankind;
> All are not fit with them to stir and toil,
> Nor is it discontent to keep the mind

> Deep in its fountain, lest it overboil
> In the hot throng, where we become the spoil
> Of our infection, till too late and long
> We may deplore and struggle with the coil,
> In wretched interchange of wrong for wrong
> 'Midst a contentious world, striving where none are strong.
>
> (653–661)

This world is a contentious and difficult one precisely because "none are strong." The image of the resistant mind deep in its fountain reminds us of the use of the Wordsworthian model of psychological depth in the "Sonnet on Chillon" to forge a space for self-construction that would allow one to distinguish oneself. In this case, this depth *explicitly* functions as a form of retreat from equality; the narrator was simply not meant to stir and toil with mankind. The fountain image itself, however, indicates the difficulty of such a retreat; it is the nature of fountains to "overboil," and it is hard to imagine this fluid mind doing anything but continually gushing up to the surface.

While location-based identity threatens to level distinctions, to eliminate the differences of race altogether, the narrator of *Childe Harold's Pilgrimage*, Canto III, is sometimes able to make a virtue of necessity and reinstate distinctions between people precisely by grounding their identity in a particular landscape. A lengthy description of the virtues of the Rhine closes thus:

> The negligently grand, the fruitful bloom
> Of coming ripeness, the white city's sheen,
> The rolling stream, the precipice's gloom,
> The forest's growth, and Gothic walls between,
> The wild rocks shaped as they had turrets been
> In mockery of man's art; and these withal
> A race of faces happy as the scene,
> Whose fertile bounties here extend to all,
> Still springing o'er thy banks, though Empires near them fall.
>
> (581–589)

The semicolon after "art" announces a turn, one that introduces an ambiguity. The words "these withal" appear at first to refer to the elements of the landscape described in the first part of the stanza, but seem by the time the reader has reached the next line to refer to the "race of faces." The following lines only sustain the confusion. It is unclear whether the "whose" of line 588 is a reference to the race or the scene, and it is even less clear whether what is "springing" in line

589 is the race, the scene, or the long-unmentioned Rhine itself. The race thus takes its features from the scene and even becomes formally conflated with it, and both proceed with their pleasant existence while "Empires near them fall."

The narrator finds other ways to subvert the levelling effects of context-based identity as well. The most common of these is the discovery of, and focus on, the ruins of the hierarchical order in the landscape. The "Gothic walls between" of the stanza quoted above is one instance among many of the sudden appearance of gothic structures in a purportedly natural scene; in that case such structures literally divide up the natural scene, draw distinctions in it. But throughout the poem the narrator has difficulty sustaining interest in the untouched nature to which he repeatedly turns in Wordsworthian style for answers to his questions about self and society:

> Maternal Nature!. . .who teems like thee,
> Thus on the banks of thy majestic Rhine?
> There Harold gazes on a work divine,
> A blending of all beauties; streams and dells,
> Fruit, foliage, crag, wood, cornfield, mountain, vine,
> And chiefless castles breathing stern farewells
> From grey but leafy walls, where Ruin greenly dwells.
>
> And there they stand, as stands a lofty mind,
> Worn, but unstooping to the baser crowd . . .   (408–416)

The focus turns almost imperceptibly from nature to culture, and the former finally comes to seem secondary, a reminder not of an original state but of the passing of culture, a green ruin. The contemplation of the landscape gives way to contemplation of a lost culture characterized by an emphasis on hierarchy. The elements of the natural landscape, serially and almost monotonously invoked, are replaced by the singular castles that seem to take on a moving emotional life of their own. It comes as little surprise that it is to these that the narrator turns for a model of the mind ("there they stand, as stands a lofty mind"). At other moments in the poem, social distinctions are inscribed directly into the natural scene itself; the Alps, for example, are described as "The palaces of Nature" (591).

It is in part in the context of the complicated effects of location-based identity that Harold's travels take on their peculiar meaning. If on the one hand Harold finds his "mind is coloured by. . .every hue" (574) of the landscape through which he travels, thereby rendering his sense of self a frail and contingent thing, on the other hand his very mobility represents an effort to break the bond between identity and place. To gain a sense of the truth that "purifies from self" (845), the narrator claims that one must experience a communion with all of one's surroundings, a communion that renders the self simultaneously null and vast:

> Not vainly did the early Persian make
> His altar the high places and the peak
> Or earth-o'ergazing mountains. . .   (851–853)

The narrator reminds us not to "fix on fond abodes to circumscribe [our] prayer" (859). Harold's/Byron's travels reflect the importance of place in the establishment of a sense of self while suggesting that Harold and Byron are not part of any place in particular and so are not finally determined by their context.

VI

In the late eighteenth and early nineteenth centuries, then, between the genealogical and individualist models of identity with which we are so familiar, there existed a Revolutionary conception of identity based on context. This conception shares a number of features with current historicist paradigms, paradigms which tend, as Alan Liu points out, both to focus on local knowledge and the influence of context and to become "determinedly depthless."[63] But one could turn to a philosopher of the middle of the twentieth century for an account of being that encapsulates the competing attractions of all three models of identity. In his "Dialectics of Outside and Inside" in *The Poetics of Space*, Bachelard struggles to define being in terms other than geometrical ones of circumscription, and determines that "man is half-open being," with his continual "movements of opening and closing."[64] He imagines that being may be something other than an inside opposed to an outside, and that inner and outer worlds may be mutually defining, both a part of being.

But even Bachelard continues to return to a notion of "a profound depth of being" (224), a point where true identity is most intensely felt. Bachelard's move toward the depths, a move associated with freedom as it is in Byron's "Sonnet on Chillon," provides a fitting coda to the movement from genealogy to context-based identity to individualism that has been described in this chapter:

We should be more indulgent if we were reading a fever chart. By following the labyrinth of fever that runs through the body, by exploring the "seats of fever," or the pains that inhabit a hollow tooth, we should learn that the imagination localizes suffering and creates and recreates imaginary anatomies. But I shall not use in this work the numerous documents that psychiatry provides...For my problem is to discuss the images of a pure, free imagination, a liberating imagination that has no connection with organic incitements. (225)

Fever charts turn us toward the "seats of fever" and localized pains, which in their turn begin to seem only imaginary. Finally, even this connection with the world through local bodily sensation comes to seem limiting, and the goal becomes the construction of an imagination freed from connection altogether, liberated and "pure" in its freely chosen relations.

CHAPTER 4

Incarnate imagination and The Cenci

In discussions of power, it is conventionally the case that those with power are said to be "represented" whereas those without power are "without representation." It may therefore seem contradictory to discover that...the Omnipotent will be materially unrepresented and that the comparatively powerless humanity will be materially represented by their own deep embodiment. But to have no body is to have no limits on one's extension out into the world; conversely, to have a body, a body made emphatic by being continually altered through various forms of creation, instruction...and wounding, is to have one's sphere of extension contracted down to the small circle of one's immediate physical presence. Consequently, to be intensely embodied is the equivalent of being unrepresented and (here as in many secular contexts) is almost always the condition of those without power.

Elaine Scarry, *The Body in Pain*[1]

The emphasis on psychological interiority in some Romantic writing is generally linked to a tendency to restrict the role of the body in the establishment of identity; as Charles Rzepka argues, the canonical Romantic model of the self is of a "self as mind."[2] The speaker's injury in "This Lime-Tree Bower My Prison," for example, limits his physical movement but thereby encourages mental exertions that increase his self-consciousness. It is significant, moreover, that the account of this injury and its physical effects is relegated to a prose headnote rather than included in the poem proper. We are reminded of Bachelard's urge to leave behind fevers and pains in order to discover a pure liberated imagination.

Perhaps no Romantic poet is better known for spiritualizing and idealizing persons than Shelley. Indeed, Shelley's typical model of the self has much in common with the canonical model: persons have an external being, which is often represented as a kind of clothing or veil, and an inner being that is a miniature of that external being but purified "of all that we condemn or despise."[3] Shelley not only organizes identity spatially in the manner of the canonical Romantic model, but in his poetry he generally concerns himself with the inner being. He does not, however, focus on this inner being consistently or uncritically, and, I will argue, in *The Cenci* in particular he reflects on the repercussions of this focus. In his discussion of *The Cenci* Alan Richardson remarks that while the "Romantics are often credited with the popularization, if not the discovery, of the unconscious" it is nevertheless true that in what Richardson terms Romantic mental theater "the mind forms itself through its dynamic relations with the social and material world, moving with an active and outward or an inward and reactive bias."[4] As Jeffrey Cox rightly notes, "*we* may feel that Shelley had a lyric temperament, but in writing key works *he* returned time and again to dramatic forms."[5]

It is my contention that in *The Cenci* Shelley deliberately magnifies the importance of external being and traces the effects of that magnification on the inner being. Specifically, I will show that the play explores the relationship of inner and outer being in terms of their resemblance to two representational modes: poetry and drama. We will see that external being is associated with masks, costumes, and theatricality, while the inner being is constructed as both an imaginative portrait of the outer being, and, like poetry, a mirror of the beautiful. The play dramatizes, in canonical Romantic fashion, the hollowness and dangers of an existence rooted in the theatrical and corporeal, and it represents Count Cenci as a playwright figure whose viciousness resides in part in his extreme interest in display and the manipulation of corporeal forms. At the same time, however, the play demonstrates through Beatrice's experience that even the "inmost spirit"[6] must make reference to the external being to ground itself, and that when it can no longer do so it becomes disorganized and unstable. In spite of Shelley's insistence that corporeal life is merely a theatrical mask, his play teaches that the circumscription of the representation of corporeal life can have profoundly pernicious consequences. Shelley suggests that it is only by overcoming the potential antagonism between embodiment and representation – the antagonism Scarry describes above – that one can hope to empower the disempowered. Unfortunately, for Shelley as for Beatrice contemporary society confines the representation of the body within certain parameters, and this denial of bodily experience limits the healing and purifying potential of the imagination. Ultimately, then, while the theatrical aspect of being is

destroyed in the figure of Count Cenci, the imaginative internal aspect
of being, in so far as it cannot be reconciled to the corporeal, is
sacrificed in the figure of Beatrice, whose capacity to imagine what she
knows about her body is tragically limited.

I

In his essay "On Love" Shelley provides a relatively extensive and
explicit account of his typical conception of the self:

We dimly see within our intellectual nature a miniature as it were of our
entire self, yet deprived of all that we condemn or despise, the ideal prototype
of every thing excellent or lovely that we are capable of conceiving as
belonging to the nature of man. Not only the portrait of our external being,
but an assemblage of the minutest particulars of which our nature is
composed: a mirror whose surface reflects only the forms of purity and
brightness: a soul within our soul that describes a circle around its proper
Paradise which pain and sorrow and evil dare not overleap. To this we
eagerly refer all sensations, thirsting that they should resemble or correspond
with it.[7]

This description of the self accords with the canonical Romantic model
in many respects. Shelley gestures toward a notion of extreme
interiority: a soul within the soul within the "external being." Moreover, this interiority, as I suggested of Romantic interiority generally in
chapter 2, defends the self from commodification and other forms of
social appropriation: the "soul within our soul…describes a circle
around its *proper* Paradise which pain and sorrow and evil dare not
overleap." One's internal paradise, at least, is one's own inalienable
property. Persons, like poetry, are a source of infinite pleasure and
wisdom but are not susceptible to commodification because the infinite
regress of their identity or meaning renders them ultimately ungrasp-
able from without. As Shelley says of "high poetry," "veil after veil
may be undrawn, and the inmost naked beauty of the meaning never
exposed."[8]
    Nevertheless, it is significant that even the inmost self is not wholly
self-created or defined but a representation or reflection of things
external to it. For all its emphasis on the depth and ideality of the

inmost being, Shelley's model ultimately defines that being as nothing but a portrait or reflection of the external. Shelley optimistically claims that the inner being is both a portrait of our external being and a mirror that reflects forms of purity. In "On Love," the potential disjunction between these two aspects of the inmost self is not an issue largely because the focus is not on the subject matter *per se* of representation or reflection but on the capacity of those imaginative procedures to reorganize that subject matter. It is the task of the intellect and the imagination to re-present to itself an image of the self that is so purified as to serve as the "ideal prototype of every thing excellent or lovely that we are capable of conceiving as belonging to the nature of man" (473–474).

The division between the external being and the internal being that is a representation of it reminds us of Scarry's description of the antagonism between embodiment and representation and suggests a potential problem. If the external or corporeal being takes on a magnified importance, its imaginative purification may become more difficult, and the ideality of the representational inner being may be threatened. At the same time, the inner being cannot afford to sever itself entirely from the external being because it relies on the external being to provide the materials for its imaginative work. *The Cenci* confronts precisely this problem. In his dedication to the play Shelley set it apart from his usual work:

Those writings which I have hitherto published, have been little else than visions which impersonate my own apprehensions of the beautiful and the just. I can also perceive in them the literary defects incidental to youth and impatience; they are dreams of what ought to be, or may be. The drama which I now present to you is a sad reality. (237)

Although all of Shelley's literary works are of course imaginative representations that also gesture toward the "real" and the corporeal, Shelley intends in this play to accent the real and external rather than the visionary and internal aspect of human character and experience. Given that it is the internal self that serves as the "ideal prototype" of human nature, it is not surprising that this piece that focuses on external being should be the "sad" account it is. Jerrold Hogle comments that the characters of *The Cenci*, "since they must be fleshed out in body-language and rhetorical assertions, rather than being pointed to by a distant narrator…are more likely to act out the

contradictory tendencies of full-bodied people."[9] As Hogle's remark
suggests, *The Cenci* focuses on external being both in its substance and
in its form. Moreover, Shelley not only chose to write in the most
corporeal of literary modes, the drama, but was also keen to have the
play produced, and even had specific actors in mind for the major
roles.

But in *The Cenci* Shelley does more than adopt a literary form that
magnifies the significance of corporeal life; he also specifically associates
corporeal life generally with that literary form. Within the play itself,
corporeal life is described as superficial and "put on." Beatrice and her
brothers repeatedly refer to their bodies as mere clothing; they speak of
their birth as having "clothed [them] in these limbs" (I. iii. 102). More
importantly, corporeality is explicitly associated with the masks and
costumes of the theater. As Shelley remarks in the preface, Beatrice's
experience and behavior in the world were but the "mask and mantle"
of her true self, implying that physical existence is fundamentally and
literally theatrical and even tragic. Corporeal life would seem to
amount to nothing more than the role one is forced by one's society to
adopt – it has no necessary connection with one's "true" inner life.
Beatrice in particular experiences her corporeal existence as little more
than a theatrical fiction, especially after being physically attacked:
"This woful *story* [of life with the Count] / So did I *overact* in my sick
dreams, / That I *imagined*...no, it cannot be!" (III. i. 48–50, my
emphasis). Of course, this fictionalizing of "real" experience serves as a
distancing mechanism for Beatrice herself, but as Shelley argues in the
preface, Beatrice's life truly *was* an overacted drama, a corporeal
fiction masking her true (and innocent) self. Unfortunately, in the world
of *The Cenci* this hollow corporeal self tends to define the whole self;
Hogle locates at least one of the Cenci's problems in the fact that theirs
is a society "that fashions personality theatrically" (157).

Corporeal life, moreover, is not only tied to social life generally but
is explicitly linked to what Shelley in this play has fixed on as the
salient feature of Renaissance social life – its domination by patriarchal power structures. In an interesting reversal of the Aristotelian
view that the relation of sperm to egg is analogous to that of idea to
matter, this play associates the initiation of material life wholly with
fathering. Cenci "clothed [his children] in these limbs" (I. iii. 102) and
his is "the form that moulded" Giacomo's (III. ii. 20). Even Cenci's
soul is described as lending Giacomo only his external form: Cenci's is
the "soul by which [Giacomo's soul] was *arrayed* / In God's immortal

likeness" (III. ii. 22–23, my emphasis). The theatricality of corporeal being is thus related both to its superficiality and to its implication in social (as opposed to inner) life: for Beatrice and her brothers, to have a body is to be brought by a father into a society that privileges fathers, from the Count to the Pope to God. As Cenci puts it, Beatrice is a "particle of [his] divided being" (IV. i. 117). Earl Wasserman goes so far as to claim that the play suggests that it is through the "father," in a broad sense, that evil enters the world in the first instance,[10] and I would argue that if this is so it is because it is fathers who are responsible for the incarnation that their children experience as a masking of their true and innocent selves. To father someone, to clothe him in limbs, is to do no less than force him to play a social role that may no more reflect his inner self than the actor's part reflects his true character. Beatrice's rape is of course the supreme example of the evil of incarnation and fathering: in that act Cenci hopes to dissolve Beatrice's inner sense of herself both by making her aware of herself as flesh, and his flesh, and by fathering in his own child another child. It is little wonder that Beatrice's act of clothing the murderer Marzio with her grandfather's "mantle" (again a reference to the "mask and mantle" of theatricality and corporeality) is such an ominously telling gesture; the patriarchal investment of someone seems unavoidably to involve a compromised investment in them.

The exposed and fragile nature of corporeal existence, and its domination by patriarchal power structures, is underscored by the play's focus on rape and torture. Moreover, it is significant that even the latter, an extreme form of corporeal magnification, does not ultimately challenge the body's superficial status in this play. Although in the final act the judge hopes to "wring the truth / Out of [his victim's] nerves and sinews, groan by groan" (v. ii. 193–194), his own language highlights the limits of the torturer's power: "Drag him away to torments; let them be / Subtle and long drawn out, to tear the folds / Of the heart's inmost cell" (v. ii. 160–162). On the one hand this image suggests the continuity of outer and inner life: an attack on the body could tear the heart's inmost cell. But on the other hand the use of the word "folds," in a play where the body is constantly associated with clothing and hence with superficiality, implies that even when the torturer appears to have penetrated the very being of his victim he has merely grasped the inessential, the folds of yet another veil. It is perhaps not surprising that Marzio responds to the judge's order by saying "Torture me as ye will: / A keener pain has wrung a higher truth / From my last breath" (v. ii. 163–165). Beatrice's response to the threat of torture demonstrates even more forcefully that the power of torture is limited when the body is like a garment:

> JUDGE: Confess, or I will warp
>   Your limbs with such keen tortures...
> BEATRICE: Tortures! Turn
>   The rack henceforth into a spinning-wheel!   (v. iii. 60–62)

For Beatrice the image of the rack, joined to the judge's "warp," seems to lead, through a chain of association, to the warp and woof of the loom, and thence to the phallic spinning wheel that produces the raw material for the weaving of the cloth that is the human body. At the same time, Beatrice's exclamation not only indicates the inefficacy of torture in her case, but also resonates with her earlier argument that torture can produce talk but not necessarily honest talk, that, in other words, one might be induced by physical pain to spin a yarn, to produce another theatrical fiction, but that is all. For Beatrice, the body may play a determining role in one's life on this earth, but it has no necessary connection to a higher order of truth. That Marzio and Beatrice speak of a truth that is rather too cleanly severed from the realm of the corporeal we shall soon see,[11] but in speaking of the body as the clothing of being they express one of the fundamental premises of the play.

II

Given that fathering resembles the playwright's production and manipulation of character and role, it is fitting that in the figure of the Count Shelley reflects on the significance of his own focus on external being in *The Cenci*. As Stuart Curran argues, "the Count is an artist, conscious of his every effect," in addition to which he is a "shrewd critic."[12] I would argue further that he specifically functions as a playwright figure. As we have seen, *The Cenci* represents a deeply theatrical world, one that, as Hogle argues, "explores how desirous beings constitute themselves as 'characters' on the stage of the world and how, in doing so, they position themselves in relation to other such performers and finally under the aegis of commanding scripts that force figures with multiple tendencies into the behaviors appropriate to certain roles" (149). The Count as wealthy patriarch not only allies himself with the power of those commanding scripts but also revises them and writes some of his own. In the first scene Camillo claims that Cenci should have his children "sitting round [him] now, / But that [he] fear[s] to read upon their looks / The shame and misery [he has] written there" (I. i. 40–42). Like a playwright, Cenci "writes" misery so that it takes a corporeal form; he produces pained expressions in others. He explains to Camillo that he actually enjoys "The sight of agony, and the sense of joy, / When this shall be another's, and that mine" (I. i. 82–83), commenting thus not only on his own personality but also on one of the cruxes of the theory of tragedy: the relation between suffering on stage and the pleasure experienced by the audience. The Count's comment modifies only slightly the model of performer/audience relations typical of the Jacobean tragedies *The Cenci* so much resembles. As the heroine of *The Duchess of Malfi* explains, tragedy pleases in part through distance:

> DUCHESS: Discourse to me some dismal tragedy.
> CARIOLA: O 'twill increase your melancholy.
> DUCHESS: Thou art deceiv'd;
>   To hear of greater grief would lessen mine.[13]

The Count is in some respects too avid a fan of the tragic; as he says, "most [men] exult / Over the tortures they can never feel – / Flattering their secret peace with others' pain. / But I delight in nothing else" (I. i. 78–81). The Count does not, however, become a theatergoer, but directs tragedy around him, incarnating his visions just as he incarnates his children:

> Any design my captious fancy makes
> The picture of its wish, and it forms none
> But such as men like you would start to know.
> Is as my natural food and rest debarred
> Until it be accomplished.   (I. i. 87–91)[14]

It is worth noting that the character most like Cenci – Orsino – explicitly confesses to trying to direct a drama around himself; he had hoped to attain his

>   own peculiar ends
> By some such plot of mingled good and ill
> As others weave; but there arose a Power
> Which graspt and snapped the threads of my device
> And turned it to a net of ruin...   (V. i. 79–83)

Here again the making of cloth, the manipulation of others, and theatricality are linked.

The third scene of the first act perfectly exemplifies the Count's theatricality. At the banquet, Cenci assembles an audience for his verbal re-creation of deaths he was not fortunate enough to have produced himself. Not satisfied, however, with performative tale-telling, wanting, that is, to be more than a mere actor, Cenci claims that his prayer influenced God's act and that he himself was therefore the author of his sons' destruction. The dinner thus becomes a sort of triumphant reprise wherein Cenci claims to have orchestrated an event and forces others to celebrate that event and its director. In so doing, he produces another scene in its own right, adroitly manipulating the sentiments and actions of his guests. The members of Cenci's "audience" thus come to play a role analogous to the role his sons played; they serve as manipulated actors in a scene of Cenci's devising. Their dismay and the limitations they feel on their action provide Cenci, in his sense of relative freedom, with the pleasurable feeling of distance enjoyed by the Jacobean viewer of tragedy.

Shelley's wish to have Cenci portrayed by Edmund Kean takes on a special significance in light of the Count's theatricality. Several commentators on *The Cenci* have found it remarkable that Shelley should want for his own play an actor whose skills he had, at least at one point, disdained. We know from Mary Shelley's journal that at an 1814 performance of *Hamlet* "Shelley [was] displeased with what he saw of Kean."[15] But Shelley's interest in that actor may have been due to more than the fact that "Kean's *métier* was the portrayal of savage and explosive violence."[16] *Hamlet* disappointed because it presented what Mary Shelley describes as "the loathsome sight of men personating characters which do not and cannot belong to them"; but the loathsomeness of palpably artificial acting would perfectly suit the impersonation of the deliberately theatrical Count. Hazlitt said of Kean's performance in *The Revenge* that while he lacked "dignified repose, and deep internal sentiment," "the very vices of Mr. Kean's general acting might almost be said to assist him in the part,"[17] and one could imagine that the same might have been true in the case of *The Cenci*. The difference between Kean's acting style and that of Eliza O'Neill, whom Shelley wanted for the part of Beatrice, further underscores this point. Miss O'Neill was specifically known for her "self-abandonment to character,"[18] and Shelley was "deeply moved...by the graceful sweetness, the intense pathos, and sublime vehemence of passion she displayed."[19] Hazlitt described the difference between the two actors thus:

Mr. Kean affects the audience from the force of passion instead of sentiment, or sinks into pathos from the violence of action, but seldom rises into it from the power of thought and feeling. In this respect, he presents almost a direct contrast to Miss O'Neill. Her energy always arises out of her sensibility. Distress takes possession of, and overcomes her faculties; she triumphs in her weakness, and vanquishes by yielding.[20]

One might say that O'Neill, unlike Kean, did make the characters she impersonated "belong" to her. While Kean's acting does not seem to be motivated from within, O'Neill's reflects her keen sensibility. This distinction corresponds to the distinction between the Count's theatricality and Beatrice's imaginative interiority. I will discuss Beatrice's association with imagination and the inner being in some detail later, but at this point it is worth noting the way this distinction is also reflected in theatrical portraiture. Even in a delicately modelled and relatively "feminine" portrait of Kean, his face is expressive of energy and directness (see fig. 12). O'Neill, on the other hand, passively receptive, displays her profile and a disengaged gaze (see fig. 13). The veils she holds in this picture and in figure 14 tempt the Shelleyan viewer to consider the link between gauzy feminine fashions and Shelley's recurrent use of the metaphor of unveiling the inner being. While Eliza O'Neill, meditative and withdrawn, stands accessible to the viewer's penetrating gaze, Kean, with his mantle, passionately projects his character outward.

Given that *The Cenci* was Shelley's first completed tragedy, and the first (and only) drama he ever hoped to have staged, it seems likely that his representation of the Count as a playwright-like manipulator serves as a metadramatic commentary on his own activity in writing the play. The character of the Count focuses a set of issues pertinent to Shelley's own situation: the proper relation of artist to audience, the desire to give one's ideas practical embodiment, and the repercussions of amplifying the corporeal aspect of being. If Beatrice's life experience was but a mask and mantle over her true self, what were the implications of representing her only in "masked" form? Like Cenci, Shelley authors the incarnation of tragedy, and Shelley's discomfort with this role is reflected in his treatment of the Count. As he demonstrates in the person of the Count, Shelley believes the human capacity to enjoy tragedy at all is the sign of a constitutional defect:

12   Edmund Kean as Macbeth.

"from an inexplicable defect of harmony in the constitution of human nature, the pain of the inferior is frequently connected with the pleasures of the superior portions of our being...Our sympathy in tragic fiction depends on this principle; tragedy delights by affording a shadow of the pleasure which exists in pain."[21] The language used in

13   Eliza O'Neill as Juliet.

Drawn at the request of a Lady of Distinction   and Engraved with her permission

MISS O'NEILL
in the Character of
Belvidera

14   Eliza O'Neill as Belvidera.

the preface to *The Cenci* to describe the workings of tragedy makes it clear that Shelley understands drama itself as an asketic form: in a dramatic composition "Imagination is as the immortal God which should assume flesh for the redemption of mortal passion" (241).

Ironically enough, however, even the preface itself, as a set of instructions for reading the play, is akin to Cencian manipulation. Shelley's direct address to the audience, in which he insists upon the Christological implications of his work, is similar to Cenci's triumphant and sacramental account of his sons' deaths: addressing a bowl of wine, Cenci announces: "Could I believe thou wert their mingled blood, / Then would I taste thee like a sacrament" (I. iii. 81–82). Just as Cenci would make a sacrament of deaths he (claims to have) manipulated from afar, Shelley assures his audience of the redemptive powers of the horrors he has reproduced. Shelley's preface, like Cenci's dramatic reprise of his sons' deaths, functions as a kind of triumphant encapsulation of the events of the play, in which the author of those events outlines his motives and methods for producing this tragedy and tries to direct our responses to it. While Cenci sacrifices his children, Shelley, in producing a play that he intends should be closely modelled on "reality," sacrifices the imagination itself and the creative forms – lyrical and visionary – it typically took for him. He pointedly states that he has "been cautious to avoid the introducing faults of youthful composition; diffuseness, a profusion of inapplicable imagery. . ."[22] For Cenci too the "playwright's" choice of horrific subject-matter is linked to the limitation of imagination; he must do ever-worse deeds to "sharpen his appetite" now that "Invention palls: – Aye, we must all grow old – " (I. i. 99). Shelley represents in Cenci the dangers of the very form of art he was himself producing: a powerful form that operates through the physical manipulation of others – a horrific form associated with the limits of the imagination.

But while Shelley's decision to focus on external being and circumscribe the refining work of his own imagination (as well as that of the characters within the play) makes him like Cenci, his faithfulness to his Renaissance sources also represents an effort to avoid the threat Cenci poses. This fidelity is not only Shelley's stated and, according to most commentators, fulfilled goal,[23] but is subtly suggested in the very language of the prefatory materials. The ambiguity of a remark in the dedication to the play – "the drama which I now present to you is a sad reality" (237) – is a case in point. The word "drama," as it is used here, hovers between referring to Shelley's play and referring to the events in the lives of the Cenci themselves, with the result that we do not even pause at the implication that Shelley's play *is* a sad reality. Throughout the preface Shelley speaks of the original events that constitute his subject matter as if they were themselves a kind of drama. He uses the word "act," for instance, in a way that brings to mind both action and performance, with the result that the original members of the Cenci family themselves seem to be actors: "Such a story, if told so as to present to the reader all the feelings of those who once acted it..." (239). The events in the lives of the Cenci are referred to as a "tragedy" (239), and the life of Beatrice in particular is described as a theatrical performance: "The crimes and miseries in which [Beatrice] was an actor and a sufferer are as the mask and the mantle in which circumstances clothed her for her impersonation on the scene of the world" (242). This language underscores the association, discussed earlier, of corporeal life and theatricality; the salient events of Beatrice's life are nothing more than a mask, and to be a person at all is merely to impersonate. But these elisions also reflect Shelley's impulse to mini-mize his role as dramatic incarnator: Cenci may literalize his visions, but Shelley merely makes a tragedy out of what already was one. The sacrifice of the imagination thus marks not only Shelley's distance from his more optimistic writings – visionary writings that tended to focus on inner being and the powers of the imagination – but also from the text that functions as a response to those writings: *The Cenci* itself.

III

The Cenci does not, however, focus exclusively on the corporeal, but uses it as a vantage point from which to interrogate the status and workings of internal being. While Count Cenci is associated with externality and theatricality, Beatrice is, at least initially, associated with the poetic imagination and the behavioral ideal provided by the "inmost spirit." The Victorian critic Walter Bagehot complained that "Beatrice Cenci is really none other than Percy Bysshe Shelley himself in petticoats."[24] Silly as this sounds, if we heed Timothy Webb's injunction that we consider Shelley's self-projection on to certain exemplary characters not as a sign of egomania but as a way of exploring aspects of the poetic vocation,[25] we see that Bagehot is not far off the mark. As William Ulmer argues, "Beatrice...emerges as the play's predominant poet-figure."[26] We see this first of all in her representation as a self-sacrificial mediator. The interest in the poet's role as mediator is of course central to canonical Romanticism, and this mediation is often presented in Christological terms not only by the more conventionally religious poets like Coleridge but also by the atheist Shelley, for whom Christ was a type of the self-sacrificing poet. Beatrice is, of course, repeatedly characterized as a Christlike mediator: as Lucretia remarks to her, "you have ever stood / Between us and your father's moody wrath / Like a protecting presence: your firm mind / Has been our only refuge and defence" (II. i. 46–49). Even after she helps to orchestrate her father's murder, Beatrice still appears to those around her to be a heavenly emissary: "She, who alone in this unnatural work, / Stands like God's angel ministered upon / By fiends" (V. i. 42–44). Like Christ too, Beatrice's selfless mediation between her father and the rest of her family culminates in her sacrifice. Cenci, who makes a sacrament of his children's blood, not only permits but performs this sacrifice: Beatrice's rape. After the threat of incest has been posed but before it has been fulfilled, Beatrice cries "Thou, great God, / Whose image upon earth a father is, / Dost thou indeed abandon me!" (II. i. 16–18), thus underscoring the parallel between Christ's death and her rape. The moment of the rape functions as the critical ascetic moment, and Cenci himself makes it clear that he commits the rape not for sexual gratification but only to make Beatrice experience even her pure inmost self in terms of corrupt and suffering flesh, "Body and soul a monstrous lump of ruin" (IV. i. 95). And Cenci's act has the effect he intends. After the rape, Beatrice laments that "These putrefying limbs / Shut round and sepulchre the panting soul / Which would burst forth into the wandering air" (III. i. 26–28).

Unfortunately, as this image of entrapment suggests, Beatrice's mediating efforts and idealism are threatened by the very incarnation that solidifies her Christlike status. The play suggests that when the importance of the body to one's sense of self is magnified, it is dangerously easy for external forces to influence even the inmost being. This is so because accenting the external being abolishes the distance that makes mediation and imaginative re-presentation possible. Christlike though it may be, in the human corporeal world of this play mediation can easily become not only a self-sacrificial act but also a self-contaminating one. It is significant that when Camillo associates Beatrice with his beloved nephew and with Christ, he cuts her role as mediator short:

I would as soon have tortured mine own nephew

. . .

As that most perfect image of God's love
That ever came sorrowing upon the earth.
She is as pure as speechless infancy!   (v. ii. 63–69)

As this play repeatedly suggests, innocence demands a kind of passive non-involvement with the world, the deliberate avoidance of dangerous contacts.

The unification so often celebrated in Shelley's poetry becomes tragedy here as Beatrice becomes too intimate with her father in an act that is dreadful precisely because it destroys all distinctions, because it is "A deed which shall confound both night and day" (ii. ii. 183). Beatrice laments that a contaminating mist

                                                    glues
            My fingers and my limbs to one another,
            And eats into my sinews, and dissolves
            My flesh to a pollution, poisoning
            The subtle, pure, and inmost spirit of life!   (iii. i. 19–23)

The accumulation of clauses beginning with "and" itself suggests a relentless agglutination and dissolution, a union and disintegration that violates Beatrice's personal integrity in both senses of the phrase. At this point, Beatrice's body and then Beatrice herself threaten to become conduits of Cenci's evil because Beatrice believes her sense of self is determined in the last instance by her body. After the rape, she feels her father's blood doubly thick in her veins – "O blood, which art my father's blood, / Circling through these contaminated veins" (iii. i. 95–96) – and later begins to behave more and more like him. As long as the body is assumed to play a primary role in the determination of self the inmost self is in danger not only of being sullied by it but also of being unable to do its characteristic work of imaginatively reconceiving it. In a thoroughly corporeal world, mediation can easily lead to destructive *immediate* contact and become a means of contamination. Beatrice suffers terribly because she believes she can no longer safely refer her inner image of herself to her external being and experience.

But the danger here extends beyond the fact that this play represents a realm of amplified corporeality, a world where one can easily make the mistake of overestimating the body's role in identity-formation. When Beatrice does *not* make reference to her body or the fact of her physical subjugation, she does not become, as one might guess, a perfect mirror of purity, the ultimate canonical Romantic self. Her imagination does to some extent come to the fore as she tries to define herself as distinct from her body, but it operates almost frantically at certain moments, while being absolutely stymied at others. Beatrice's sense of self becomes profoundly disorganized once she can no longer ground her imagined inner sense of self in her external being. This becomes clear upon her reappearance on stage after the rape. Whereas the ideal canonical Romantic individual engages in a form of self-reflection wherein the self as consciousness enjoys a stable point from which to view the self as object, Beatrice as a disembodied subject feels herself reeling while her bodily, objectified form remains still; she says "I see a woman weeping there, / And standing calm and motionless, whilst I / Slide giddily as the world reels" (III. i. 10–12). Beatrice's detachment from her physical experience and self ironically leaves her, not free and unbound, but even more painfully disoriented than she might otherwise be.

Nevertheless, throughout the first scene of the third act Beatrice repeatedly tries to divorce herself from her corporeal being:

> ...Do you know
> I thought I was that wretched Beatrice
> Men speak of, whom her father sometimes hales
> From hall to hall by the entangled hair;
> At others, pens up naked in damp cells
> Where scaly reptiles crawl, and starves her there,
> Till she will eat strange flesh. (III. i. 42–48)

When she does make an effort to accept her physical existence and determine her identity on that basis, she finds she is unable to do so: "This is the Cenci palace; / Thou art Lucretia; I am Beatrice. / I have talked some wild words, but will no more. / Mother, come near me: from this point of time, / I am..." (III. i. 64–68). The unfortunate result of this incapacity to imaginatively connect inner and outer being is the thoroughgoing destabilization of Beatrice's identity. Her cry, "O, God! What thing am I?" (III. i. 38), could serve as the refrain for the scene. At times even Beatrice herself recognizes that her inability to accept what has happened to her body renders her almost mentally incapacitated: "My God! I never knew what the mad felt / Before; for I am mad beyond all doubt!" (III. i. 24–25). Her persistent question – "Oh, what am I? / What name, what place, what memory shall be mine?" (III. i. 74–75) – never finds a satisfactory answer because she can never fully imagine what she knows to be true of her external being.

As resistant as the body may be to imaginative idealization, Beatrice finds that when she tries to divorce her sense of self from her body altogether she cannot imaginatively represent herself either to herself or to anyone else:

> Horrible things have been in this wide world,
> Prodigious mixtures, and confusions strange
> Of good and ill; and worse have been conceived
> Than ever there was found a heart to do.
> But never fancy imaged such a deed
> As. . .   (III. i. 51–56)

Of course, Cenci's fancy did image such a deed, but for Beatrice to do so would entail, it seems, the unbearable recognition of a loss of integrity. Ironically, Beatrice's effort to screen her inner sense of self from her external self leaves her imagination bereft of material and therefore incapable of producing the distinctions (between innocent victim and guilty assailant, herself and Cenci, good and evil) she might find useful; she so obscures her knowledge of what has happened that she can't refashion it: "What is this undistinguishable mist / Of thoughts, which rise, like shadow after shadow, / Darkening each other?" (III. i. 170–172). Beatrice responds to Lucretia's inquiries by insisting that she has told all she knows of her experience, but this is true only because she has not permitted knowledge of her experience to take the form of concrete thoughts in the first place:

> . . .I hide them [sufferings] not.
> What are the words which you would have me speak?
> I, who can feign no image in my mind
> Of that which has transformed me. I, whose thought
> Is like a ghost shrouded and folded up
> In its own formless horror.   (III. i. 106–111)

In an effort to keep her former sense of self intact, Beatrice relinquishes her imaginative powers; but to do so is to relinquish the very faculty that originally characterized her self. "Ask me not what it is, for there are deeds / Which have no form, sufferings which have no tongue" (III. i. 141–142) – Cenci has managed to silence a woman known for her powerful understanding and fearless eloquence.

Beatrice's complete separation of her inner and outer self transforms her into a character who, throughout the rest of the play, remains enigmatic to herself, to those around her, and to the viewer/reader. She vacillates between appearing to be a reproduction of her father –

her identity as defined by her bodily contamination – and appearing to be a pure and Christlike figure – her inner identity as it was formerly defined. At one moment she pays a murderer with gold in Cencian fashion, at the next she pleads her essential innocence, and viewers and readers of the play find themselves unable to do anything but engage in an "anatomizing casuistry"[27] in an effort to understand her. Interestingly enough, this tension is visible even in the portrait of *La Cenci* so beloved by Shelley (see fig. 15). Pictured just prior to her execution, Beatrice's features suggest the tender pathos of O'Neill's delicacy, while at the same time she seems laden down with her prison garb, the sign of her guilty involvement in the corporeal theatrical world of her father. Because, after the rape, Beatrice is unable to accept her corporeal being, she is also unable to frame imaginatively what has happened to that being and to mediate between it and her inner sense of purity. The result is a bifurcated character whose inner purity is so thoroughly divorced from its external actions that the former cannot curb the viciousness of the latter.

But the fact that Beatrice's inability to mediate imaginatively between her inner and outer selves is paralleled by her inability to communicate with others about her state of mind and body suggests that she is responding not just to a personal but to a broadly social problem. Although innocently meant, Lucretia's questions to her after the rape resonate imagistically with the Count's act and hint at the extent to which it is Beatrice's whole world that renders her situation unspeakable and unimaginable:

> LUCRETIA: ...Speak to me,
> Unlock those pallid hands whose fingers twine
> With one another.
> BEATRICE: 'Tis the restless life
> Tortured within them. If I try to speak
> I shall go mad.   (III. i. 82–86)

Given that Beatrice entered the scene wondering how her hair had come to be undone when she had "tied it fast" (III. i. 8), we are hardly surprised that she is unwilling now to unlock her hands. Lucretia's request that Beatrice not hide her suffering "in proud impenetrable grief" (III. i. 105) resounds unpleasantly in the reader's ear and renders Beatrice's response perfectly fitting: "Of all words, / That minister to mortal intercourse, / Which wouldst thou hear?" (III. i. 111–113). For Beatrice, all intercourse and penetration, even of a strictly verbal sort,

15 *Beatrice Cenci*, engraved by Johann Heinrich Lips after Guido Reni, attrib., published in J. C. Lavater's *Physiognomische fragmente* (1778).

is suspect. As Hogle remarks, "any concrete utterance will turn around to oppress the 'I' and skew its aims with a configuration of the words according to the confining standards attributed to the father" (153). For Beatrice to find a word for her violation would be to repeat it, but in an even more public form:

> If I could find a word that might make known
> The crime of my destroyer; and that done
> My tongue should like a knife tear out the secret
> Which cankers my heart's core; aye, lay all bare
> So that my unpolluted fame should be
> With vilest gossips a stale mouthed story. (III. i. 154–159)

Beatrice can still think of herself as "unpolluted" and suggests that she might use her tongue to purify herself, to "tear out" the knowledge of her bodily experience that she alternately suppresses altogether or believes to have soiled her inmost soul. But this imagined possibility cannot be realized in a society like Beatrice's in which certain bodily acts cannot easily be represented. In fact, so unrepresentable is Beatrice's rape that when she describes herself as the subject of gossip she speaks as if it were her pure and not her raped self that will be discussed: "my *unpolluted fame* should be / With vilest gossips a stale mouthed story."

IV

Of course, the reluctance to speak of the body and the social ban on the representation of certain bodily functions, acts, and experiences are not problems peculiar to Beatrice or her time. Much canonical Romantic poetry, in its concern with mental life, neglects corporeal life. In many of his own writings, Shelley himself focuses on the metaphysical or ideal aspects of being, as he suggests in his preface to *The Cenci*. He does this not only at the level of content but also at the level of style, through the implementation of an array of peculiarly Shelleyan rhetorical techniques. The first of these is the use of images drawn from thought processes to describe events in the material world. Shelley explicitly and self-consciously describes this method in the preface to *Prometheus Unbound*: "The imagery which I have employed will be found in many instances to have been drawn from the operations of the human mind, or from those external actions by which they are expressed."[28] As William Keach points out, this technique inverts typical metaphoric practice; a mental operation becomes the vehicle in a metaphor whose tenor is physical.[29] Shelley's frequent use of reflexive imagery has a similar effect, in that it imitates "verbally [the] impulse of the mind to invest nature with its own reflexive activity" (83). Most notably, Shelley's verse is often characterized by a rapid metaphoric turnover that continually destabilizes the solidity of any given image. This creates the effect Keach describes as Shelley's speed, and he notes, moreover, that "throughout Shelley's poetry the pre-eminent figurative standard for speed is the action of thought or spirit" (174). It is perfectly appropriate that C. S. Lewis should have found in Shelley's poetry an airy quality: "You know...the air and fire of Shelley, the very antithesis of the Miltonic solidity, the untrammeled, reckless speed through pellucid spaces which makes us imagine while we are reading him that we have somehow left our bodies behind."[30]

Given Shelley's *meta*physical leanings, it is not surprising that in *Prometheus Unbound* Panthea's dream represents Prometheus' renewal after recalling his curse in terms of leaving a body behind:

> . . . his pale, wound-worn limbs
> Fell from Prometheus, and the azure night
> Grew radiant with the glory of that form
> Which lives unchanged within, and his voice fell
> Like music. . .   (II. i. 62–66)

The body falls away and whatever the form may be that emerges is marked only by its radiance – and then the voice alone comes to the fore. It almost seems that Demogorgon's role is to take on the burden of incarnation so that he, and not Prometheus, can effect the physical counterpart to the retraction of the curse – the removal of Jupiter:

> Two mighty spirits, mingling, made a third
> Mightier than either – which unbodied now
> Between us, floats, felt although unbeheld,
> Waiting the incarnation. . .   (III. i. 43–46)[31]

While Beatrice ultimately elicits an "anatomizing casuistry" and thus becomes a preeminently "dramatic character" (240), Prometheus, because he does not encourage "pernicious casuistry" remains a preeminently "poetical" one (133).

Given that *The Cenci* was written during the composition of *Prometheus Unbound*, there is every reason to believe that it represents a sort of commentary on the idealizing view of subjectivity represented in that more optimistic play. In *The Cenci* Shelley not only writes a drama for the stage, but focuses on bodily events and refuses to employ stylistic techniques that have the effect of spiritualizing matter. Barbara Gelpi argues that both the rape of Thetis and the rape of Beatrice can be read as displacements on to women's bodies of Shelley's anxieties regarding his ideal of an open and embracing subjectivity.[32] However comforting such a displacement may be, it is significant that in *The*

Cenci Shelley makes the rape the central event of the play, has its victim function as the play's protagonist, and denies himself the consolation of a happy ending. Beatrice's rape does not spawn a Demogorgon who will remove the murderous patriarch, and her own guilty orchestration of Cenci's "removal" is proved ironically superfluous by the arrival of the Pope's emissary. In her world, Beatrice's effort to shed her "wound-worn limbs" necessarily involves self-deception. Beatrice announces right after the murder of her father that she is "as universal as the light; / Free as the earth-surrounding air; as firm / As the world's centre" (IV. iv. 48–50). She can imagine herself universal, free, and firm – but only after her worst act. In the corporeal world of *The Cenci*, the individual drive toward unity with the world at large is exposed as an egoistic self-extension that involves the negation of others.

In *The Cenci*, then, Shelley sets himself the task of facing directly the issue of the role of corporeality in subjective and, by extension, public life. We see in Beatrice that if persons can ill afford to accept the corporeal as constitutive of subjectivity, neither should they sever their sense of self from their bodies entirely. Beatrice's failure to link internal and external being, a failure of the imagination to manage the corporeal, carries the neglect or verbal sublimation of the body to its logical extreme. As William Ulmer argues, "Shelley *is* on trial in *The Cenci*, and with him the poetic imagination as a means of moral renovation" (123). Beatrice's inability to name what happened to her body, like Shelley's inability to name incest on the public stage of the early 1800s, signals a circumscription of the corporeal that leads to imaginative failure.[33]

Unfortunately, this circumscription appears, finally, to be definitive. The fate of the inner being in the theatrical world of the body is perhaps most painfully though subtly exposed in the parallels established at the metadramatic level between Beatrice and the imagination. Beatrice, the poet figure whose face Shelley describes as expressive of "imagination and sensibility" (242), is not only initially characterized by a powerful imagination but also plays a role analogous to it. As the obvious Christ figure within the play and the victim of an asketic penetration, she clearly has affinities with the imagination and poetic imagery Shelley describes in his preface:

In a dramatic composition the imagery and the passion should *interpenetrate* one another, the former being reserved simply for the full development and illustration of the latter. Imagination is as the *immortal God which should assume flesh* for the redemption of mortal passion. (241, my emphasis)

In the rape, the Christlike Beatrice is reminded of her own corporeality – she assumes flesh. But Beatrice's fate exposes the difficulties inherent in the confident assertions of the preface; her example suggests that the noble faculty of the imagination cannot be made incarnate without being threatened in its very nature. Imagery and passion, imagination and flesh, must interpenetrate one another, but in the play that interpenetration leads only to death and seems to have little redemptive power.

The tendency to read *The Cenci* in terms of Shelley's more optimistic and canonical works and the desire to make his work self-consistent has often led to the perception of Beatrice's rape and the play's other pessimistic representations as no more than dark parodies of the imagery used in texts like *Prometheus Unbound*, rather than as serious criticisms of those texts. But the notion of parody doesn't quite do justice to the relentless pessimism of *The Cenci*. Earl Wasserman ends his chapter on *The Cenci* by commenting that "although [Shelley] offered *Prometheus Unbound* and *The Cenci* as independent, self-sustaining works with confident postures, they represent, taken together, the antinomies of the skeptical contest as it was waged in Shelley's own mind" (128). But as he himself remarks of Beatrice, "however closely her innocence and wrongs are brought together, they refuse to accommodate them-selves to each other" (125), and one could argue that this refusal of accommodation characterizes the two plays as well. The amplification of the role of corporeality in human affairs destabilizes the political and philosophical system, however skeptical it may be, that undergirds much of Shelley's poetic work. Shelley calls into question the efficacy and durability of the poetic imagination itself in the "real world" of persons who experience themselves, at least in part, in terms of their bodies and the physical actions of bodies.

v

By way of conclusion, I would like to make a detour to set Shelley's rumination on subjectivity in *The Cenci* in dialogue with the work of a contemporary who, like Shelley, conceives of subjectivity in generic terms, but whose perception of gender and history affords her a different view of the relation of body to spirit: Mary Shelley. During the same period that Percy wrote *The Cenci* Mary composed her own account of father–daughter incest: *Mathilda*, a piece remarkable in its use of genre in developing an argument about the nature of character.

The reader of *Mathilda* notices immediately that Mary, like Percy, tends to associate drama with material action, social as opposed to private life, and suffering: she uses the language of the drama, and/or alludes to specific dramas at moments when decisive action is pending. Thus, for instance, when Mathilda is a girl, she spends most of her time in solitary Wordsworthian nature-worship or (Percy) Shelleyan dreaming: "I wandered for ever about these lovely solitudes. . .singing as I might the wild melodies of the country, or occupied by pleasant day dreams."[34] But when she longs for company – especially that of her absent father – and considers taking physical action to change her life, Mathilda thinks in terms of drama:

I was a solitary being, and from my infant years, ever since my dear nurse left me, I had been a dreamer. I brought Rosalind and Miranda and the lady of Comus to life to be my companions, or on my isle acted over their parts imagining myself to be in their situations. Then I wandered from the fancies of others and formed affections and intimacies with the aerial creations of my own brain – but still clinging to reality I gave a name to these conceptions and nursed them in the hope of realization. . .[my] unhappy, wandering father was the idol of my imagination. . .My favourite vision was that when I grew up I would leave my aunt, whose coldness lulled my conscience, and disguised like a boy I would seek my father through the world. My imagination hung upon the scene of recognition. . .I reproached myself bitterly for [delaying this pilgrimage]. . .but this weakness returned upon me whenever the critical moment approached, and I never found courage to depart. (185)

This passage outlines a set of associations that informs the whole of *Mathilda*. Mathilda's private dreams, engrossing as they are, are always pushing outward for material realization; for Mathilda the pleasures of the imagination are clearly complicated, substitute pleasures rather than basic, simply "natural" ones (a point to which I will return later). This push towards the social and material is linked to drama: dramatic characters serve as imagined companions and finally suggest a way to bring about a real meeting with another person – through the adoption of a paradigmatically Shakespearean boy-heroine role. That action taken to fulfill what seems one's own proper destiny should require disguise, and in particular a masculine disguise, is telling. More telling still, Mathilda is never able to bring herself to act.

Unlikely as this particular action – the journey in search of the father – seems, there is something disheartening, painful, in Mathilda's failure to act. This "failure" is repeated much later in the novel, when

Mathilda, who longs to rejoin her now dead father in the afterworld, stages a suicide scene:

I planned the whole scene with an earnest heart and franticly set my soul on this project. I procured Laudanum and placing it in two glasses on the table, filled my room with flowers and decorated the last scene of my tragedy with the nicest care. (235)

The friend who is to serve as audience and fellow actor in this scene, a Shelleyan poet, responds to it with a poetic speech of optimism. Indeed, while Mathilda's carefully-chosen paraphernalia suggests that a kind of necessity stands behind her actions, as in a tragic drama, she herself offers *poetic* allusions that define her action as wrong: she speaks like Milton's Eve to Adam ("we are about to become gods; spirits free and happy as gods" [236]) and like Spenser's Despair to the Red Cross Knight. Woodville, her friend, picks up on the latter, and says he will play the part of Una to lead her to hope. As with Count Cenci, Mathilda's dramatic leanings signal an ethical waywardness. But her inability to realize her dramas reveals Mathilda's difference from the Count: the failure of her effort to play a genuinely dramatic, tragic role is explicitly linked to her gender. Mathilda as actor is like a girl disguised as a boy, Eve dictating to her husband, a woman acting the part of Despair rather than Una. Critical action on Mathilda's part repeatedly appears as simply overdramatic and wrongheaded, as mere female presumption rather than genuine hubris.

For both Percy and Mary, then, drama and the materiality to which it is linked are highly problematic. Percy, of course, does have Beatrice act, but primarily in the form of a reaction, and one which he condemns. As he explicitly remarks in his preface, it is her act of revenge that makes Beatrice so very dramatic a character; but for him that is, ethically speaking, no desideratum, and the performance of the act is wrong. For Mary, on the other hand, self-assertive action – ideologically the prerogative of men – would seem to be a rare and forbidden pleasure whose charms are not so easily denied. The male domains of drama and materiality, which meet with so much (often defensive) antagonism from male Romantic poets, are ostensibly condemned by Mary as well, and yet the narrative and Mathilda herself are unmistakably drawn to them. Of course, the very fact that the dramatic would seem generally to be the domain of men suggests that its renunciation is similarly a male virtue: Woodville's assumption of Una's role marks him as generous, whereas in Mathilda the quiet feminine attendance on others would be unremarkable. The views of Mary and Percy in relation to gender and subjectivity form, then, a sort of ideological chiasmus. Percy's ideal subject is forgiving, patient, and even passive, an idealized being whose spiritual center is ambiguously revealed through its veils – a "feminine" subject in the terms of the gender ideologies of the day. Mary, on the other hand, is drawn to a more masculine ideal of the subject, a subject expressive of will and capable of action. During these difficult years in their lives and their marriage, she, like Mathilda, seeks to justify responding to Percy's assumption of Una's role with the voice and in the character of Despair.[35]

It is significant, then, that Mathilda does, at the single most critical moment, act: when her father's resolve is weakened she urges him to divulge the secret that has so deeply disturbed him. The result is indeed tragic: he confesses his incestuous love for her, commits suicide, and leaves her to a life of mourning and guilt. As narrator, Mathilda might have represented her role in this drama as negligible; instead, she does just the opposite:

> I! I alone was the cause of his defeat and justly did I pay the fearful penalty. I said to myself. . .I will win him to me; he shall not deny his grief to me and when I know his secret then will I pour a balm into his soul and again I shall enjoy the ravishing delight of beholding his smile, and of again seeing his eyes beam if not with pleasure at least with gentle love and thankfulness. This will I do, I said. Half I accomplished; I gained his secret and we were both lost for ever. (197)

Mathilda's acceptance of responsibility for this revelation, so destructive to her peace, might be taken as a sign of an unfortunate eagerness to blame herself for the wrongdoings of another. But Mathilda shows elsewhere that she understands well enough that her father is guilty in his feelings for her; by making herself an actor at that critical moment, she makes herself an actor in the larger sense, and for that she is willing to pay a high price in personal suffering and remorse. It is not insignificant that the passage above is thick with the word "I." Mathilda's quintessentially feminine act of consolation gradually becomes almost masculine in its assertion of self – "this will I do" – and for this definitive action Mathilda suffers for the rest of her life. But from the moment she extracts her father's confession, Mathilda occupies not only a moral high ground relative to him but a position of control. He must beg her forgiveness, and later in her own room she loads on him "a daughter's curse" (204).[36] In her dream of that evening she finds him "dead-lily pale" "in flowing garments of white" (205) and pursues him over the fields – an inversion not only of their familial roles but of gender roles more generally.

In this Mathilda achieves something that Beatrice Cenci does not: she makes the "mask and mantle" that she wears in life her own. As she tells us at the outset "my fate has been governed by necessity" (176), but it is the necessity that governs the life of the classical tragic hero, a fate that is linked to character, not arbitrarily imposed. Percy tends to waffle a bit on the issue of the relation of poetry to history: at times he admits the influence of historical social setting on the poet and his poetry and at times he imagines the poetic as a thing distinct from the world of contingencies. Similarly, in *The Cenci*, he tries to make Beatrice both an expression of her time and something essentially separate from it. Like Beatrice, Mathilda's very being is marked by history, but unlike Beatrice, the reader can never imagine Mathilda any other way; the history defines the person – there is no rift between ideal and real. Much as she has to struggle to do it, Mary's heroine manages to make her being and her material existence classically whole.

If we turn to the poetic, that other major generic and characterological category in *The Cenci*, we see that for Mary as for Percy it is set in opposition to the dramatic. As we saw above, Mathilda's early life is comprised largely of the activity one associates with canonical Romantic character-formation: the solitary worship of an idealized nature combined with an absorption in the ethereal products of one's own imagination. But Mathilda, as we have seen, comes increasingly to crave dramatic action, and longs to see her dreams realized. It is in Woodville, then, that the poetic is most purely represented: a figure for Percy, Woodville is a gifted poet, gentle, imaginative, and optimistic. Mathilda is full of praise for Woodville and his words. But this landscape of praise is riddled with fault lines. In the course of the six paragraphs that introduce Woodville Mathilda mentions three times that he was a poet: "He was a Poet" (223); "I have said that he was a poet" (224); "Woodville was a Poet" (225). The incantatory quality of this repetition simultaneously marks the special value accorded this role and its near impalpability. That is, this fact – Woodville was a poet – seems at once vastly important and easy to forget. Woodville is represented in the narrative as Mathilda's best friend and her only source of sympathy, a person with consolation forever on his tongue. But his efforts to solace Mathilda are by no means entirely successful.

Just as Lucretia, in her request that Beatrice explain her distress, unwittingly suggests a re-enactment of her rape, Woodville's request that Mathilda unburden her secret to him calls for a repetition of the disastrous revelation of her father; he asks her to "utter one word" (231), just as Mathilda had demanded of her father, "a word! – I demand that dreadful word" (201). Although the admission that she is unhappy initially affords some relief to Mathilda, she eventually realizes that her unwillingness or inability to tell Woodville her entire story makes her feel worse than she had previously (239).

Most telling of all, Woodville, for all his poetry and his salutary lessons in optimism, not only cannot ultimately save Mathilda, but indirectly advances her death. During their final visit before Woodville makes a journey to his dying mother, Mathilda hears his "last lessons" and accompanies him toward the town. As she walks home Mathilda loses herself in a Dantean daydream: "I was so entirely wrapt in this reverie that I wandered on, taking no heed of my steps until I actually stooped down to gather a flower for my wreath on that bleak plain where no flower grew, when I awoke from my day dream and found myself I knew not where" (241). This poetic reverie, a dream of flowers on a barren plain, not only has no correspondence in the material world but also leaves Mathilda lost in it, with the result that she is forced to spend the night outside and contracts a consumption from which she soon dies. In a terrible irony, the absorption in solitary imaginings provokes a dangerous contact with nature that leads to the death Mathilda has so long sought. Now, through poetic indirection rather than dramatic action, her end is accomplished.

Mary Shelley's first draft version of the story, as its title, *Fields of Fancy*, suggests, is even more obviously focused on the relation between imaginative and material life. It differs from *Mathilda* primarily in its inclusion of a frame-story, in which the spirit Fantasia seeks to console the grieving narrator by transporting her to fairy lands. In a Dantean Elysium, the frame-narrator meets Plato's Diotima, who teaches a (Percy) Shelleyan creed, encouraging those around her in intellectual and moral development (a project represented as requiring centuries to accomplish); "Poetry seemed seated on her lips."[37] This frame-story then, would seem to be a tribute to the poetic and lyric ideal of character absorbed in vision. I would argue that one reason Mary eliminated this frame is because the authority it granted to the poetic, even in the female figure of Diotima, became unacceptable. Even as it stands, the frame-story shows signs of a conflict between poetic ideals and "sad realities." The narrator repeatedly reproaches Fantasia for abandoning her at the moments of her most intense grief and need, and Mathilda, in her response to Diotima, suggests that the latter's lovely words are only possible because she has not experienced deep passion and misery: "Diotima you know not how torn affections & misery incalculable misery – withers up the soul."[38] Mathilda's story becomes a narrative explanation, as it were, of her recalcitrant sadness, and it reveals the limitations of Diotima's creed. It is no small irony that it is in a field of fancy that Mathilda contracts the illness that will kill her.

In *Mathilda*, then, Mary Shelley tests the limits of the internalized, poetic character in a world of material suffering. For her, as for Percy, the imaginative and the material self are at odds. But whereas Percy struggles to define this conflict as a contingency of history, for Mary it is an aspect of being more generally, and hence not susceptible to amelioration. This difference is signalled in the way the two reflect upon the gothic in their work. For Percy in *The Cenci* gothicism is historicized; that is, it describes an historically-specific set of circumstances and possibilities for being. In *The Cenci*, Italy, the setting for many a gothic novel, is not rendered timeless but quite the opposite; Shelley insists in his preface that what we have in *The Cenci* is the sad reality of life in Catholic Renaissance Italy. Gothic lives are the products of changeable historical circumstance. For Mary, on the other hand, history itself is gothic. To suffer and to accrue memories even in modern Italy or England is to lead a gothic life. Ordinary modern life is itself sufficiently full of danger and distress, and to live in time is to accumulate painful memories, to be haunted by ghosts.

Moreover, while Mary, like Percy, links the gothic to the dramatic and material aspects of life, she also shows that even the poetic has gothic underpinnings. This connection is revealed first of all at the structural level: Mathilda's story, full of gothic events[39] – the threat of incest, supernatural signs, suicide – is initially represented as an extended visionary fantasy. But within the story itself the gothic and the poetic are often indistinguishable; both, after all, emphasize passion and the visionary/ghostly. Mathilda says of her father,

Even at that time I shuddered at the picture he drew of his passions: he had the imagination of a poet, and when he described the whirlwind that then tore his feelings he gave his words the impress of life so vividly that I believed while I trembled. I wondered how he could ever again have entered into the offices of life after his wild thoughts seemed to have given him affinity with the unearthly. (189)

The skill of the poet is here indistinguishable from that of the gothic storyteller, and Mathilda's father is at once a man of imagination and a ghost. Similarly, Woodville perceives Mathilda as a kind of vision, but a gothic one: she resembled "a being, who for some penance was sent from the Kingdom of Shadows" (245). For Mary Shelley, visions and dreams are not so easily distinguished from suffering ghosts. Moreover, happy dreams are revealed as the least truthful ones, so that they are, in effect, more superficial in their meaning than the gothic itself, that quintessentially superficial genre. Mathilda lives "like Psyche" (190) during her first blissful months with her father; but in retrospect she realizes that during that time she "hardly noticed more than the bare surface of events as they passed around me" (191). The happy spirit, so often figured by Percy in images of depth, is here revealed as superficial – without depth itself and unaware of the depths that surround it. For Mary Shelley, visionary life does not develop interiority; it simply hampers intersubjectivity and the assertion of self in action.

In fact, Mary Shelley is able to avoid some of the difficulties that trouble Percy because she does not construct subjectivity along an axis of depth but along an axis of time. Since for her life is composed of alternate periods of (poetic) stasis and (dramatic) action, character can only be understood as the sum and the history of those moments. In her final account of her life Mathilda encapsulates its generic vicissitudes:

Again and again I have passed over in my remembrance the different scenes of my short life: if the world is a stage and I merely an actor on it my part has been strange, and, alas! tragical. Almost from infancy I was deprived of all the testimonies of affection which children generally receive; I was thrown entirely upon my own resources, and I enjoyed what I may almost call unnatural pleasures, for they were dreams and not realities. The earth was to me a magic lantern and I [a] gazer, and a listener but no actor; but then came the transporting and soul-reviving era of my existence: my father returned and I could pour my warm affections on a human heart; there was a new sun and a new earth created to me; the waters of existence sparkled. joy! joy! but, alas! what grief! My bliss was more rapid than the progress of a sunbeam on a mountain. (245)

The pleasures of solitary reverie amid scenes of nature, vividly described earlier in the narrative, are now frankly termed, ironically enough, unnatural. Again, the poetic reverie is linked to the gothic – here, through the metaphor of the magic lantern, used during this period in the production of "ghost-shows."[40] Retrospectively, this early part of Mathilda's life – her childhood steeped in nature – seems static, passive, immaterial, and ghostly. Then, with change, the dramatic/ tragic comes to the fore in the image of a "new sun and a new earth," an allusion to the "new heaven, new earth" of *Antony and Cleopatra*[41] – an allusion that proleptically suggests that gratification will only come with death. And, indeed, this period of bliss proves to be just another light-effect, immaterial and ephemeral.

What we learn from Mathilda's story, then, is that life is, in its very nature, generically impure. The gothic is not only of the past but also of the present, and it infiltrates both the dramatic and the poetic. The poetic tells one kind of truth about life and human character, but if character were limited to its "poetic" mode, it would be static and superficial. The dramatic introduces not only materiality but also change; it is dangerous, but the action it entails is necessary to the expression and development of character – Mary perhaps understood better than Percy the hazards of feminine passivity. The prose narrative, in its capacity to contain and order these various genres, becomes perforce the only means of representing character. Mary deliberately calls attention to the narrative structure of the tale, its capacity to reproduce events over time and to mimic the passage of time itself: "I wander from my relation – let woe come at its appointed time; I may at this stage of my story still talk of happiness" (189); "I would pause for ever on the recollections of these happy weeks; I would repeat every word, and how many do I remember, record every enchantment of the faery habitation. But, no, my tale must not pause; it must be as rapid as was my fate" (190). The subsumption of other genres is, of course, not unconflicted; in particular, Mary is clearly anxious that her narrative prose will not do justice to poetry: "The poetry of [Woodville's] language and ideas which my words ill convey held me enchained to his discourses" (229); "These words are shadowy as I repeat them" (238). On one level this would appear to be the fault of the prose medium, a sign of its weakness. On another, however, it is suggested that prose reveals the truth of Woodville's words: the pleasures they afford are both imprisoning and ephemeral. And, again, the limitations of poetry are analogous to the limitations of poetic subjectivity: Woodville offers affection and sympathy, but no more substantive solace. He, occupied with "shapes copied from nature that dwelt in his mind with beauty greater than their own" (230), is unable to help Mathilda with the material realities that shape her being.

Not only does the prose narrative reveal Mathilda to us but it also permits her to make herself. Like Beatrice, Mathilda hears "one word" which changes not only her life but her identity: "infamy and guilt was mingled with my portion; unlawful and detestable passion had poured its poison into my ears and changed all my blood, so that it was no longer the kindly stream...[I was] a wretch on whom Nature had set her ban" (229). But unlike Beatrice, who is never able to reassemble the constituent parts of her life and her self into any coherent whole, Mathilda finds in narrative a generic solution to her need to reveal the truth of herself. The story we read is her own account of her life, written in the last days of it. Unfortunately, since it is history that defines identity here, and that history can only be complete at the end of life, Mathilda's story can only be told from what one might call a posthumous perspective – and hence it is only in death that Mathilda is able to reclaim her life.

Thus, we see that even given Cencian premises regarding subjectivity and genre, it is possible to develop a theory of both that is quite different from what we have in *The Cenci*. And yet the quandaries and contradictions explored in *The Cenci* are by no means easily avoided or resolved, however they are confronted. Although for Mary gender and history transform the significance of drama and poetry, she can ultimately only imagine her heroine dead. Similarly, *The Cenci* cannot finally offer what Wasserman calls "positive moral analysis,"[42] much less an *answer* to Percy's concerns about the subject and style of his more optimistic poetry. The play can only offer the Count and Beatrice as expiatory victims, tragic figures for the playwright and the imaginative poet; like *Mathilda*, *The Cenci* offers a sacrifice where it cannot offer a solution to the difficulties posed by the canonical Romantic opposition of spirit and body.

CHAPTER 5

Centrality and circulation in The Heart of Mid-Lothian

> *The Heart of Midlothian.* . .purported to be. . ."collected". . .[by the] parish-clerk of Gandercleugh. Gandercleugh, according to the introduction to the first series of *Tales*, is "the central part – the navel. . .of this our native realm of Scotland."[1]

In this final chapter we return to the novel and the problem of the relation of persons to a market economy, focusing in this case not on the commodification of identity but on the apparent effect of the dynamism of early industrial capitalism on the stability of even the innermost aspect of identity. Unlike the gothic novel, Scott's realistic *Heart of Mid-Lothian*, as its title suggests, is very much concerned with characterological depth and social centrality. Its plot is driven by two linked impulses: to determine what lies at the heart of social life, and to reveal the heart, the inner core, of individual people. These related mysteries of the heart, we learn, have a common solution; the novel finally locates the motive for social action in the hidden personal motives of a single man, a man who, moreover, has strong ties to the Heart of Midlothian: George Staunton. Oddly enough, however, Staunton appears only infrequently in the pages of the novel, pages which encourage an almost complete absorption in the character and fate of Jeanie Deans. This discrepancy reflects the fact that Staunton embodies the fundamental threat the novel aims to neutralize: the centrality of circulation to both social and personal life within a market economy. Staunton is not only the dynamic center of the novel's linked narratives but is also a figure for the dynamism of circulation itself, a dynamism visible in the rapidly developing networks of exchange and transportation of Scott's day and the increased mobility – physical, social, and characterological – that was their result. This excessive circulatory energy is represented as being at once fascinating and repulsive, and the characters, like Staunton, who are most closely associated with it are marked by a fluidity that is presented as both erotic and threatening.

As we shall see, the novel makes use of a variety of strategies for managing its knowledge that the heart of personal identity and the heart of society are not stable entities but merely the nodal points of circulation. These strategies range from the marginalization of characters like Staunton, to the use of a realistic narrative form that imposes a literally straightforward structure on circulation, to the employment of childbirth metaphors that represent circulatory energy as *re*productive. Ultimately, however, the novel solves the problems circulation poses by shifting its focus away from a market society altogether and to a colonial one defined by a patronage system of exchange relations. Within this colonial framework the novel strives to create, in the image of the Roseneath community, an idealized vision of an economic self-sufficiency that would render exchange relations simply unnecessary. *The Heart of Mid-Lothian* suggests, ultimately, that for Scott the canonical Romantic notion of deep interiority introduces the fluidity of a marketplace economy into human identity itself. The novel teaches, therefore, that two-dimensionality is the ideal state of being for both society and the individual, for as long as either is understood to have a heart, it will be involved in circulation.

I

One can trace in *The Heart of Mid-Lothian*'s prefatory and framing materials minor versions of the fundamental task of the novel – the management of what could be called circulatory energy. The first edition of the novel opens with a letter to the reader from a schoolmaster who claims that the text that follows was written by one Peter Pattieson, and the first chapter of the book functions as a frame-story in which Pattieson explains how he came upon the tale that forms the body of the novel. As we shall see, these two pieces foreground the issue of marketplace circulation – in the form of movement, exchange, and fluidity – as well as suggesting several strategies for harnessing or controlling this circulation. These strategies range from the metaphoric containment of circulatory energy in images of controlled reproductivity to the superimposition of a patronage system of exchange on a marketplace one. The novel's prefatory materials, then, establish the terms in which the problems of circulation will be both posed and resolved.

Pattieson's introductory frame-story opens with a discussion of the
significant recent changes in forms of circulation: "The times have
changed in nothing more...than in the rapid conveyance of intelligence
and communication betwixt one part of Scotland and another" (13).
The narrator suggests that the increase in the speed and extent of the
transportation of news, goods, and people poses a vague threat: "in
both [England and Scotland] these ancient, slow, and sure modes of
conveyance, are now alike unknown; mail-coach races against mail-
coach, and high-flyer against high-flyer, through the most remote
districts of Britain" (13). The very existence of these new coaches marks
the extension of market relations, a significance underscored in their
description: transportation now seems a race, a competition, and it also
seems less "sure." The expansion of transportation networks had not
only changed the landscape from the time of the novel's setting to the
time of the frame-story; it was continuing at an accelerated pace in
Scott's own day, as he was well aware. In letters written during the
period of the composition of *The Heart of Mid-Lothian*, Scott speaks of
the improvement and extension of Scottish roads and discusses plans
for the establishment of Scottish rail lines. In one, for instance, he
mentions talking to his "country neighbours" about a subject of
common interest: "an intended rail road to connect us with the coal
and lime works of Lothian."[2] The importance of circulation in the
form of transportation to the development of an industrial economy
was clear.

The changes in transportation that occurred between the period of
the novel's setting and the time of its composition were indeed
remarkable; as Roy Porter notes, "road improvement axed travelling
times," and the trip from Edinburgh to London that took an average of
256 hours in 1700 took only 60 in 1800.[3] Improved transportation
meant improved market circulation generally, and furthered capitalist
expansion. Agriculturalist and social commentator Arthur Young
applauded

The general impetus given to circulation; new people – new ideas – new
exertions – fresh activity to every branch of industry; people residing among
good roads, who were never seen with bad ones, and all the animation...and
industry, which flow with a full tide...between the capital and the provinces.[4]

Increased and improved circulation was associated with the production
of novelty of all kinds, and even seemed to bring new populations into
being. As Porter argues, during the eighteenth century the principal

incitement to growth was not technological and industrial development but the increased circulation of goods and capital: "[the growth of British industry] did not hinge on revolutionary innovations in entre-preneurship or technology, but on the steady sucking of wealth into circulation, better use of labour reserves, and new techniques for making exchange of goods and services easier, faster, and more reliable. The heroes of this march of commercial capitalism are largely anonymous, not least the rank-and-file distributors, hauliers, shippers, transporters..." (210). In the late eighteenth and early nineteenth centuries capitalist development was particularly visible in the form of movement, circulation in all its modes, ranging from the increasing opportunities for recreational travel to the faster and cheaper transpor-tation of newspapers that spread the market for London fashions to the provinces.[5] The circulation of money, of course, had for some time been associated with the generation of wealth. As Jon Klancher notes, "in his *Political Arithmetic* Young himself joined the tradition of economic thinking, from Aristotle to Condillac, Hume, and Adam Smith, that locates surplus wealth in the circulation of money," and during the eighteenth century in particular "'circulation' had acquired meta-phorical resonances as a symptom of national growth."[6] Scott was well aware of the almost productive capacity of monetary circulation, as is evidenced in advice he gave to Joanna Baillie in 1817 regarding the abundance of money, the medium of circulation: "if you want to sell the poems I think it almost certain that the Trade would give the thousand pounds and well they might. I do not know that this could be done two years since but money is now plenty and commerce in all its branches feels its vivifying influence" (*LWS*, 25–26). It is characteristic of capitalist circulation to appear inherently productive; as Antonio Negri points out, "even though circulation does not produce surplus value, it nonetheless enables capital to produce surplus value at every point of the circulation."[7] It comes as little surprise, then, that circulation should seem to acquire an agency of its own, a capacity for expansion that exceeds its reproductive aims. In the early phases of British industrial capitalism circulation in the material form of trans-port and exchange was an arena in which economic growth was both particularly promoted and particularly visible; circulation seemed therefore not simply to redistribute value (its ostensible function) but to generate a surplus of it.

The frame-story to *The Heart of Mid-Lothian* initially represents the accelerated speed of circulation as fascinating but potentially disruptive.

The narrator explains that he walked out on the highway to meet with a coach he expected to bring him a favorite periodical, and then proceeds to confess that it was not only the immediate receipt of his journal that interested him: "It was with such feelings [of impatience] that I eyed the approach of the new coach, lately established on our road, and known by the name of the Somerset, which, to say truth, possesses some interest for me, even when it conveys no such important information" (14). We soon learn, however, that the swiftly moving coach, interesting though it is to watch, is not as secure a mode of transportation as it might be; the narrator remarks that there are occasions when "the Insides and Outsides [of a coach], to use the appropriate vehicular phrases, have reason to rue the exchange of the slow and safe motion of the ancient Fly-coaches" (13–14). Such swiftness of movement has, in fact, the potential to turn the world upside down: "the Somerset had made a summerset in good earnest, and overturned so completely, that it was literally resting upon the ground, with the roof undermost, and the four wheels in the air" (15). This chaos, however, is made the opportunity for a metaphoric birth: " 'the guard and coachman'...were now proceeding to extricate the *insides* by a sort of summary and Caesarean process of delivery, forcing the hinges from one of the doors which they could not open otherwise. In this manner were two disconsolate damsels set at liberty from the womb of the leathern conveniency" (15–16). This description exemplifies one of the novel's principal strategies for the recovery of what could be called excess circulatory energy: the use of an image of birth to render reproductive an energy that might otherwise be disruptive. It is perfectly fitting that this recuperative gesture should have a comic tone. This "birth" is one that brings life out of death; the "two ladies" are also described as having been "disinterred" (16).

This is not the only instance in the frame-story of the association through metaphor of circulation, death, and birth. I quote at length a passage in which this connection is made much more subtly:

"He looks as if he were just about to honour with his residence the HEART OF MID-LOTHIAN."

"You are mistaken – he is just delivered from it...Pray, Mr Pattieson, have you been in Edinburgh?"

"Then you must have passed...through a narrow intricate passage, leading

out of the north-west corner of the Parliament Square, and passing by a high
and antique building, with turrets and iron grates,

> Making good the saying odd,
> Near the church and far from God" –

Mr Halkit broke in upon his learned counsel, to contribute his moiety to
the riddle – "Having at the door the sign of the Red Man" –

"And being on the whole," resumed the counsellor, interrupting his friend
in his turn, "a sort of place where misfortune is happily confounded with guilt,
where all who are in wish to get out" –

"And where none who have the good luck to be out, wish to get in," added
his companion.

"I conceive you, gentlemen," replied I; "you mean the prison."   (19)

This description, which, as a riddle, formally suggests its own multi-
valence, clearly conjures images of hell and death. But the language
here – of being delivered, moving through a narrow intricate passage,
getting out of a place that has at the door the sign of the Red Man, and
conception – suggests that movement or circulation around the
Tolbooth has affinities with birth. What might be imagined as random
movement is imagined instead as the regulated movement of a
reproductive process.

The vague threat of violence and the suggestion of birth here at the
first mention of the Heart of Midlothian are no accident, for the
circulation or movement that gives rise to images of both disruption
and birth is continually connected in the novel with the notion of a
heart. The Tolbooth's very name signals the building's association with
trade and tax, and reminds us that a tolbooth typically serves as the
heart of exchange, the center of circulation.[8] But of course, at the
moment of the novel's action, the Heart of Midlothian is anything but
a circulatory organ: "'a prison is a world within itself, and has its own
business, griefs, and joys, peculiar to its circle'" (20). Circulation is
contained within the small circle of the prison: "'how many hearts
have throbbed within these walls...?'" (22). The Tolbooth thus serves
as the perfect emblem of the status of circulation in the novel: it is
represented as necessary, literally central, but in need of delimitation.

The use of the metaphor of biological circulation to describe economic circulation is not only suggested in reference to the Tolbooth but pervades the entire frame-story and reflects the contemporary significance of circulation. The "elder lawyer" refers to "'the gentry, shut up in their distant and solitary mansion-houses, nursing their revengeful passions just to keep their blood from stagnating'" (23). The lawyer implies that circulation of various kinds – trade, intermarriage, physical and social mobility – all stand in contrast to the relative stasis and self-sufficiency of an older order. It is not by chance that Deleuze and Guattari use language that punningly draws upon biological imagery in their description of Marx's concern with the role of circulation in capitalism: "At the *heart* of *Capital,* Marx points to the encounter of two 'principal' elements:...the deterritorialized worker ...and...decoded money...these two *flows*: *flows* of producers and *flows* of money."[9] The aptness of the metaphor was not lost on Marx himself: "The circulation of capital is at the same time its becoming, its growth, its vital process. If anything needed to be compared with the circulation of the blood, it was...the content-filled circulation of capital."[10] Circulation is functionally central to a capitalist economy; the establishment of capitalist relations depends on its intensive and extensive development. The focus on the Heart of Midlothian represents both an expression of this knowledge and a suppression of it.

Circulation has yet another aspect in the frame-story, one that, once again, is linked to the Tolbooth. During the composition of *The Heart of Mid-Lothian* in 1817 Scott wrote to Robert Johnstone that he would like to "embrace your kind offer of once more troubling you for another *rake* of the Old Heart of Midlothian & for Creeches lintel whereof you gave me so entertaining an account" (*LWS*, 14–15). As H. J. Grierson points out in his notes to Scott's letters, "'Creech's Land,' a tenement at the east end of the Luckenbooths, in the Tolbooth, was a great haunt and centre of the Edinburgh literati of the eighteenth century...It was here [that Allan Ramsay] established the first circulating library in Scotland" (*LWS*, 15).[11] Ramsay's, in fact, appears to have been the first real circulating library in all of Britain.[12] Scott was markedly sensitive to the desires of reading audiences of his day; he wrote to Constable that he was "delighted with Mathurines success – he is a clever fellow – I have some fear, however (commercially speaking) of his sermons. They are not – the more's the pity – exactly the current coin of our day" (*LWS*, 131). At the same time, however, he tried to distance himself from the market economy that book sales and circulating libraries represented. As he mentioned in a letter to John Ballantyne, he was "afraid the people [would] take [him] up for coining. Indeed these novels while their attractions last are something like it."[13] As in his letter to Baillie, Scott takes the medium of circulation – money – as the sign of the surplus value to which circulation seems, almost unaccountably, to give rise. The extent of Scott's own commercial success was unprecedented: the popularity of his novels led to an increase in price that eventually extended to all novels.[14] As he wrote in a letter of 1818 to John Morritt: "the public taste or rather voracious appetite for fictitious narrative has done for me what your kind and well judging relative has performd for you and have enabled me to make a spacious accession of territory" (*LWS* 48). This popularity naturally made Scott's work staple fare for the circulating libraries: in an investigation in the later nineteenth century of the holdings of ten of the London circulating libraries the London Statistical Society created a separate category for novels by Scott or in imitation of him, and this group was second in size only to "Fashionable Novels, well known," and "Novels of the lowest character."[15] This form of circulation around the Tolbooth is, then, conceived in terms of the same problematic we have already seen at work: in this case, an increase in the circulation of fiction not only gives rise to an increase in its production, but also determines in part the nature of that production and its value. Once again, the increase in circulation leads to a generation of surplus value that destabilizes whatever inherent value fiction seemed to have.

As Richard Altick points out, "the hostility to novels which had been building up for several decades reached its peak in the early nineteenth century. The primary target was the circulating-library novel..." (123). In the frame-story of *The Heart of Mid-Lothian*, Scott suggests the formal distance of his novel from such circulating novels. One of the lawyers within the story refers to the " 'half-bound and slip-shod volumes of the circulating library' " (23), and his companion argues that law cases would better satisfy the public's appetite for narrative because of their true novelty: " '[with novels] I read and swear till I get to the end of the narrative. But not so in the real records of human vagaries – not so in the State Trials, or in the Books of Adjournal, where every now and then you read new pages of the human *heart*, and turns of fortune far beyond what the boldest novelist ever attempted to produce from the *coinage* of his brain' " (21–22, my emphasis). The legal tale, based on "real" events, which comprises the novel proper is thus implicitly established as a text that is more exciting and therefore marketable than the purely fictional novel, while at the same time being exempt from the taint of simple commercialism.[16] Fittingly enough, true tales of this sort, such as accounts of the gentry who committed crimes " 'to keep their blood from stagnating' " (23), serve to *obstruct* circulation in their readers: " 'the blood of each reader shall be curdled' " (23).

The novel's techniques for regulating the surplus energies of circulation thus range from the use of birth images that make movement appear visibly and controllably reproductive, to the definition of its own genre as one distinct from that of the circulating novel while still being marketable. But the novel also tries to redefine the very nature of capitalist circulation by overlaying it with a patronage system of exchange. This overlay takes a comic form in Cleishbotham's prefatory letter in acknowledgement of his "patron": "To the best of patrons, a pleased and indulgent reader, Jedediah Cleishbotham wishes health, and increase, and contentment" (9). The productive capacity of circulation is refigured here as the natural escalation of the value of the gifts exchanged in a patronage system: "We [Cleishbotham and the reader] do therefore lie, in respect of each other, under a reciprocation of benefits, whereof those received by me being the most solid, (in respect that a new house and a new coat are better than a new tale and an old song,) it is meet that my gratitude should be expressed with the louder voice and more preponderating vehemence" (9).

Of course, the comedy of the letter arises from its petty bourgeois tone; the fact that Cleishbotham works entirely within a market economy makes his appropriation of the language of patronage – a mode of financing literary production in the absence of a sufficient market for it – laughably inappropriate. Moreover, Cleishbotham gracelessly displays his commercial interests: he goes on at length about the new coat he has bought with his past earnings and the land he hopes to buy with future ones. As a man who sells the tales of others in order to purchase goods and land for himself, Cleishbotham has obvious affinities with Scott. By displaying his own techniques and interests in such an extreme form, by parodying his own role, Scott establishes his distance from Cleishbotham – that Scott could never be like Cleishbotham is proved by his ability to recognize him for what he is. In Cleishbotham, Scott, the anonymous author behind him, plays out some of the contradictions of his own methods and situation.

After he does reveal himself as the author of *The Heart of Mid-Lothian* and other novels, Scott appends his own introduction to the book, an introduction in which he, unlike Cleishbotham, offers a seamless and satisfying representation of a patronage relationship. In that introduction, Scott serves as patron to Mrs. Goldie, the woman who provided him with the story of Helen Walker that he reproduced as the story of Jeanie Deans. While Walker's experience and Goldie's retelling of it provide Scott with source material he takes to market, the women's relationship to him is represented as one involving the generous and open-ended reciprocation of benefits:

"Mrs Goldie was extremely anxious to have a tombstone and an inscription upon it...and if Sir Walter Scott will condescend to write the last, a little subscription could be easily raised in the immediate neighbourhood, and Mrs Goldie's wish be thus fulfilled."

It is scarcely necessary to add, that the request of Miss Goldie will be most willingly complied with, and without the necessity of any tax on the public. Nor is there much occasion to repeat how much the author conceives himself obliged to his unknown correspondent, who thus supplied him with a theme... (6)

Scott, unlike Cleishbotham, knows how to participate in and describe a patronage relationship; the emphasis here is on the free gift of goods with no expectation of recompense.

The replacement or subsumption of a market relationship by something resembling a patronage relationship appears repeatedly in the novel, as in the following small moment from the frame-story. A ragged old man who was at one time a client of one of the lawyers is taken into their company out of kindness. But after being "in the company of his superiors," and "declining all entreaty to partake of the wine, which circulated freely round, he...modestly withdrew" (19). The circulation of wine that began with its purchase is redefined as an economy wherein the enjoyment of goods is based on personal connections rather than money. In this case, the old man's sense that the lawyers are his true superiors is so acute that he cannot even enjoy the generosity of his patrons.

Scott's use of a quotation from Cowper's *The Task* similarly suggests the replacement of a market relationship by a patronage relationship:

I expected by the coach a new number of an interesting periodical publication, and walked forward on the highway to meet it, with the impatience which Cowper has described as actuating the resident in the country when longing for intelligence from the mart of news:

– "The grand debate,
       . . .
And the loud laugh, – I long to know them all; –
I burn to set the imprison'd wranglers free,
And give them voice and utterance again."   (14)

In *The Task*, Cowper's speaker goes on to describe the newspaper as "a map of busy life, / Its fluctuations, and its vast concerns" but remarks that "surveying thus at ease / The globe and its concerns, I seem advanced / To some secure and more than mortal height."[17] Fittingly then, in Scott's piece one's purchase from the mart of news is imagined to be a generous condescension to liberate those discussed in the newspaper; to whatever extent people are trapped for sale by the paper, they are figured as being freed again by the consumer. One almost becomes a literary patron – one who finances the speech of others – through the purchase of a commodity.

The novel's effort to define and delimit agency at both a social and an individual level leads it again and again to the question of circulation – the various social exchanges and movements that increasingly seem to take on an agency of their own. As we have seen, the novel's framing materials foreground this problem and suggest two strategies for its solution: the channeling of surplus circulatory energy into images of controlled reproductivity – birth, the retelling of a true tale – and the superimposition of a patronage system of circulation on the market system. We shall see that in the central tale itself the Heart of Midlothian will be associated with a proliferation of value and meaning very much in need of the regulatory structures of birth, realism, and patronage – a proliferation anticipated by the punning which the name "Heart of Midlothian" gives rise to in the frame-story:

"the metropolitan county may...be said to have a sad heart..."
"and a close heart, and a hard heart..."
"And a wicked heart, and a poor heart..."
"And yet it may be called in some sort a strong heart, and a high heart...You see I can put you both out of heart..."
"I have played all my hearts..." (20)

II

Just as the high speed of modern coaches leads to an accident that results in the recounting of the central tale of *The Heart of Mid-Lothian*,[18] the main plot of that tale is set in motion by an entry into circulation.

As dissenters and country folk of an earlier period than the frame-story, the Deanses initially lead a life that is preeminently static. Not only, as David Deans puts it, do they not "'trinquet and traffic wi' courts'" (192), but they barely trinquet or traffic with anybody. The act that disrupts that stasis is sending Effie to be a shopgirl in the urban center of Midlothian – where, "for some inconceivable reason, our ancestors had jammed [the Luckenbooths (shops by the Tolbooth)] into the *midst* of the *principal street* of the town" (56, my emphasis) – with the result that she becomes involved in commerce of both an economic and a sexual kind. Thus drawn into the center of circulation (she travels to the city, works in trade, circulates her own body), Effie is suddenly swept up in its mysterious excesses. This circulation yields a "product" that was neither foreseen nor intended, a "product" whose fate and maker (father) are alike shrouded in mystery – Effie's baby. The legal system becomes strangely productive itself in response to the unregulated and therefore not truly *re*productive energies of Scotland's women: the law that would condemn Effie was designed "'to prevent the horrid delict of bringing forth children in secret – The crime is rather a favourite of the law, this species of murther being one of its ain creation'" (55).

The focus on the dangers of unregulated circulation is not limited to the main plot. The Tolbooth prison that serves to limit Effie's circulation ties her story to the novel's secondary plot, which focuses on the Porteous riots. In that narrative, contraband trade – circulation that does not go through official channels – leads to the unpopular execution that triggers mob violence. The criminal world of unregulated trade finds its counterpart in unregulated and violent mob action, and the mob's activity, like Effie's pregnancy, has no definable agent. At Wilson's execution and in the Porteous riot, movement escalates and leads to results that seem to have no author: "The crowded populace, as if their motions had corresponded with the unsettled state of their minds, fluctuated to and fro without any visible cause of impulse" (42).

The novel thus juxtaposes two cases of unregulated circulation leading to problems of indeterminate identity and agency: that of the anonymous Porteous mob and that of the anonymous father of Effie's child. The first case presents a historical-social problem: "The secret history of the Porteous Mob has been till this day unravelled; and it has always been quoted as a close, daring, and calculated act of violence, of a nature peculiarly characteristic of the Scottish people. Nevertheless, the author, for a considerable time, nourished hopes to have found himself enabled to throw some light on this mysterious story."[19] In spite of the fact that Scott's research yielded nothing to indicate that the riot was an organized event led by a small group of men, his impulse in the novel is always to argue that it was: the narrator refers to "the mob, or rather, we should say, the conspirators" (63). In fact, in Scott's fictional account, the agency of the unaccountable mob is given a center in a single character, George Staunton. Moreover, we learn that Staunton is also the father of Effie's child.

Given Staunton's role as the link between the novel's two plots and the person whose connections to the Heart of Midlothian are strongest (as one who was imprisoned himself, leads the storming of the Tolbooth as part of the Porteous riot, and plans to release Effie from prison), it comes as little surprise that he should be involved in the various forms of circulation that drive the novel. He comes, in fact, to be powerfully associated with the most threatening aspects of capitalist life. The contraband trade he participates in functions as the dark double of legal trade, characterized by exaggerated forms of the most troublesome features of a rapidly growing market: it is unregulated, it attenuates and shrouds the connection between producer and consumer, and it has a fraudulent air about it. The narrator remarks that "Contraband trade, though it strikes at the root of legitimate government, by encroaching on its revenues, – though it injures the fair trader, and debauches the minds of those engaged in it...was almost universal in Scotland in the reigns of George I. and II." (28).

Moreover, Staunton's physical and social mobility allows him to go from being an aristocrat, to being a wanderer and contraband trader by the name of Robertson, to posing as an aristocrat – now under false pretenses – in the latter part of the novel. "'The chances of a wandering life'" (325) carry him not only from one place to another but also from one role to another. Staunton's mobility and his involvement in trade pervade his very character, a fact that is signalled by his association with theatricality. As Jean-Christophe Agnew argues in *Worlds Apart*, from the seventeenth century onward the theater was powerfully associated with the marketplace because both were imagined to be arenas of imposture. At the same time, the imitability of status in theatrical representation came more and more to signify the fluid and theatrical nature of social character generally under capitalism. Increased social mobility made one's current stature no more than a temporary role: self-help manuals "kept to the theme of a newly-discovered, Protean social world, one in which the conventional signposts of social and individual identity had become mobile and manipulable reference points."[20] Complaints about this social world were part of an effort to "give practical and figurative form to the very principles of liquidity and exchangeability that were dissolving, dividing, and destroying form..." (9). Agnew traces the growing sense of the theatricality of social relations from the first puritan attacks on the theater to the notion of the theatricality of moral sentiments in the writings of one of "the age's countless itinerants" (188), Adam Smith. As Agnew puts it:

In accordance with this widespread awareness of social bargaining, public and private life assumed an extraordinarily theatrical style as classes, factions, and individuals maneuvered for position on a cultural terrain that years of violent upheaval and slow economic change had steadily defamiliarized. Popular consciousness was adapting, to recur to Pocock's phrase, "to a world of moving objects" and, we might add, to an increasingly detached and mobile population. (188)

Staunton's representation as a masked actor (especially in the mob scene, where he and others are in concealing costumes) links him with the anonymity and untrustworthy qualities of market relations and the potential for social mobility within capitalist society. Staunton's theatricality is at times made quite explicit: a magistrate is tempted to throw aside a letter Staunton wrote "as the production of a madman, so little did 'the scraps from playbooks,' as he termed the poetical quotation [cited in the letter], resemble the correspondence of a rational being" (182–183). Not only do Staunton's manners and speech seem to be inordinately affected, but both Madge Wildfire and Ratcliffe mention that he literally was at one time "a play-actor" (161); Madge once went with him "to see him act upon a stage, in fine clothes" (302). David Deans's suspicion of the theater – he considered meetings for the purpose of dancing or "dramatic representations, as one of the most flagrant proofs of defection and causes of wrath" (100) – is reminiscent of puritan prohibitions of earlier times. In fact, the seventeenth-century puritan notion that "all changes and extravagances of dress were a species of transvestism,"[21] highlights the way Staunton's literal transvestism represents the ultimate in shape-shifting. As Madge Wildfire explains, "Gentle Geordie Robertson put my ilka-day's claise on his ain bonny sell yestreen, and gaed a' through the town wi' them; and gawsie and grand he lookit, like ony queen in the land" (165).

Staunton's travesty foregrounds the ways the urban riot he leads has an
element of that old marketplace event, the carnival – the world turned
upside down.[22]

But unlike the theatrical personae of Agnew's study, Staunton's
character is not without interiority. And unlike the characters of the
gothic novel, whose mysterious public identities are sharply distinguished from their static and obvious private identities, Staunton's
role-playing is represented as an aspect of his inner character;
theatricality and canonical Romantic inwardness combine in him. It is
as if the exchange value that is associated with social identity in the
gothic has been driven into the inner depths that canonical Romantic
subjectivity originally offered as a safe haven from the world of
market relations. Here, interiorized Romantic identity, precisely
because of its hiddenness and changeability, comes to be associated
with the incomprehensibility and unpredictability of market relations.
It is the mystery and unknowability of Staunton's character that make
that character the deep, high Romantic thing that it is, a point to
which I will return later. For Scott, characterological fluidity runs
deep, and is all the more dangerous for doing so.

We see then that not only does rapid circulation seem to signify an
economy driven by barely contained forces, but the movement of
circulation both gives rise to and becomes a metaphor for a social life
wherein everything from value to individual identity is characterized by
continual flux. It is not without reason that Staunton stands at the center
of both a social and a personal mystery; the excesses of circulation are at
work on both a social and an individual level. Marx argues that under
capitalism value increasingly appears to be "endowed with a motion of
its own."[23] For Deleuze and Guattari, this unaccountable flux characterizes more than just value; they refer to "the fundamental capitalist
phenomenon of *the transformation of the surplus value of code into a surplus value
of flux*" (228). As ever more things become commodified and are made
equivalent to the standard of value represented in money, a value
subject to market fluctuations, they lose their fixed and discrete character. Values and identities are produced in excess and are constantly
changing. Moreover, as Pocock argues, the development of a credit
economy led during the eighteenth century to a sense that "property –
the material foundation of both personality and government – [had]
ceased to be real and [had] become not merely mobile but imaginary."
Pocock reminds us "that it was the hysteria, not the cold rationality, of
economic man that dismayed the moralists."[24]

We can perhaps better understand the significance of this flux, as it is figured in Staunton, by turning to Bataille's notion of expenditure.[25] In so far as this concept describes for Bataille the unregulated and unproductive release of energy it has much in common with Staunton's frighteningly and fascinatingly unchanneled excesses. He is associated with the violent and unaccountable energies of the mob, his eroticism is not channelled into social reproduction, and he responds to events around him with a theatrical surfeit of emotion. Bataille's drive to imagine what Derrida calls "a negativity without reserve,"[26] a form of activity so resolutely outside a restricted Hegelian economy that it cannot be recuperated by it, provides an insight into the function of Staunton's character within the novel's structure. For Bataille, this negativity arises from within the restricted economy itself although it threatens it; he describes the way a disruptive tendency of this type is displayed in gambling: "It is true that this circulation of money profits a small number of professional bettors, but it is no less true that this circulation can be considered to be a real *charge* of the passions unleashed by competition and that, among a large number of bettors, it leads to losses disproportionate to their means; these even attain such a level of madness that often the only way out for gamblers is prison or death" (119). Located at the very heart of the novel's market economy, Staunton represents the destructive potential of the energies that drive it, their capacity to disrupt that economy altogether. Staunton's passionate nature involves him in expenditures that make him funda- mentally criminal in Bataille's sense: "the boundless refuse of activity pushes human plans – including those associated with economic opera- tions – into the game of characterizing universal matter; matter, in fact, can only be defined as the *nonlogical difference* that represents in relation to the *economy* of the universe what *crime* represents in relation to the law" (129). Indeed, in addition to being responsible for the death of Porteous and others, Staunton has, by his own admission, " 'been the destruction of the mother that bore me – of the friend that loved me – of the woman that trusted me – of the innocent child that was born to me' " (152). He is possessed of a kind of demonic energy that challenges all order: he refers to himself at one point as " 'the devil' " (111) and Jeanie fears upon first meeting him that he is " 'the Great Enemy' " (150).

The threatening excesses of Staunton's character, and the erotic and violent "charge" of those excesses, are suggested even in minor details of the language of the narrative. In a chapter that opens with a discussion of demonology and witchcraft, Jeanie's journey to her moonlight rendezvous with Staunton at a site that commemorates a man's murder of his wife is described thus: "like Christiana in the Pilgrim's Progress, when traversing with a timid yet resolved step the terrors of the Valley of the Shadow of Death, she glided on by rock and stone, 'now in glimmer and now in gloom,' as her path lay through moonlight or shadow, and endeavoured to overpower the suggestions of fear..." (150). The relatively submerged allusion to Coleridge's "Christabel" has sinister overtones that counteract the more optimistic reference to *The Pilgrim's Progress*.[27] Jeanie meets up with Robertson just as Christabel's midnight walk leads her to befriend Geraldine, a satanic and erotically charged shape-shifter who is, like Staunton, a seducer of innocent women.

This allusion points to another attribute of Staunton's (and of the characters like him): they are not only characterized by Romantic psychological depth but are also associated with high Romanticism generally. Staunton himself, of course, is a Byronic figure (a type Scott himself had earlier helped to fashion in works like *Marmion*). Like Manfred, the eponymous hero of the Byron play that had appeared the year before Scott's composition of *The Heart of Mid-Lothian*, Staunton loudly laments the destruction of himself and those he loves, oscillating between proclaiming his own guilty part in this destruction and blaming the world for misunderstanding him. Moreover, Staunton's aristocratic origins, seductiveness, and theatricality all associate him with the Byronic hero.

But Staunton does not stand alone in opposition to Jeanie, who, we are repeatedly told, "was no heroine of romance" (251). Effie, Madge Wildfire, and Meg Murdockson all have qualities in common with Staunton, including their association with the Romantic. Effie, for instance, very definitely *is* a heroine of romance, and a character whose role and fate in the novel we imagine would be quite different were this not largely an anti-Romantic novel. Called "the Lily of St Leonard's, a name which she deserved as much by her guileless purity of thought, speech, and action, as by her uncommon loveliness of face and person" (97), she nevertheless is somewhat spoiled from childhood on and never learns to channel properly her emotions or desires. The following encounter with her sister is typical:

Here the songstress stopped, looked full at her sister, and, observing the tear gather in her eyes, she suddenly flung her arms round her neck, and kissed them away. Jeanie, though hurt and displeased, was unable to resist the caresses of this untaught child of nature, whose good and evil seemed to flow rather from impulse than from reflection. (99)

Jeanie, although less intelligent and attractive than her sister, displays throughout the novel a character firmly grounded in principle, and against this foil Effie, the child of nature and impulse, appears particularly Romantic. When Effie goes to the city to become a shop-girl her uncontrolled impulsiveness results in a mysterious production, "the mystery of the birth" (221), that jeopardizes her well-being and that of those around her. But right up to the end of the novel she retains her Romantic qualities:

Gifted in every particular with a higher degree of imagination than that of her sister, she was an admirer of the beauties of nature, a taste which compensates many evils to those who happen to enjoy it. Here her character of a fine lady stopped short...with the two boys for her guides, she undertook long and fatiguing walks among the neighbouring mountains...It is Wordsworth, I think, who, talking of an old man under difficulties, remarks, with a singular attention to nature,

> " – whether it was care that spurred him,
> God only knows; but to the very last,
> He had the lightest foot in Ennerdale."   (477–478)

Here Wordsworth is invoked for his special insight into a nature such as Effie's, a typically high Romantic nature characterized by a lively imagination and a taste for the natural world. Once again, Scott reminds us of the dangers of this Romanticism: Effie urges her guide to take her on to a crag overlooking a waterfall where the precariousness of her footing "had so powerful an effect on the senses and imagination of Lady Staunton, that she called out to David she was falling, and would in fact have dropped" (479). As James Kerr argues, "In *The Heart of Midlothian*, a romantic imagination is no longer simply a remediable weakness of vision, but a flaw that is both self-destructive and dangerous to the integrity of the family and the nation."[28] This is the case because in this novel a Romantic nature is a sign, not of an adolescent absorption in fantasy (as, for example, in *Waverley*), but of an undisciplined and changeable character that links one to the unchanneled energies of a market economy.

Before considering further the implications of Scott's representation of the Romantic, it should be noted that Staunton has an even more fitting female analog in Madge Wildfire. Madge is explicitly associated with Martha Ray of Wordsworth's "The Thorn":

they had gained the deepest part of a patch of woodland. The trees were a little separated from each other, and at the foot of one of them, a beautiful poplar, was a variegated hillock of wild flowers and moss, such as the poet of Grasmere has described in his verses on the Thorn. So soon as she arrived at this spot, Madge Wildfire, joining her hands above her head, with a loud scream that resembled laughter, flung herself all at once upon the spot [where her child was buried]. (296–297)

Scott mentions in his notes to the novel that he took the first conception of Madge's character from an account of a wandering maniac named Feckless Fanny, whose life was "altogether like a romance" (535). Like Staunton, Madge is not only a Romantic but also a highly erotic character:

a tall, strapping wench of eighteen or twenty, dressed fantastically, in a sort of blue riding-jacket, with tarnished lace, her hair clubbed like that of a man, a Highland bonnet, and a bunch of broken feathers, a riding-skirt...Her features were coarse and masculine, yet at a little distance, by dint of very bright wild-looking black eyes, an aquiline nose, and a commanding profile, appeared rather handsome. She flourished the switch she held in her hand, dropped a curtsy as low as a lady at a birth-night introduction... (163)

Unlike the fair Effie, the dark-eyed Madge fantastically signals many different and usually contradictory things by her costume (with her riding-jacket, Highland bonnet, and feathers) in addition to, like Staunton, gendering herself both male and female, with mannish hair and features and a skirt. The excessive number and intensity of these signs is directly linked to her eroticism: she both flourishes a switch and drops an extremely low curtsy. Her nature tends fundamentally toward excess; when she attends to her toilette in imitation of Jeanie, she only makes "her appearance ten times more fantastic and apish than it had been before" (306). It is fitting that Madge is first seen dressed in a riding outfit, given that this gypsy wanderer is involved in uncontrolled movements of various kinds. Madge's attractive yet repulsive multiplicity makes her a witch to Staunton's Satan, and she herself makes reference to the "broomstick" that would be a sign both of her unnatural phallic power and of her freedom of movement:

Come, naggie, trot awa, man, an as thou wert a broomstick, for a witch rides thee –

> "With my curtch on my foot, and my shoe on my hand,
> I glance like the wildfire through brugh and through land" (282)

Madge, described as resembling Hecate (286) and the witches of Macbeth (188), is, like Effie, a songstress, although a wilder one, and is at heart a "performer" (164), whose name of Wildfire is of her own creation. She even sings a song in celebration of her own mobility and energy: " 'I'm Madge of the country, I'm Madge of the town, / And I'm Madge of the lad I am blithest to own...I am Queen of the Wake, and I'm Lady of May...The wild-fire that flashes so fair and so free, / Was never so bright, or so bonny, as me' " (303). As with Staunton, Madge's shape-shifting extends to her mind, which is characterized by "a doubtful, uncertain, and twilight sort of rationality" (295). Only on her death-bed is her excess energy finally tamed: "Madge was...singing her own wild snatches of songs and obsolete airs, with a voice no longer over-strained by false spirits...She was still insane, but was no longer able to express her wandering ideas in the wild notes of her former state of exalted imagination" (394). A second allusion to "Christabel," this one involving Madge, reminds the reader of the parallel suggested between Jeanie's nighttime meeting with Staunton and Christabel's with Geraldine. Chapter 31 opens with the following epigraph: "So free from danger, free from fear, / They cross'd the court – right glad they were" (302). The chapter describes Jeanie's journey with Madge finally reaching a safe conclusion, and so, once again, Jeanie is associated with Christabel while Madge, like Staunton, functions as a Geraldine figure.

Given that the Romantic imagination is repeatedly represented as wandering, as errant, it comes as little surprise that "Romantic" characters like Staunton, while they set the novel's two plots in motion, should appear only occasionally within the narrative, and seem, in fact, to obstruct its forward progress, much as Madge waylays Jeanie on her journey to see the Queen. While characters like Staunton, Effie, and Madge are associated with fiction generally – Jeanie thinks they have gained "distinction by undue paths, and the outworks and bulwarks of fiction" (458)[29] – the fictions they produce are specifically marked by their discontinuity and digressiveness. The narrator remarks of road thieves and contrabanders that they supply "their broken phrases by shrugs and signs, as is usual amongst those of their disorderly profession" (291). Effie's energetic impatience makes it difficult for her to lend an ear to the steady pace of narrative: at one point she speaks "with the most ruthless disregard to the narrative which she mangled by [her] interruptions" (476). This disruption of straightforward narrative occurs not only at the level of language but informs the very lives of these characters; as Staunton says to Jeanie: "'I will tell you more of my story than I have told to any one. – Story did I call it? – it is a tissue of folly, guilt, and misery'" (324). The narrator himself finally interrupts to impose a narrative structure on Staunton's speech: "At the risk of being somewhat heavy, as explanations usually prove, we must here endeavour to combine into a distinct narrative, information which the invalid communicated in a manner at once too circumstantial, and too much broken by passion, to admit of our giving his precise words" (324). The reliable characters, like Jeanie, are not associated with fiction of any kind, and their lives are susceptible of an orderly narrative account. It is worth noting that the narrator apologizes at the points in his own narrative when he has had to interrupt the procession of events in Jeanie's or Reuben's life: "We have been a long while in conducting Butler to the door of the cottage at St Leonard's; yet the space which we have occupied in the preceding narrative does not exceed in length that which he actually spent on Salisbury Crags" (108). Superfluous speech, like superfluous activity, is foreign to the virtuous characters, and when they do speak unnecessarily it is presented as an implicitly comic anomaly:

On this occasion David Deans was delivered of his first-born joke; and apparently the parturition was accompanied with many throes, for sorely did he twist about his physiognomy, and much did he stumble in his speech, before he could express his idea, "That the lad being now wedded to his spiritual bride, it was hard to threaten him with ane temporal spouse in the same day." He then laughed a hoarse and brief laugh, and was suddenly grave and silent, as if abashed at his own vivacious effort. (439–440)[30]

We see then that just as, according to the frame-story, speedy transportation leads to the production of the novel itself, the actions and energies of Effie, Robertson, and Madge fuel the novel's internal events. But these characters can only comfortably be construed as peripheral to the narrative economy whose own internal tendencies they actually represent. Just as Staunton is silenced so that the narrator can combine the events of his life into a regular narrative, the novel's circular structure and realistic style strive to impose a grid of quid pro quo exchanges and regulated circular movement on a world where circulation appears to be wayward and productive of unexpected surpluses.

III

> The uterus is to the Race what the heart is to the Individual: it is
> the organ of circulation to the species...Ages are the channels in
> which created beings circulate; and man passes continually from
> the womb of his mother onwards to the womb of time...Parturi-
> tion is the systole of the uterus, the unimpregnated state its
> diastole, and the living beings which flow on in countless numbers
> are as inconsiderable in the great stream of life as the myriads of
> globules revealed by the microscope are in the circulation of the
> blood.
>
>   From W. Tyler Smith's 1847–8 lecture series on obstetrics[31]

It is not only the realistic narrative form that lends order to circulation;
as we saw in the frame-story and even in the account of Deans's joke,
the excess energy of circulation can be recovered through the imposi-
tion of a birth metaphor. Birth holds a privileged place in the
metaphoric dynamic of *The Heart of Mid-Lothian*: it provides a way of
both recuperating erotic energy and imagining production as merely a
form of reproduction. The ideal pole of perfect reproduction is, of
course, exemplified in the most general sense in Jeanie's activity. With
the exception of her journey – the decision to attempt such a trip had
"something of romance" in it (268) – Jeanie is thoroughly anti-
circulatory, and as soon as her journey is done she returns to the arms
of her father and her childhood sweetheart to continue living her life in
pastoral stasis. Moreover, Jeanie shows through her journey that if one
must circulate one can do so and remain unchanged; when she marries
Reuben near the end of the novel she has "the same firm mind and
affectionate disposition, – the same natural and homely good sense,
and spirit of useful exertion, – in a word, all the domestic good qualities
of which she had given proof during her maiden life" (447–448). Given
that art involves, in Bataille's words, "*symbolic* expenditure" (120), it is
perfectly fitting that Jeanie is the resolutely anti-fiction character that
she is; she will not tell a fiction to save her sister or for any other
purpose: "instantly feeling ashamed of the fiction to which she had
resorted, for her love of and veneration for truth was almost quaker-
like, she corrected herself" (265). Jeanie will never be involved in the
proliferation of meanings and values that surround the Romantic
characters; as she puts it, " 'I hae but ae word to bestow on ony body,
and that's aye a true one' " (258). The notion of surplus or market gain

is so foreign to Jeanie that it is not surprising that "she did not understand how to secure the money which came into her hands otherwise than by saving and hoarding it" (466).

Fittingly, Jeanie embodies the purely reproductive capacity of childbirth. Her children represent a continuation of earlier generations:

It is especially necessary to mention, that, in the course of five years, Mrs Butler had three children, two boys and a girl, all stout healthy babes of grace, fair-haired, blue-eyed, and strong-limbed. The boys were named David and Reuben, an order of nomenclature which was much to the satisfaction of the old hero of the Covenant, and the girl, by her mother's special desire, was christened Euphemia...But from some feeling, I know not of what kind, the child was never distinguished by the name of Effie, but by the abbreviation of Femie. (448–449)

The difficulties in reproducing Jeanie's generation are registered only in the need to call the second Euphemia by a different nickname. This Euphemia will make, we assume, an honest designation of her name – she will be "well reputed" – rather than, like her aunt at the end of the novel, enjoying a high status simply because she is "fair of speech" – the other connotation of "euphemious."[32] While the children are given the names of close family members Jeanie points out to Reuben that "'You are Bible Butler now, as weel [*sic*] as your forbear'" (466). Significantly, Scott includes in the notes he wrote for the 1829 Magnum edition of the novel a reproductive genealogy of his own that runs on for several pages: he traces generations of Walters down through his paternal lineage.[33]

But birth can range from being an ideal reproductive process to being little more than the refuse of eroticism, as it is in the case of Madge's childbirth. The birth of Effie's child stands between these two poles, as an unsanctioned form of production that not only arises out of Effie's own involvement in circulation but that is, from the outset, swept up in circulation and exchange. Meg is paid to serve as midwife to Effie, but Madge carries the baby off, believing it to be her own, and then sells it to a female stroller. This woman makes the child "the companion of her wanderings and her beggary" until "she sold him in her turn to Donacha dhu na Dunaigh" (501). Donacha intends, initially, to sell the child into servitude in America, but decides he likes him too much to part with him. Later, however, he does indeed sell him as a slave (506). This son is thus unable to continue his family line at all: "But where was the youth who might eventually be called to the honours and estates of this ancient family? On what heath was he *wandering*, and shrouded by what mean *disguise*? Did he gain his precarious bread by some petty *trade*, by menial toil, by violence, or by theft?" (486–487, my emphasis). Staunton's family line comes to an end as his child is lost to the forces of circulation themselves.

Thus, both metaphors of birth and birth itself, while they are useful in their capacity to reclaim erotic energies for the purposes of reproduction, are also particularly threatening due to their potential to be drawn into the realm of freely circulating goods and energies – a danger epitomized by Effie's unwed pregnancy and the loss and sale of her child. As we saw in chapter 1, in the late eighteenth and early nineteenth centuries childbirth continually threatened to become linked to commodity production. In *The Heart of Mid-Lothian*, as in the epigraph to this section, the uterus appears at times to be, like the heart, an organ of circulation.

Madge Wildfire's mother, Meg, represents the worst aspects of motherhood. Like her daughter, "the old woman" (284) has phallic attributes, but hers are associated with her role as midwife and mother: "'Come, come, Mother Blood' said the tall man...'we are bad enough, but not such as you would make us – devils incarnate.' ...said the old woman, 'if you call me Mother Blood again, I'll paint this gully' (and she held a knife up as if about to make good her threat) 'in the best blood in your body, my bonny boy'" (284). While Madge's masculine attributes render her erotic, her mother's masculinity renders her directly and violently threatening. Meg's motherly nature is described as violently uncivilized; she acts on maternal instincts like that of the "she-wolf and lioness" (486). While ostensibly tending to Madge's welfare, she kills Madge's child and Madge's sanity with it. She also, we remember, nursed Staunton "'at this withered breast'" (293), and he later comments that "'the source from which I derived food, when an infant, must have communicated to me the wretched – the fated – propensity to vices that were strangers in my own family'" (323).

In all her characteristics Meg is, of course, diametrically opposed to Jeanie, in whom Scott offers a comforting image of maternity. Not only is Jeanie unerotic and lawfully reproductive, but she is also associated with maternal nurture as opposed to parturition (it is significant that her children are introduced to us after they have all been born): while Jeanie is in Madge's custody Madge announces that she likes her because she once gave her a "'drink o' milk'" (297), and Jeanie's cheese-making skills arise from her understanding of "the milky mothers" (434). Jeanie draws on her sense of the high value of motherhood when she begs of road thieves: " 'as you were born of woman, dinna ask me to leave the road! rather take all I have in the world' " (283). She would deflect the threat of sexual violence by emphasizing the sanctity of kindly maternal reproduction, the female world as she understands it. But the vulnerability of Jeanie's more positive model of motherhood is reflected not only in the fact that her plea here goes unanswered, but also in the fact that Scott chose to have Jeanie live alone with her *father*. A minor and rather comic figure, Deans is a good and reliable parent. Even when torn by his own desires, he gives Jeanie his paternal benediction for her trip, while when Madge asks for a maternal blessing she receives only a violent benediction:

"Mammie, hear me say my prayers before I go to bed, and say God bless my bonny face, as ye used to do lang syne."

"The deil flay the hide o' it to sole his brogues wi'!" said the old lady, aiming a buffet at the supplicant...

The blow missed Madge, who, being probably acquainted by experience with the mode in which her mother was wont to confer her maternal benedictions, slipt out of arm's length... The hag then started up, and, seizing a pair of old fire-tongs, would have amended her motion, by beating out the brains either of her daughter or Jeanie... (286)

Meg is prevented from using this new phallic weapon by one of the men present, who calls her " 'Mother Damnable' " (286).

In spite of Jeanie's role as the novel's heroine, Madge threatens to dominate the category of woman – the narrator refers to her, even after she has been introduced, as "the female" (172) – and Mother Blood threatens to dominate the category of mother: "Madge Wildfire broke out of the noisy circle of tormentors who surrounded her, and clinging fast to the door of the calash, uttered, in a sound betwixt laughter and screaming, 'Eh, d'ye ken, Jeanie Deans, they hae hangit *our* mother?' " (392, my emphasis). It is worth noting that after giving a several-page account of his own paternal lineage of "Walters," Scott mentions his maternal lineage in one sentence and then concludes thus: "as in the play of the Anti-Jacobin, the ghost of the author's grandmother having arisen to speak the Epilogue, it is full time to conclude, lest the reader should remonstrate that his desire to know the Author of Waverley never included a wish to be acquainted with his whole ancestry" (512). A discussion of maternal ancestry would seem to lend the genealogical project an absurd quality. In the context of this novel, one suspects that it is not only an investment in a traditional patriarchal social structure that makes an image of maternal ancestry unsettling; " 'the facility and pliability, of the female sex' " (221) threaten to render childbirth productive in the commercial sense rather than reproductive of a genealogical line.

IV

The final third of the novel functions as a celebration of Jeanie's reproductivity and details its many rewards. The deaths of Madge Wildfire and her mother, and Effie's decision to go to a convent, represent appropriate punishments for their waywardness as women and mothers. At the same time, however, a new strategy for the management of circulatory energy is put into play. By superimposing first a more typical, and later a more unusual, type of colonial social structure on to the market economy, a way is found of managing both to regulate circulation overall and to account for its tendency to generate surplus value.

    In the first case, colonial relations are used to reconceive market expansion. By the lights of imperialism, the extension of circulatory networks signals, not mysterious and uncontrolled development, but the planned development of the uncontrolled, the imposition of civilization on the uncivilized. As de Certeau argues, imperialism changes the very structure of knowledge; in the nineteenth century "The organizing framework is not the medieval one of ascension, nor that of the dictionary, which prevailed during the eighteenth century. The order of knowledge takes the form of a circular voyage."[34] Although it does not take the form of a perfect circle, Jeanie's voyage does circumscribe a world; as Kerr argues, "the range of Jeanie's experience on the road is designed to include every reach in the social hierarchy" (803). Jeanie's journey, although a journey of the colonized, empowers her (and the narrative) as if she were the colonizer: on the voyage out she is accosted, waylaid by Madge and others, and taken through wilderness, while on the voyage back she rides in a carriage and watches from a distance while Meg is hanged and Madge is ducked.

The point is not that Scott would have London be a Scottish colony but that he would use the *structure* of colonial relations to regulate circulation and exchange, even if those relations were historically designed to increase trade. It comes as little surprise that, in this context, contraband trade should be presented as particularly pernicious. It is not without reason that the good Reuben Butler exclaims that " 'It is impossible...to conceive...the difficulty I have had with my poor people, in teaching them the guilt and the danger of this contraband trade – yet they have perpetually before their eyes all its dangerous consequences. I do not know any thing that more effectually depraves and ruins their moral and religious principles' " (496).

It is within this colonial structure that the patronage relationships discussed earlier find their place in the modern world of Scott's day. Jeanie's interview with the Queen provides the model for a patronage relationship while reaffirming the "colonial" bond between England and Scotland that the Porteous riots (which originally occurred due to Scottish sympathy with contraband trade) had challenged. The Queen not only tends to Jeanie's request but also gives her a housewife case as a token of their encounter. Jeanie, the ideal colonial subject, is so grateful for the souvenir that she tries to return the fifty-pound bill in the pocket, which she considers almost, although not quite, superfluous by comparison. Even this monetary transaction, since it is literally enclosed by the sign of the patronage relationship, can in no way be mistaken for commercial exchange. It is the structure of the patronage relationship that is important here, and we find, in fact, that this kind of exchange characterizes the "good" exchanges of money in the novel regardless of the agents involved. Jeanie, for instance, leaves money for Reuben wrapped in a paper in his Bible between pages where she has marked two passages: " 'A little that a righteous man hath, is better than the riches of the wicked.' – 'I have been young and am now old, yet have I not seen the righteous forsaken, nor his seed begging their bread' " (269). The faith that God will provide for His servant parallels that which set Jeanie on her journey in the first place: the faith that the Queen will provide for her subjects. To exchange money within the framework of such beliefs is to purify both exchange and money of all sordid connotations: "Deeply impressed with the affectionate delicacy which shrouded its own generosity under the cover of a providential supply to his wants, he pressed the gold to his lips with more ardour than ever the metal was greeted with by a miser" (269).

It is a mark of Jeanie's honor that this is the only kind of exchange she will be involved in. She is willing to finance her trip to London by begging (that is, she will participate in a non-reciprocal exchange, accept a freely given gift), but she will not marry the Laird of Dumbiedikes in order to obtain his money. It is not only her sense of her family's dishonor and her preference for Reuben that prevents Jeanie from accepting the Laird; Dumbiedikes proposes while showing Jeanie his silver and thus connects the proposal of marriage to an offer of financial support – a connection that seems perfectly reasonable to him and rather offensive to her.

The patronage/colonial relationship not only replaces market exchange with a form of exchange that seems both safely traditional (patronage) and sufficiently modern (colonial), but also accounts for the unexpected increase generated by contemporary exchange relations. The novel teaches that giving without the expectation of recompense will ultimately be amply rewarded, as it is for Mrs. Goldie. Jeanie's generosity towards others is more than repaid in the form of the goods she receives from her patrons the Queen and the Duke of Argyle. In the realm of commercial exchange, surplus value is generated through a variety of processes other than simple labor, as Scott was well aware; as he noted in the aforementioned letter to Baillie, the mere increase of money in circulation has the effect of revivifying trade and raising prices. But *The Heart of Mid-Lothian* attempts to reconceive the increase in wealth as the result of a more traditional and comprehensible dynamic.

Scott explores a second and more unusual colonial structure at the very end of the novel, a structure that suggests not just an alternative interpretation of the increase in wealth, but an alternative to the necessity of exchange itself. We can approach this second structure by turning to Scott's account of his own colonial project, for his conception of a colonial economy finds expression not just in his view of the relationship of England to Scotland but also in his view of the economy of Abbotsford. That Scott put the considerable proceeds from the sale of his books into the increase and development of his own property is a fact that has not been lost on either his contemporary or his modern critics: "on his Border estate of Abbotsford, Scott exchanged the ungentlemanly earnings of novel writing and various clandestine business ventures for the solid representations of lineage and paternal authority."[35] Throughout the period of the composition of *The Heart of Mid-Lothian* Scott was busy with extensive remodelling projects at Abbotsford, a fact clearly evidenced in his letters. But Scott conceived the goal of these efforts according to a social model more specific than a traditional image of landed gentry; he conceived it in colonial terms. As he wrote in a letter to Lady Compton:

Finding myself something richer by the extrication of funds which the late distressing times placed in rather a precarious state I have made considerable additions to Abbotsford and am over boots over shoes in draining ditching and planting so the property will in a few years be very valuable and in the meantime having enough to live with decency and hospitality I am not anxious for any immediate return...[Abbotsford] defies all rules of architecture being built on the principle of an old English hall such as a squire of yore dwelt in. So it is a bravura stile of building or if you will what a romance is in poetry or a melo-drama in modern theatricals...It is a sort of pic-nic dwelling for its ornaments have been pillaged from all sort of old buildings...[including] the tolbooth of Edinburgh...I have in the person of my steward a man of great genius...*Item* I have for my spiritual consolation a Cameronian preacher whom I intend to dub my chaplain...Lastly I am negociating [*sic*] for the presence of a celebrated Border piper so that since the days of Robinson Crusoe there never was a colony so queerly peopled. (*LWS*, 91–93)

This passage hints at the complex structure of Scott's ideal economy. His interest in establishing a colony like Crusoe's perfectly expresses his divided attitude toward circulation: he is simultaneously driven to obtain all goods in circulation and to rediscover a primitive form of self-sufficiency and isolation. In this case Scott's imperialism takes the form of a movement inward rather than outward: he is constantly bringing in goods from outside, but with the ever-distant goal of achieving static self-sufficiency. As is clear from the quotation above, this second imperial dynamic encompasses both the realm of commodities *per se* and people, as Scott's use of the word "Item" in his listing of his colonists indicates. Scott was to comment in a letter to William Laidlaw that he had "no notion of the proprietor who is only ambitious to be lord of the 'beast and the brute,' and chases the human face from his vicinity. By the by, could we not manage to have a piper among the colonists?" (*LWS* 40).

The very architecture of Abbotsford expresses this dual relation to circulation. Scott does not simply reinvest circulating value in the land in order to stabilize it; while his investment in building does gesture toward a more stable past – the structure is "such as a squire of yore dwelt in" – it is also specifically designed to show the traces of its own origins in contemporary circulation. Its very gesture toward the past marks it with a surplus of style, a kind of "bravura" that aligns it with romance and melodrama. The excesses of romance and melodrama are thus not shunned altogether but are used to lend a charge to a static structure, much as the "Romantic" characters of *The Heart of Mid-Lothian* lend the narrative energy and color. In fact, this "pic-nic" dwelling is reminiscent of Madge Wildfire's "pic-nic" manner of dress. Scott is frankly proud of the pastiche quality of his building, its deliberate and visible appropriation of pieces of other buildings, pieces that announce the circulation that brought them to Abbotsford. At the same time that he imagines Abbotsford as self-sufficient like Crusoe's island society, he knows that his construction of it relies fundamentally on the development of contemporary trade and transportation.[36] Scott's particular interest in appropriating a piece of the Tolbooth itself shows this same impulse – a fascination with circulation and a desire to freeze it. As he writes in his own note on the Tolbooth in *The Heart of Mid-Lothian*,

[a friend] procured for the Author of Waverley the stones which composed the gateway, together with the door, and its ponderous fastenings, which he employed in decorating the entrance of his kitchen-court at Abbotsford. "To such base offices may we return." The application of these relics of the Heart of Mid-Lothian to serve as the postern gate to a court of modern offices, may be justly ridiculed as whimsical; but yet it is not without interest, that we see the gateway through which so much of the stormy politics of a rude age, and the vice and misery of later times, had found their passage, now occupied in the service of rural economy. Last year, to complete the change, a tom-tit was pleased to build her nest within the lock of the Tolbooth. (513)

It is significant that Scott focuses on circulation through the Tolbooth rather than on its containing function. Scott maintains the threshold status of his artifact, but puts it "in the service of rural economy."

It is on this type of Crusoe-inspired island colony that *The Heart of Mid-Lothian* ultimately focuses. Jeanie's patron, the Duke of Argyle, brings her to live on an estate that is not only secluded but literally on an island – the isle of Roseneath. As in the frame-story, the issue of the contemporary increase in the extent and speed of circulation arises: "The islands in the Frith of Clyde, which the daily passage of so many smoke-pennoned steamboats now renders so easily accessible, were, in our fathers' times, secluded spots, frequented by no travellers, and few visitants of any kind" (406). Jeanie can now serve as an ideal tenant/colonist such as Scott was concerned to procure for Abbotsford.[37] In this setting, she can safely lead the "uniform life" (449) for which she is so well suited.

This new economic setting redefines the characters of the novel in terms of colonial relations. The "Romantic" characters, as I have called them, are now defined in terms of their literally peripheral relationship to the stable and honest characters centering around Jeanie, and they are also figured as wild and dark-skinned. The highland banditti that threaten the peaceful existence of the Roseneath community are explicitly compared to "savage tribes" (494). "The Whistler," Effie and Staunton's son (although his parentage is not generally known), is discovered with an unknown man in a remote glen, and the two of them are described in terms that precisely ally them with the cannibal natives of Crusoe's narrative: "a human face, black, and having grizzled hair hanging down over the forehead...looked down on them...'It is The Enemy!' said the boy, who had very nearly become incapable of supporting Lady Staunton...The face glared at them...another, that of a young lad, appeared beside the first, equally swart and begrimed, but having tangled black hair" (479). One recognizes colonialism here not only in the Crusoe-esque quality of the encounter, but also in the conflation of forms of wildness and Blackness. It comes as little surprise when we learn at the end of the narrative that the Whistler was finally sold into slavery in America, from which he escaped only to join "the next tribe of wild Indians" (506). The Whistler acts as a figure for the "native" generally, defined by the logic of colonialism as both a threat to the colonial project and its reason for being. The stability of the patronage economy that Scott delineates requires that the world outside the "colony" that bears down upon it appears to be not the modern world of developing capitalism but the wild world of lawless dark-skinned savages. The "colony" then becomes the stronghold of both traditional patronage relationships and modern civilization.

Just as the boy becomes Black, as it were, by being the object and the subject of illegal trade and part of the world threatening the colony of Roseneath, so his father too is ultimately associated with both slavery and Blackness. We learn that "the father of George Staunton...during service in the West Indies, had married the heiress of a wealthy planter...George...passed the first part of his early youth under the charge of a doting mother, and in the society of negro slaves, whose study it was to gratify his every caprice" (341). Back in Scotland, "the young men of his own rank would not endure the purse-proud insolence of the Creole" (342).

Thus, it is not simply that the latter part of the novel represents a straightforward change in genre or even a protracted celebration of the rewards of virtue. This final section of the novel marks a change in the novel's geographical and economic center, a shift from the heart of the busy city of Edinburgh to the isolated island of Roseneath. The novel sets out to do no less than redefine society in terms of a rural "colonial" economy rather than an urban market one. Cleishbotham's brief envoy, in which he tells of the moving of the Tolbooth, suggests the significance of the novel's own change of setting: "The Heart of Mid-Lothian is now no more, or rather it is transferred to the extreme side of the city, even as the Sieur Jean Baptiste Poquelin hath it, in his pleasant comedy called *Le Médecin Malgré lui*, where the simulated doctor wittily replieth to a charge, that he had placed the heart on the right side, instead of the left, '*Cela étiot autrefois ainsi, mais nous avons changé tout cela*'" (508). This change of heart speaks not only to the moving of the Tolbooth but also to a shift in the novel's focus that amounts to a thoroughgoing generic transformation. The novel turns from a realistic mode interrupted by (and enlivened by) Romantic elements – a mode that reflects a formal effort to regulate a market economy – to what could be called a colonial pastoral. This redefinition of economic relations allowed Scott to go from describing the novel as a "mournful story" (*LWS* 67) and a specifically "Bourgeoise tragedy" (*LWS* 135) to referring to it as a book out of which "we could hammer a neat *comedie bourgeoise*" (*LWS* 148).

v

Ultimately, then, the novel simply abandons the notion of a heart since it necessarily functions as the center of circulation, a place of dangerous fluidity. In the novel's final installment, Scott gradually eliminates the depth model with which the book began and moves toward an ideal world wherein there would be no need to distinguish a core from a periphery or a surface because circulation would not be necessary to social life and individual persons would be utterly static and straightforward. The social structure that serves as the novel's ideal – the island colony – aspires to an isolation and self-sufficiency that would ideally and ultimately make any "peripheries" drop out altogether. Similarly, the ideal subject would be, like Jeanie Deans, so thoroughly honest that no distinction could be drawn between her inner and outer self. Although the world of circulation and hearts has its fascinations, they are ultimately relinquished for the sake of achieving both social and characterological stability.

The three-dimensionality of both social relations and individual character is thus flattened, made as two-dimensional as possible – we return to a notion of character resembling what we saw in the gothic novel. In the case of the gothic, flatness, with its attendant qualities of insubstantiality and mystery, signaled a growing sense of character as an exchange value. In the context of that problem, the notion of personal depth provided a model of character as resistant to commodification. But Scott interprets the depth model as describing and permitting an internal and mysterious fluidity that parallels the fluidity of market relations and values, and he offers his two-dimensional characters and society as a remedy for the superfluity and fluctuation of value and meaning encouraged by circulation and exchange. "For," as Bachelard puts it:

in reality, the experiences of being that might justify "geometrical" expression are among the most indigent...And if we want to determine man's being, we are never sure of being closer to ourselves if we "withdraw" into ourselves, if we move toward the center of the spiral; for often it is in the heart of being that being is errancy.[38]

Epilogue

It should by now be clear that the notion of internal depth served as only one of many models of subjectivity during the Romantic period. Here we have touched on just a few competing conceptions of the self and explored their workings and motives; there were, of course, numerous others. Hannah More, for instance, expresses a common late eighteenth-century belief when, in her poem "Sensibility," she suggests a diffusion of the moral self throughout the body, arguing that "feeling is diffus'd through ev'ry part," and that "what would seem compassion's moral flow, / is but a circulation swift or slow."[1] William Blake, in his own more idiosyncratic formulations, similarly eschews a body/soul dichotomy, claiming that "Man has no Body distinct from his Soul"[2] and underscoring the importance of the surface that divides person from world, a surface he graphically magnified in the form of the "bounding outline." Coleridge, in his late poem "Self-Knowledge" asks "What is there in thee, Man, that can be known? – / Dark fluxion, all unfixable by thought, / A phantom dim of past and future wrought,"[3] expressing in rather darker – even somewhat gothic – terms the concern we saw in Godwin, Bichat, and Byron with the mutability of that thing often fixed on as "true character."

The list could go on and on, for during the period these conceptions were themselves in "dark fluxion." And not only were various models available, but similar models were often used to serve quite different ends, as we saw in comparing the flatness of gothic characterization to the flatness of Scott's characters. These shifts and metamorphoses were by no means limited to the domain of those models of subjectivity uncanonized by modern criticism; it is not that they varied while the depth model stood strong. For proof of this we turn briefly to the major practitioner of depth psychology in Romantic poetry, Wordsworth.

In his play *The Borderers*, Wordsworth directly confronts the issue of depth psychology, but his treatment of it is not at all what the reader of

The Prelude would tend to expect. Originally composed in 1797–1799, *The Borderers* is one of the first of many works in which Wordsworth tries to come to terms with his own Revolutionary enthusiasm and his involvement in French politics during the 1790s. As a product of political and personal disillusionment, we might expect *The Borderers* to represent in some way the turn inward for which Romanticism is currently so renowned. Indeed, the play is very much concerned with an inward turn; but it represents that turn not as natural and healthy – or even simply as inevitable – but as pathological and founded on a false notion of human character.

The play documents the seduction of Mortimer, the noble leader of a vigilante band, by an Iago-like character who, having morally fallen himself, is led by a sort of wanton spite to destroy others. Rivers convinces Mortimer that the father of his beloved Matilda is an imposter using her for his own gain, and urges Mortimer to kill him. Mortimer does eventually abandon the blind old man and so, indirectly, leads to his death. For our purposes, what is most remarkable is that Rivers achieves his evil end largely by convincing Mortimer that the appearances he has long trusted conceal rather than reveal the truth: Rivers argues that not only does Herbert, the old man, have a wicked internal being that is entirely at odds with his external appearance, but most men do. Rivers convinces Mortimer that it is the task of the intelligent and good to sound those depths, to be undeceived by what they see on the surface.

This theory of psychological depth, then, leads directly to the tragedy of the play: Mortimer abandons Herbert, and thereby also destroys his own and Matilda's chances for happiness, because he wrongly believes that there is a depth to Herbert's personality that has previously gone unperceived. In fact, Herbert is what he appears to be: a helpless old man who is deeply concerned for his daughter's welfare. The reader/viewer realizes fairly early in the play that the very notion of depth psychology, and especially of internal depths opposed to superficial appearances, seems to be largely an idea – one might even say a "superstition" – of Rivers's. Not only does he wrongly apply this model to Herbert, but he says of Mortimer that "This stripling's mind, / It hath been rudely shaken, and the dregs / Float on the surface – yea, the very dregs – " (III. ii. 20–22).[4] Rivers would have us believe that he is bringing out the deep truth of Mortimer's character, effacing his own vicious role in producing Mortimer's current behavior. But while the confusion that Mortimer experiences throughout the bulk of the play could in some respects be considered a magnification of the moral ambiguity of his role as a Robin Hood-style vigilante, Mortimer's character and moral standing initially appear in an unambiguously good light; the band of borderers and Matilda believe in his superlative goodness. Thus, Rivers's claim that he is exposing the previously unseen depths of Mortimer's character sounds to the reader like a justification for what in fact amounts to *forging* a depth that previously did not exist.

Interestingly, Rivers's own language hints at the process actually at work here; he remarks that "Thoughts and feelings will sink deep, but then / They have no shape. – Let a few minutes pass, / And something shall be done which memory / May touch when she looks back upon it" (III. ii. 29–32). Mortimer's current thoughts and feelings do not spring from depths within but "sink" in deep; it sounds as if they are in fact introduced from without and forced underneath by their conflict with his typical character. The very fact that Rivers's underlying aim is to make Mortimer a mirror of himself, an embittered, fallen man, shows the extent to which Rivers's efforts to realize the truth of Mortimer's character are self-serving rather than revelatory and productive of individuality. Tellingly, even after his fall Mortimer – while he does learn something about himself and others – does not become deceptive and his character does not become "deep": he simply leaves a monument openly to record his story and banishes himself from the community.

The Borderers teaches that an individual's true self is displayed on the surface – even Rivers is recognized for what he is by the members of Mortimer's band, if not by Mortimer himself. For Wordsworth at this point, *looking into* the depth of human souls amounts to *forging* a depth in human souls; it is not about finding the deep truth of human character but destroying the character outwardly displayed, the one meaningful not only to the community but also to the individual. It is, by implication, the work of the corrupt Revolutionary, the man led by *ressentiment* to encourage innocent men to destroy venerable patriarchs.

The various difficulties attendant upon the use of the depth model – Tennyson in 1832 speaks punningly of "the abysmal deeps of Personality"[5] – are, of course, easy to forget when one reads a poem like *The Prelude*. The Wordsworth of *The Prelude* offers a vision of the depths so convincing in itself, and so effective as a solution to political disillusionment, that, in retrospect, its importance in the period is magnified, and its usefulness and later canonization appear inevitable. But in the period itself, and even for Wordsworth himself, the meaning and value of that vision of the depths were anything but obvious. No wonder, then, that so many should have struggled with and chosen quite different conceptions. That the depth model itself can be so differently conceived by a single author underscores the impossibility of providing any monolithic account of Romantic subjectivity.

The Romantic era was a time of profound social change. With new ideas reshaping almost every realm of human endeavor – politics, economics, science, religion, aesthetics – it is hardly to be expected that notions of identity and character would be anything but varied and diverse, as men and women, poets and doctors, philosophers and statesmen, rushed to redefine selfhood in a world of fresh and open possibilities. Critics since Hazlitt have attempted to define a spirit of the age, and, particularly in our post-Freudian world, that definition has included an insistence on the importance of depth psychology. But that insistence, while it brings one strain of the Romantic achievement into sharp focus, also limits our view of the real richness of Romantic conceptions of subjectivity. Even Hazlitt himself, whose wide-ranging work played such an important role in paring Romanticism down to a manageable, if formidable, monolith, remarks with delight in his essay "On Personal Identity": "What a Proteus is the human mind!"[6]

Notes

INTRODUCTION
FROM COINS TO HEARTS: ROMANTIC FORMS OF SUBJECTIVITY

1   William Wordsworth, *The Prelude*, eds. Jonathan Wordsworth, M. H. Abrams, and Stephen Gill (New York: W. W. Norton, 1979), 1805 version, book XII, lines 159–167.
2   M. H. Abrams, *Natural Supernaturalism* (New York: W. W. Norton, 1973), 28.
3   Harold Bloom, *The Ringers in the Tower* (Chicago: University of Chicago Press, 1971), 18.
4   Jerome McGann, *The Romantic Ideology* (Chicago: University of Chicago Press, 1983), 91.
5   *Ibid.*, 67–68.
6   Clifford Siskin, *The Historicity of Romantic Discourse* (Oxford: Oxford University Press, 1988), 13.
7   See Marjorie Levinson, *Wordsworth's Great Period Poems* (Cambridge: Cambridge University Press, 1986), especially chapter 1, "Insight and Oversight: Reading 'Tintern Abbey.'"
8   See *Historicity*, part III: "Desire and Discipline: The Politics of Mind."
9   Slavoj Žižek, *The Sublime Object of Ideology* (New York: Verso, 1989), 72.
10 Michael Taussig, *The Nervous System* (London: Routledge, 1992), 147.
11 See Charles Rzepka, *The Self as Mind: Vision and Identity in Wordsworth, Coleridge, and Keats* (Cambridge, Mass.: Harvard University Press, 1986).
12 Gaston Bachelard, *The Poetics of Space*, trans. Maria Jolas (Boston, Mass.: Beacon Press, 1969), 215.

1   DOLL-MACHINES AND BUTCHER-SHOP MEAT: MODES OF CHILDBIRTH
IN THE EARLY STAGES OF INDUSTRIAL CAPITALISM

1   Joseph Needham, *Chemical Embryology* (Cambridge: Cambridge University Press, 1931), I, 7–8.
2   Considerable attention has been paid to the medicalization of the female body and the replacement of female midwives by male ones during the

eighteenth and nineteenth centuries. (See, for instance, Judith Walzer Leavitt, *Brought to Bed: Childbearing in America, 1750 to 1950* [Oxford: Oxford University Press, 1986]; Emily Martin, *The Woman in the Body: a Cultural Analysis of Reproduction* [Boston: Beacon Press, 1987]; William Ray Arney, *Power and the Profession of Obstetrics* [Chicago: University of Chicago Press, 1982]; Jacques Gélis, *La sage-femme ou le médecin* [Paris: A. Fayard, 1988]; Mary Poovey, " 'Scenes of an Indelicate Character': the Medical 'Treatment' of Victorian Women," in *The Making of the Modern Body*, eds. Catherine Gallagher and Thomas Laqueur [Berkeley: University of California Press, 1987], 137–168.) But theories of embryological growth and birth together form a complicated network of meanings that cannot be divorced from one another or understood in terms of gender constructs alone.

3 See, for instance, Lawrence Stone, *The Family, Sex and Marriage in England 1500–1800*, abridged edn. (New York: Harper and Row, 1979), 164, *passim*.

4 Daniel Defoe, *The Fortunes and Misfortunes of the Famous Moll Flanders*, ed. Juliet Mitchell (New York: Penguin Books, 1978), 76.

5 Robert Erickson, *Mother Midnight: Birth, Sex, and Fate in Eighteenth-Century Fiction* (New York: AMS Press, 1986), 61.

6 Lois Chaber, "Matriarchal Mirror: Women and Capital in *Moll Flanders*," *PMLA* 97.2 (March 1982): 221. Chaber's parenthetical allusion to the industrialization of weaving has a special resonance in this context given the traditional representation of pregnancy as a form of spinning or weaving within the womb. As Erikson notes of a late seventeenth-century midwife, Jane Sharp's "observations on sexual anatomy have more the texture of the woolen manufacture than of the medical textbook...Her language is full of 'seams,' 'wrinkles,' 'strings fast knit,' 'bridles,' 'coats,' 'woven networks,' and allusions to 'hollow weaving' and 'Weaver's Shuttles.' She has much to say about the inward and outward layers or 'membranes' of the womb itself, and within the womb the two further outward and inward coats: 'The first thing Nature makes for the child, is the *Amnios* or inward skin'; next comes 'the outward or *Chorion* which...wraps the Infant round, and this membrane is like a soft Pillow for the Veins and Navel-arteries of the Child to lean upon...but the inward Coat which is wonderful soft and thin...is loose on each side...These two Coats grow so close together that they seem to be but one garment' " (16). By the end of the century, textile manufacture, long one of the most important trades in Britain, and one that tended to employ women – the wife of Bath comes to mind as a literary example – had been undomesticated. As Marx notes, "manufacture seize[d] hold initially not of the so-called urban trades, but of secondary occupations, spinning and weaving" (*Grundrisse: Foundations of the Critique of Political Economy* [Harmondsworth: Penguin, 1973], 511). Moll's weaver nurse is, as Chaber points out, "tied to the disappearing economic mode of cottage industry" (219). The increasing industrializa-

tion of textile manufacture, coupled with the mechanization of the maternal body discussed later in this chapter, threatened to link metaphorically childbearing to industrial production – in an age increasingly devoted to and suspicious of such production.

7 Juliet Mitchell, *Women, the Longest Revolution* (*New Left Review*, November–December 1966; rpt. Boston: New England Free Press, 1967), 11, quoted in Chaber, "Matriarchal Mirror," 221.

8 Of course, even as early as 1729 Jonathan Swift made economic and political oppression visible by making the metaphorical commodity-child literal in "A Modest Proposal." There, children are explicitly (and bitterly) referred to as "saleable commodities" ("A Modest Proposal," in *The Writings of Jonathan Swift*, eds. Robert Greenberg and William Piper [New York: Norton, 1973], 502–509).

9 Ornella Moscucci, *The Science of Woman: Gynaecology and Gender in England, 1800–1929* (Cambridge: Cambridge University Press, 1990), 43, 50.

10 William Smellie, *A Set of Anatomical Tables*, 2nd edn. (London: n.p., 1761) (first published 1754), preface.

11 Martin, *The Woman in the Body*, 57.

12 William Smellie, *A Treatise on the Theory and Practice of Midwifery*, 2nd edn. (1752), vol. 1: 87–88.

13 William Smellie, *A Collection of Cases and Observations*, 2nd edn., 2 vols. (London: Printed for D. Wilson and T. Durham, 1758), 291, my emphasis.

14 *Ibid.*, 4.

15 *The Life and Opinions of Tristram Shandy*, ed. Graham Petrie (New York: Penguin, 1967), 72.

16 On the connection between Slop and Burton, see Arthur Cash, "The Birth of Tristram Shandy: Sterne and Dr. Burton," in *Sexuality in Eighteenth-Century Britain*, ed. Paul-Gabriel Boucé (Manchester: Manchester University Press, 1982), 198–224.

17 *A Letter to William Smellie, M. D.* (n.p., 1753), 117.

18 Elizabeth Nihell, *A Treatise on the Art of Midwifery. Setting Forth various Abuses therein, especially as to the Practice with Instruments. . .* (London: A. Morley, 1760), preface, i.

19 It is worth noting that the use of instruments and involvement in mechanized instruction in midwifery were not strictly limited to men. As Moscucci notes in *The Science of Woman*, "Margaret Stephen, a midwife who delivered Queen Charlotte, ran a school of midwifery in London in the 1790s where she demonstrated the forceps on a wooden manikin, and it is possible that she may have employed the forceps herself" (48).

20 The differences in the engravings, although not entirely attributable to differences between the authors, reflect their distinct intentions far more than one might suppose. Smellie's plates were engraved by Charles Grignion from original drawings "made mainly by Jan van Rymsdyk and Petrus Camper." Rymsdyk was also the principal artist for *The Gravid Uterus*. In both cases the artist worked as an employee of the author and

under his direction, with the result that in terms of both subject matter and style the drawings almost appear to be the work of two different hands.

21   L. J. Jordanova, "Gender, Generation, and Science," in *William Hunter and the Eighteenth-Century Medical World*, eds. W. Bynum and Roy Porter (New York: Cambridge University Press, 1985), 388.

22   Jane Oppenheimer points out that

> the specific connections between the Hunters [William and his brother John] and the romantic movement were not so remote as might seem on first thought. On the literary side, John and William's sister Dorothea was the mother not only of Matthew Baillie the pathologist, but also of Joanna Baillie, the distinguished poetess and dramatist who was for a half century the close friend of Sir Walter Scott (himself, by the way, the grandson of a distinguished Scottish physician). William Hunter seems to have been a friend of Allan Ramsay the younger, whose father, like the Hunters born in Lanarkshire, was one of the heralds of the literary romantic movement in England. Robert Burns was an admirer of poems written by Mrs. John Hunter; and in fact, some of her own poems…were themselves lyrics with a strong romantic undertone. On the scientific side, John's significance for the fate of transcendental anatomy in England could hardly have been more direct, since the one English anatomist who was most influenced by *Naturphilosophie* and who spoke up most strongly for it was none other than Richard Owen, who…derived his intellectual descent almost immediately from [John Hunter]. (*Essays in the History of Embryology and Biology* [Cambridge, Mass.: MIT Press, 1967], 316)

23   William Harvey, "Anatomical Exercises on the Generation of Animals," in *The Works of William Harvey*, trans. Robert Willis (Philadelphia: University of Pennsylvania Press, 1989), 153.

24   From a letter to Cullen. Quoted in Harvey Graham, *Eternal Eve: the History of Gynaecology and Obstetrics* (Garden City: Doubleday and Company, 1951), 319.

25   William Smellie, *A Set of Anatomical Tables*, preface.

26   William Hunter, *The Anatomy of the Human Gravid Uterus* (London: Sydenham Society Reprint, 1851) (first published 1774).

27   See Naomi Schor, *Reading in Detail: Aesthetics and the Feminine* (New York: Methuen, 1987), 3.

28   Quoted in Graham, *Eternal Eve*, 319.

29   Quoted in John L. Thornton and Patricia Want, "William Hunter and His Contributions to Obstetrics," *British Journal of Obstetrics and Gynaecology* 90.9 (1983): 790.

30   *Ibid.*, 787.

31   Moscucci argues that this can, in part, be explained in terms of the changes male-midwifery was undergoing: "as man-midwifery moved away from emergency to onset-call practice, the surgeon-accoucheur had an opportunity to attend an increasing number of normal births: this influenced the way he saw both the processes of birth and his role at the delivery" (*The Science of Woman*, 49).

32 This bifurcation of the feminine is encapsulated in comments like the following by an anonymous writer of the middle of the nineteenth century: "The relations of woman are twofold; material and spiritual – corporeal and moral" (quoted in Moscucci, *The Science of Woman*, p. 35).

33 Angela Carter, *The Sadeian Woman and the Ideology of Pornography* (New York: Pantheon Books, 1978), 138.

34 Marquis de Sade, "Philosophy in the Bedroom," ("La philosophie dans le boudoir") in *The Marquis de Sade*, trans. Richard Seaver and Austryn Wainhouse (New York: Grove Press, 1965), 249–250.

35 Julia Kristeva, *Powers of Horror*, trans. Leon Roudiez (New York: Columbia University Press, 1982), 10, my emphasis.

36 Barbara Schapiro, *The Romantic Mother* (Baltimore: Johns Hopkins University Press, 1983), xii.

37 Quoted in Joseph Needham, *A History of Embryology* (New York: Abelard-Schuman, 1959), 200.

38 See Elizabeth Gasking, *Investigations into Generation 1651–1828* (Baltimore: Johns Hopkins Press, 1967), chapter 4.

39 Shirley A. Roe, *Matter, Life, and Generation: Eighteenth-Century Embryology and the Haller-Wolff Debate* (Cambridge: Cambridge University Press, 1981), 150.

40 Jane Oppenheimer, *Essays in the History of Embryology and Biology*, 132.

41 Quoted in Needham, *History of Embryology*, 201, my emphasis.

42 It is important to bear in mind that some embryologists proposed theories of development that combined epigenetic and preformationist models, and that eighteenth-century embryology underwent considerable vicissitudes. Around 1760, for instance, the preformation theory, which had become somewhat less popular in the previous thirty years, was given a boost that was to carry it for another thirty by three of the most influential naturalists of the time: Haller, Spallanzani, and Bonnet – all of whom were converts to preformationism (see Gasking, *Investigations*, 107).

43 Needham, *History of Embryology*, 220.

44 Roe, *Matter*, 151.

45 See Gasking, *Investigations*, 98.

46 Quoted in *ibid.*, 152.

47 Immanuel Kant, *The Critique of Judgement*, trans. James Creed Meredith (Oxford: Clarendon Press, 1928), 85.

48 See Jordanova, "Gender, Generation, and Science," 406, n. 31.

49 From *Eighteenth-Century Women Poets: an Oxford Anthology*, ed. Roger Lonsdale (Oxford: Oxford University Press, 1989), 482–483.

50 Anna Laetitia Barbauld, *Works*, ed. Lucy Aikin, 2 vols. (London: Longman, 1825), vol. 1, 199–201.

51 Kristeva, *Powers of Horror*, 10.

52 Clifford Siskin, *The Historicity of Romantic Discourse*, 12.

2   "AN EMBARRASSING SUBJECT": USE VALUE AND EXCHANGE VALUE IN
EARLY GOTHIC CHARACTERIZATION

1   Charles Rzepka, *The Self as Mind*, 16.
2   *Ibid.*, 26.
3   Georg Lukács, *History and Class Consciousness*, trans. Rodney Livingstone
    (Great Britain: The Merlin Press, 1971), 124.
4   Luce Irigaray, *This Sex Which Is Not One*, trans. Catherine Porter (Ithaca:
    Cornell University Press, 1985), chapter 9.
5   Jean-Christophe Agnew, *Worlds Apart: the Market and the Theater in Anglo-
    American Thought, 1550–1750* (Cambridge: Cambridge University Press,
    1986), 13.
6   William Reddy, *Money and Liberty in Modern Europe* (Cambridge: Cam-
    bridge University Press, 1987), 6.
7   J. G. A. Pocock, *Virtue, Commerce, and History* (Cambridge: Cambridge
    University Press, 1985), 108–109.
8   David Hume, *An Inquiry Concerning the Principles of Morals* (New York:
    Macmillan, 1957), 61.
9   Jerome Christensen, in an interesting and subtle argument, suggests that
    Hume "essays a *communication* theory of value in an economics almost
    completely deontologized" (168), claiming that for Hume use value itself
    can vary according to the passion with which a given object is invested
    (148). (*Practicing Enlightenment: Hume and the Formation of a Literary Career*
    [Madison: University of Wisconsin Press, 1987].) I would argue that while
    the logic of Hume's arguments may tend in that direction, his language
    still reflects an investment in an Enlightenment ideal of utility, and that
    this investment in "real," tangible good is particularly important in a
    discussion of a topic as contentious and delicate as ethics. As Duncan
    Forbes writes, for Hume "utility is crucial in men's moral sentiments and
    judgements" (*Hume's Philosophical Politics* [Cambridge: Cambridge Univer-
    sity Press, 1975], 107).
10 Adam Smith, *The Theory of Moral Sentiments*, eds. A. L. Macfie and D. D.
    Raphael (Oxford: Oxford University Press, 1976), 179.
11 Henry Mackenzie, *The Man of Feeling*, ed. Kenneth Slagle (New York: W.
    W. Norton, 1958), 26, my emphasis. These are the words of a "misan-
    thropist," but even Harley recognizes the truth in them.
12 See Lukács, *History*, 83–222.
13 "The English, like antient medals, kept more apart, and passing but few
    peoples hands, preserve the first sharpnesses which the fine hand of
    nature has given them – they are not so pleasant to feel – but in return,
    the legend is so visible, that at the first look you see whose image and
    superscription they bear" (Laurence Sterne, *A Sentimental Journey*, ed. Ian
    Jack [Oxford: Oxford University Press, 1984], 90).
14 As Barbara Herrnstein Smith points out, the "central axiological move of
    Hume's argument" is "to ground the standard of taste in (naturally, one

might say) *nature*: specifically, the presumed psychophysiological nature of all human beings" (*Contingencies of Value* [Cambridge, Mass.: Harvard University Press, 1988], 59).

15 Edmund Burke, *Reflections on the Revolution in France* (Garden City: Anchor Books, 1973), 67.

16 Frank Fetter, *Development of British Monetary Orthodoxy 1797–1875* (Cambridge, Mass.: Harvard University Press, 1965), 2.

17 David Hume, "Of Money," in *David Hume: Writings on Economics*, ed. Eugene Rotwein (Madison: University of Wisconsin Press, 1970), 35.

18 Adam Smith, *An Inquiry into the Nature and Causes of the Wealth of Nations*, ed. Edwin Cannan (New York: The Modern Library, 1937), 305.

19 Fetter, *Orthodoxy*, 12.

20 *Ibid.*, 14.

21 *Ibid.*, 21.

22 *Ibid.*, 19.

23 Later gothic novels such as *Frankenstein* and *Melmoth the Wanderer* tend to fuse early gothic characterization with characterization in terms of depth.

24 Given the longtime critical tendency to argue for the psychological depth of gothic characters, it may be useful to note here that I would argue (as will become clear in my discussion of the bifurcation of identity in the gothic) that gothic characters are remarkable for their lack of depth. In 1972 Kiely wrote that for Lewis "the proper metaphor for personality was not...one of depth, but of surfaces," and that "in the context of Freudian psychology, this sounds naive and superficial." Nevertheless, Kiely argues, "too many modern critics have tried to rescue [*The Monk*] from the rubbish heap by claiming profundity for it, but this is doing no favor to Lewis, who knew rubbish when he saw it" (Robert Kiely, *The Romantic Novel in England* [Cambridge, Mass.: Harvard University Press, 1972], 107). Most commentators on the gothic have indeed set out to discover depth not only in its texture but also in its characters, assuming from the outset that identity must be generated from within. Even a recent commentator like William Patrick Day, who says that he intends to look only at the text itself, since "the surface of the Gothic fantasy is its substance," and who argues that the gothic is the *forerunner* of Freudian psychoanalysis and not simply its ideal testing ground, treats the problem of identity from the inside out, offering a psychological reason for the fragmentation of identity: the fusion of fear and desire within an originally whole individual causes self division (*In the Circles of Fear and Desire: a Study of Gothic Fantasy* [Chicago: University of Chicago Press, 1985], 14). I would argue that it is the powerful emotional charge of the issues the gothic treats – family relations, death, sex – more than its characterization *per se* that has made it so available to psychologizing criticism. In the gothic itself, when the mind is defined as deep it is described as capable of being filled primarily by conventions and from without; St. Aubert teaches Emily that "the vacant mind" should be "store[d]...with ideas," especially those of the

best poets (Radcliffe, *Udolpho*, 6). And as Adela Pinch argues in her chapter on the gothic in *Strange Fits of Passion: Epistemologies of Emotion, Hume to Austen*, emotions in the gothic seem not to originate with specific persons but to be passed about among members of a group (Stanford: Stanford University Press, forthcoming). Roughly ten years after Kiely, Eve Sedgwick again directed our attention back to surfaces; the features of gothic personality may make "Gothic characters seem devitalized or two-dimensional" ("The Character in the Veil: Imagery of the Surface in the Gothic Novel," *PMLA* 96.2 [1981]: 256), but we do not do justice to the gothic by simply ignoring these features. In my discussion of the gothic I follow Sedgwick's lead in focusing unabashedly on that super-ficiality that seems finally to define the form.

25 Ann Radcliffe, *The Italian*, ed. Frederick Garber (Oxford: Oxford University Press, 1968), 5, 86.
26 Ann Radcliffe, *The Mysteries of Udolpho*, ed. Bonamy Dobrée (Oxford: Oxford University Press, 1966), 262.
27 Horace Walpole, *The Castle of Otranto*, ed. W. S. Lewis (Oxford: Oxford University Press, 1964), 41.
28 Radcliffe, *Udolpho*, 515.
29 See Jean Baudrillard, "For a Critique of the Political Economy of the Sign," in *Selected Writings*, ed. Mark Poster (Stanford: Stanford University Press, 1988), 57–97.
30 Ann Radcliffe, *The Romance of the Forest*, ed. Chloe Chard (Oxford: Oxford University Press, 1986), 36.
31 It is not insignificant that similar terms are used in the context of the American money debates of the late nineteenth century; as David Wells argued, paper could no more be money than "a shadow could be the substance" (quoted and discussed in Walter Benn Michaels, *The Gold Standard and the Logic of Naturalism* [Berkeley: University of California Press, 1987], 146).
32 Terry Castle, "The Spectralization of the Other in *The Mysteries of Udolpho*," in *The New Eighteenth Century*, eds. Felicity Nussbaum and Laura Brown (New York: Methuen, 1987), 231–253. See also Castle's further work on the topic, where she examines the popularity of the "magic lantern," analyzes the terms used to understand "spectral technology," and argues that "if ghosts were thoughts, then thoughts themselves took on – at least notionally – the haunting reality of ghosts" ("Phantasmagoria: Spectral Technology and the Metaphorics of Modern Reverie," *Critical Inquiry* 15.1 [1988]: 52).
33 See Karl Marx, *Capital*, ed. Frederick Engels, trans. Samuel Moore and Edward Aveling, 3 vols (New York: International Publishers, 1967), vol. 1, part 1; and Irigaray, *This Sex*, chapter 9.
34 Irigaray, *This Sex*, 172.
35 *Ibid.*, 175.
36 *Ibid.*, 176.

37 Day, *Circles of Fear and Desire*, 45.
38 Irigaray, *This Sex*, 179.
39 Elaine Scarry, *The Body in Pain* (Oxford: Oxford University Press, 1985), 14.
40 Comparison of the status of the body in the texts of Hume and Smith with, for example, the medieval conception of the body as little more than the site of sin and temptation highlights the more positive role of the sensible body in the eighteenth century.
41 Irigaray, *This Sex*, 177.
42 *Ibid.*, 186.
43 This is, of course, considered by many feminist theorists to be the quintessential masculine activity; as Judith Butler puts it: "reason and mind are associated with masculinity and agency, while the body and nature are considered to be the mute facticity of the feminine, awaiting signification from an opposing masculine subject" (*Gender Trouble: Feminism and the Subversion of Identity* [New York: Routledge, 1990], 37).
44 See Gayle Rubin, "The Traffic in Women: Notes on the 'Political Economy' of Sex," in *Toward an Anthropology of Women*, ed. Rayna Reiter (New York: Monthly Review Press, 1975); and Irigaray, *This Sex*, chapters 8 and 9.
45 Naomi Schor, *Reading in Detail*, 19–20.
46 On the problem of woman's "lack of essence" (and the strategic usefulness of Irigaray's "essentialism") see Diana Fuss, *Essentially Speaking* (New York: Routledge, 1989), 72.
47 Lukács, *History*, 208, 137.
48 Norbert Elias, *The Court Society*, trans. Edmund Jephcott (Oxford: Basil Blackwell, 1969), 86.
49 Marx, *Capital*, vol. III, 830.
50 Robert Kiely, *The Romantic Novel*, 1.
51 Agnew, *Worlds Apart*, 13.

3   FROM "RACE" TO "PLACE" IN "THE PRISONER OF CHILLON"

1 William Godwin, *Enquiry Concerning Political Justice* (1798) (New York: Penguin Books, 1985), 97.
2 As Thomas Balfour Elder points out, later editions of *Political Justice* tend to speak somewhat more of the mind's capacity for self-generated activity ("Godwin and 'The Great Springs of Human Passion,'" *Ariel: a Review of International English Literature* 14. 1 [1983]: 15–31). As biographers like William St Clair point out, Godwin's experience educating his own children encouraged him to revise his earlier view that children were born without innate talents or propensities (*The Godwins and the Shelleys* [Baltimore: Johns Hopkins University Press, 1989], 298). Even in its final version, however, *Political Justice* makes strong arguments for the passivity of the mind; the quotations used here are all from that final version.

3   The distinction between Godwin's work and the physiological texts
    treated in the next section is not as great as our current disciplinary
    boundaries might lead us to expect. Godwin's method derives largely
    from the methods and principles of Newtonian natural science and relies
    on the parallel workings of what we would distinguish as natural and
    human sciences. Furthermore, that he should specifically touch upon the
    political significance of issues in embryology is entirely in keeping with the
    central role embryological and developmental studies were beginning to
    play within the domains of physiology, pathology, and especially natural
    history. German *Naturphilosophie*, for example, looked to embryological
    studies as a source of knowledge not only of current distinctions between
    species but also their historical relations and (for some) even their capacity
    for transmutation – all of which had serious theological as well as social
    implications.
4   See, for example, Lynn Hunt, *Politics, Culture, and Class in the French
    Revolution* (Berkeley: University of California Press, 1984).
5   Fielding Garrison, *An Introduction to the History of Medicine*, 4th edn.
    (Philadelphia: W. B. Saunders Company, 1929), 407.
6   *Ibid.*, 407.
7   Erwin Ackerknecht, *A Short History of Medicine* (Baltimore: Johns Hopkins
    University Press, 1982), 130.
8   Michel Foucault, *The Birth of the Clinic*, trans. A. M. Sheridan Smith (New
    York: Vintage, 1975), 6.
9   Sydenham, quoted by Sauvages in his *Nosologie méthodique* (source
    Foucault, *Birth of the Clinic*, 7).
10 Garrison, *History of Medicine*, 444.
11 L. S. Jacyna, "Romantic Thought and the Origins of Cell Theory," in
    Romanticism and the Sciences, eds. Andrew Cunningham and Nicholas
    Jardine (Cambridge: Cambridge University Press, 1990), 162.
12 J. B. Demangeon quoted by Foucault in *Birth of the Clinic*, 31.
13 Given the political implications of context-based identity it is telling that
    contagion is a popular theme and motif in British Romantic writing, and
    often expresses a conservative resistance to the mingling of classes.
    Moreover, as Adela Pinch argues, Romantic writing often expresses a
    concern that even non-physical states of being, like emotions, sometimes
    appear to be mobile and "contagious" (*Strange Fits of Passion*).
14 See Elizabeth Haigh, *Xavier Bichat and the Medical Theory of the Eighteenth
    Century* (London: Wellcome Institute for the History of Medicine, 1984), 81.
15 *Ibid.*, 69.
16 *Ibid.*, 67.
17 *Ibid.*, 80.
18 *Ibid.*, 81. Cabanis does, however, admit to variation on the basis of factors
    such as age and sex.
19 Quoted inWilliam Randall Arlbury, "Experiment and Explanation in the
    Physiology of Bichat and Magendie," *Studies in History of Biology* 1 (1977), 101.

20 Xavier Bichat, *Physiological Researches on Life and Death* (1827), trans. F. Gold (New York: Arno Press, 1977), 10–11. For the purposes of this chapter, I have quoted from this early British translation. References to the language of the French original will be drawn from *Recherches physiologiques sur la vie et la mort* (Paris: Charpentier, 1859).

21 Bichat, *Physiological Researches*, 13; page 3 in the French.

22 In this instance, the word "revolution" is properly the English translator's (the original sentence ends "reviennent à l'animal et en ressortent ensuite" [4]). The word "revolution" does, however, appear in the original in similar contexts; it is, for instance, used in the original of the upcoming quotation in the main text.
    It is perhaps worth noting that German Romantic medicine or *Naturphilosophie* had as one of its prime tenets the idea that the world is in continual flux (see Jacyna, "Romantic thought," 164). That this should be so is not terribly surprising given that, as Philip Rehbock says, "*Naturphilosophie* was German philosophical idealism yielding to French political radicalism" ("Transcendental Anatomy," in *Romanticism and the Sciences*, eds. Andrew Cunningham and Nicholas Jardine [Cambridge: Cambridge University Press, 1990], 146).

23 John Pickstone, "Bureaucracy, Liberalism and the Body in Post-Revolutionary France: Bichat's Physiology and the Paris School of Medicine," *History of Science* 19 (1981): 130–131.

24 *Ibid.*, 132.

25 *Ibid.*, 137.

26 It may be worthwhile to note some contemporaneous developments in British medicine: John Brown developed a theory of stimulation that focused on the importance of maintaining a balance between over- and under-stimulation (see Nelly Tsouyopoulos, "Doctors *contra* Clysters and Feudalism: the Consequences of a Romantic Revolution" in *Romanticism and the Sciences*, eds. Andrew Cunningham and Nicholas Jardine [Cambridge: Cambridge University Press, 1990], 107). Brown's theories were quite popular; in his study of mesmerism Nigel Leask remarks that "mesmerism, like the Brunonian system so popular amongst English and German Romantics, rejected the complex nosologies and (to use Michel Foucault's term) 'noso-politics' of the medical establishments" ("Shelley's 'Magnetic Ladies': Romantic Mesmerism and the Politics of the Body," in *Beyond Romanticism*, eds. Stephen Copley and John Whale [New York: Routledge, 1992], 63).
    John Hunter, a prominent English physiologist and natural historian, speaks like Bichat of the role of the body in matters of "consciousness": "Custom arises from external impressions, either in the mind or body. . .I have used the word *consciousness*, because we have no language existing answerable to all my views on the animal oeconomy. . .There are actions in the body which come the nearest to consciousness of the mind of anything that I can conceive" (quoted in Stephen Cross, "John Hunter,

the Animal Oeconomy, and Late Eighteenth-Century Physiological Discourse," *Studies in History of Biology* 5 [1981]: 48). Cross suggests that "Hunter minimizes the role of the *sensorium* and will in regulation of animal functions" (75). Like Bichat, Hunter stresses interdependence: "The more complicated a machine is, the more nice its operations are, and, of course, the greater dependence each part has upon the other; and, therefore, there is a more intimate connexion through the whole. This holds good in society. It also holds good in the animal oeconomy" (quoted in Cross, 76). Cross associates these features with the political economic theories of Adam Smith, although he does not show how the concept of liberalism figures in Hunter.

27 F. J. V. Broussais, *A Treatise on Physiology Applied to Pathology*, trans. John Bell, MD and R. La Roche, MD (Philadelphia: H. C. Carey and I. Lea, 1826), 11.

28 Indeed, this was one of the principal complaints of François Magendie, a physiologist who produced his major work in the 1810s and 1820s (see Haigh, *Xavier Bichat*, 117). Some of Bichat's followers were to place more and more emphasis on interaction: "empirical knowledge now began to appear as a system of internal relations between organized units that were not simply reducible to their component parts and that functioned together as a totality" (Arlbury, "Experiment," 88).

29 F. J. V. Broussais, *Principles of Physiological Medicine*, trans. Isaac Hays, MD and Eglesfeld Griffith (Philadelphia: Carey and Lea, 1982), iv.

30 Broussais, *Treatise*, 12.

31 Broussais, *Principles*, iv.

32 Ackernecht, *History of Medicine*, 148.

33 Broussais, *Principles*, iv.

34 Broussais, *Treatise*, 10.

35 *Ibid.*, 37.

36 *Ibid.*

37 William Wordsworth, *The Prelude*, 1799 version, Part 1, lines 67–68.

38 See, for instance, Marjorie Levinson, "Insight and oversight: reading 'Tintern Abbey,' " in *Wordsworth's Great Period Poems*, 14–57.

39 "The Dantean Politics of *The Prisoner of Chillon*," *Keats-Shelley Journal* 35 (1986): 23–29.

40 See McGann's notes in *Lord Byron: The Complete Poetical Works*, ed. Jerome J. McGann, 7 vols (New York: Oxford University Press, 1986), vol. IV, 449.

41 *Ibid.*, 4, lines 1–4. All subsequent references to "Sonnet on Chillon" and "The Prisoner of Chillon" will be from this edition, pages 3–16, and will be cited by line number in parentheses in the text.

42 *Ibid.*, 451.

43 *Byron and the Ruins of Paradise* (Baltimore: Johns Hopkins University Press, 1967), 191.

44 *Ibid.*, 193.

45 Lord Byron, *The Oxford Authors: Byron*, ed. Jerome J. McGann (Oxford: Oxford University Press, 1986) 123–124, lines 617–622. All subsequent references to *Childe Harold's Pilgrimage*, Canto III, will be to this edition, pages 104–145, and will be cited by line number in parentheses in the text.

46 Gleckner, *Byron and the Ruins of Paradise*, 193, n. 21.

47 William Wordsworth, *The Poems*, ed. John Hayden, 2 vols. (New Haven: Yale University Press, 1981), vol. I, 444, line 30. All subsequent references to "The Seven Sisters" will be to this edition and will be cited by line number in parentheses in the text.

48 Byron, "Prisoner," *Complete Works*, line 15.

49 Medwin, *Life of Percy Bysshe Shelley*, quoted in McGann's notes in Byron, *Complete Works*, 450.

50 Significantly, it is at this moment that the prisoner frees himself of the chain linking him to the gothic column (although he remains trapped within his prison).

51 *Seventeenth-Century Prose and Poetry*, 2nd edn., ed. Alexander Witherspoon and Frank Warnke, (New York: Harcourt Brace Jovanovich, 1982), 948, lines 25–32. Subsequent references to this poem will be to this edition and will be given by line number in parentheses in the text.

52 Jerome McGann, *Fiery Dust: Byron's Poetic Development* (Chicago: University of Chicago Press, 1968), 171.

53 *Byron: a Poet Before his Public* (Cambridge: Cambridge University Press, 1982), 88, 89.

54 "Experiments in the Narrative of Consciousness: Byron, Wordsworth, and *Childe Harold*, Cantos 3 and 4," *ELH* 53.1 (Spring 1986): 136.

55 "The Social Other: *Don Juan* and the Genesis of the Self," *Mosaic* 22.2 (1989): 34–35.

56 *Poetic Form and British Romanticism* (New York: Oxford University Press, 1986), 40.

57 Wordsworth, *Poems*, 586, lines 1–5. All subsequent references to the sonnet will be given by line number in parentheses in the text.

58 Sigmund Freud, "Negation," in *The Standard Edition of the Complete Psychological Works*, trans. and ed. James Strachey, 24 vols. (London: The Hogarth Press, 1974), vol. XIX, 235–240.

59 W. D. Ian Rolfe, "William and John Hunter: Breaking the Great Chain of Being," in *William Hunter and the Eighteenth-Century Medical World*, eds. W. F. Bynum and Roy Porter (Cambridge: Cambridge University Press, 1985), 300.

60 Alexander Pope, *Poetical Works*, ed. Herbert Davis (Oxford: Oxford University Press, 1978), 248, lines 237–246.

61 William Hunter, for instance, whose work in obstetrics I discussed in chapter 1, demonstrated that at least two species had become extinct, and therefore, as Rolfe puts it, "broke the Great Chain of Being twice" ("William and John Hunter," 315).

62 See Harold Perkin, *Origins of Modern English Society* (New York: Ark, 1985), for a discussion of England's transformation from a society based on vertical affiliations to one based on horizontal affiliations.

63 Alan Liu, "Local Transcendence: Cultural Criticism, Postmodernism, and the Romanticism of Detail," *Representations* 32 (Fall 1990): 94, 98.

64 Gaston Bachelard, *The Poetics of Space*, 222.

4 INCARNATE IMAGINATION AND *THE CENCI*

1   Elaine Scarry, *The Body in Pain*, 207.

2   Charles Rzepka, *The Self as Mind*.

3   Percy Bysshe Shelley, "On Love," in *Shelley's Poetry and Prose*, eds. Donald Reiman and Sharon Powers (New York: W. W. Norton, 1977), 473.

4   " 'Self-Anatomy' and Self-Consciousness in *The Cenci*," in *A Mental Theater* (University Park: Pennsylvania State University Press, 1988), 116.

5   *In the Shadows of Romance: Romantic Tragic Drama in Germany, England, and France* (Athens: Ohio University Press, 1987), 140.

6   Percy Bysshe Shelley, *The Cenci, Shelley's Poetry and Prose*, III. i. 23. All subsequent references to the play and its prefatory materials will be to this edition and will be cited by act, scene, and line number in parentheses in the text.

7   Shelley, "On Love," 473–474.

8   Shelley, "A Defence of Poetry," *Shelley's Poetry and Prose*, 500.

9   Jerrold Hogle, *Shelley's Process: Radical Transference and the Development of His Major Works* (New York: Oxford University Press, 1988), 148.

10 Earl R. Wasserman, *Shelley: a Critical Reading* (Baltimore: Johns Hopkins University Press, 1971), 87.

11 Even Marzio's metaphor of wringing the truth out of one's breath – as if the spirit were itself a cloth – reflects the ultimate impossibility of completely divorcing spirit and body.

12 Stuart Curran, *Shelley's* Cenci: *Scorpions Ringed with Fire* (Princeton: Princeton University Press, 1970), 73.

13 John Webster, *Three Plays*, ed. D. C. Gunby (New York: Penguin Books, 1972), IV. ii. 8–10.

14 The misleading syntax of line 90 nicely demonstrates the antagonistic relation of Cenci's fancy and its physical embodiment: his fanciful designs appear at first to be his natural food but slide into becoming his torment as they push forward towards accomplishment. And it is perhaps not by chance that the Count associates those designs with fancy – a faculty that, in the Coleridgean scheme at least, is merely the poor relation of the imagination proper.

15 *Mary Shelley's Journal*, ed. Frederick L. Jones (Norman: University of Oklahoma Press, 1947), 20.

16 Curran, *Shelley's* Cenci, 169.

17 William Hazlitt, *A View of the English Stage*, in *Complete Works of William*

Hazlitt, ed. P. P. Howe, 21 vols (London: J. M. Dent and Sons, 1930–1934), vol. v: 228.

18   Joseph W. Donohue, *Dramatic Character in the English Romantic Age* (Princeton: Princeton University Press, 1970), 166.

19   From Mary Shelley's note on *The Cenci*, in *Complete Poems of Keats and Shelley*, eds. Bennett Cerf and Donald Klopper (New York: Modern Library, n.d.), 364.

20   Hazlitt, *Complete Works*, vol. v: 210.

21   "Defense of Poetry," *Shelley's Poetry and Prose*, 501.

22   Quoted in Mary Shelley's note on *The Cenci*, 366.

23   See, for instance, Curran, *Shelley's* Cenci, 40.

24   Quoted in *ibid.*, 23.

25   See Timothy Webb, *Shelley: A Voice Not Understood* (Atlantic Highlands: Humanities Press, 1977), 33–74, *passim*.

26   William Ulmer, *Shelleyan Eros: the Rhetoric of Romantic Love* (Princeton: Princeton University Press, 1990), 123–124.

27   From the preface to *The Cenci, Shelley's Poetry and Prose*, 240.

28   Shelley, *Shelley's Poetry and Prose*, 133. Subsequent references to *Prometheus Unbound* and its preface will be cited in parentheses in the text. Quotes from the preface will be given by page number, and quotes from the play will be given by act, scene, and line number.

29   William Keach, *Shelley's Style* (New York: Methuen, 1984), 44.

30   Quoted in *ibid.*, 154.

31   After taking incarnate form and removing Jupiter from the scene, Demogorgon drops out of sight, leaving the relatively disembodied and unbound Prometheus innocent of the self-interested act of eliminating his oppressor. Although Prometheus and Demogorgon could be argued to be representative aspects of a larger entity, such as human nature or human destiny, it is nevertheless significant that they function as separate beings in the play, and that Prometheus is the play's hero.

32   Barbara Charlesworth Gelpi, *Shelley's Goddess: Maternity, Language, Subjectivity* (New York: Oxford University Press, 1992), 239–241.

33   In this respect it is worth noting that the account from which Shelley drew his play says only that Cenci *tried* to "debauch" his daughter while explicitly stating that he was several times convicted of sodomy. Incest, unspeakable as it was in Shelley's day, may to some extent represent a displacement of the quintessential unspeakability of sodomy, the "Unspeakable, Unmentionable...'love that dare not speak its name'" (Eve Sedgwick, *Epistemology of the Closet* [Berkeley: University of California Press, 1990], 202). Ironically, Shelley's supreme non-closet drama, for all its efforts to recognize the corporeal, makes incest what Sedgwick would call an "open secret" and the world of the Cenci family a dangerous and fragile "glass closet."

34   *Mathilda*, in *The Mary Shelley Reader*, eds. Betty Bennett and Charles E. Robinson (New York: Oxford University Press, 1990), 184; unless

otherwise noted, all subsequent references to *Mathilda* will refer to this
edition.

35   Shelley composed *Mathilda* in 1819 during the severe depression she
experienced following the death of her son William. This death, and the
antagonistic emotional needs it elicited in Mary and Percy, put a great
strain on the marriage; as Emily Sunstein argues, "the terrible second
shock of William's death, coming so soon after Clara's, decisively divided
the Shelleys" (*Mary Shelley: Romance and Reality* [Baltimore: Johns Hopkins
University Press, 1989], 170).

36   It is perhaps worth noting that during the period in which Mary was
mourning the death of her son her father "deliberately…intensified
Mary's sense of shame and failure" (Sunstein, *Mary Shelley: Romance and
Reality*, p. 174). The curse thus enacts not only a reversal but also a
vicarious retribution.

37   *The Fields of Fancy*, in *Mathilda*, ed. Elizabeth Nitchie (Chapel Hill:
University of North Carolina Press, 1959), 94.

38   *Ibid.*, 99.

39   As Anne Mellor notes, the very name "Mathilda" is common to gothic
fiction (*Mary Shelley: Her Life, Her Fiction, Her Monsters* [New York:
Methuen, 1988], 196).

40   As Terry Castle has argued, the metaphor of the magic lantern was rich
in meaning during this period; as she suggests, it links the ghostliness of
the gothic worldview to the spectralization of material life founded in the
privileging of canonical Romantic interiority ("Phantasmagoria").

41   *Antony and Cleopatra*, in *The Complete Works of Shakespeare*, ed. David
Bevington (Glenview, Illinois: Scott, Foresman and Company, 1980),
I. i. 17.

42   *Shelley: a Critical Reading*, 119

5   CENTRALITY AND CIRCULATION IN *THE HEART OF MID-LOTHIAN*

1   Walter Scott, *The Heart of Midlothian*, ed. Claire Lamont (Oxford: Oxford
University Press, 1982), 542, note for p. 9. Subsequent references to the
novel and Scott's and Lamont's notes to it will be to this edition and will
be given in parentheses in the text.

2   H. J. C. Grierson, ed., *The Letters of Sir Walter Scott*, 12 vols, vol. v (London:
Constable and Co., 1933; rpt. New York: AMS Press, 1971), 116 (this
volume hereafter cited in the text as *LWS*).

3   Roy Porter, *English Society in the Eighteenth Century* (New York: Penguin,
1982), 209.

4   Quoted in Porter, *ibid.*

5   See Porter, *English Society*, 241.

6   Jon Klancher, *The Making of English Reading Audiences, 1790–1832* (Madison:
University of Wisconsin Press, 1987), 32.

7   Antonio Negri, *Marx Beyond Marx*, trans. Harry Cleaver, Michael Ryan,

and Maurizio Viano, ed. Jim Fleming (New York: Autonomedia, 1991), 112.

8   The first definition given for the word "tolbooth" in *The Scottish National Dictionary* is the following: "Orig. a booth or office where tolls, market dues and other local imposts were paid to the municipality" (*The Scottish National Dictionary*, eds. William Grant and David Murison [Edinburgh: Scottish National, Dictionary Association, 1974], vol. IX: 359).

9   Gilles Deleuze and Félix Guattari, *Anti-Oedipus*, trans. Robert Hurley, Mark Seem, and Helen Lane (Minneapolis: University of Minnesota Press, 1983), 225, my emphasis.

10   Quoted in Negri, *Marx*, 112.

11   Grierson's remark gives the impression that the Luckenbooths formed part of the Tolbooth; it should perhaps be noted, however, that by all other accounts, including Scott's own (on page 56 of the novel), the Luckenbooths abut, but are not part of, the Tolbooth.

12   Richard D. Altick, *The English Common Reader* (Chicago: University of Chicago Press, 1957), 59.

13   Grierson, *Letters*, vol. I: 522.

14   See Altick, *Reader*, 262–263.

15   *Ibid.*, 217–218.

16   Of course, *The Heart of Mid-Lothian* enjoyed immense commercial success, and was, in fact, a popular circulating-library novel.

17   *Selections from the Poetical Works of William Cowper*, ed. James Murray (Boston: Ginn and Company, 1898), "The Task," IV, lines 55–56 and 94–96.

18   See Scott, *Midlothian*, 26.

19   *Ibid.*, 522 (Scott's note). It is telling that Scott should refer to this "secret history" as something *un*ravelled rather than as a knot to be untied; his interest is in binding and controlling history, tying it back together.

20   Jean-Christophe Agnew, *Worlds Apart*, 9.

21   *Ibid.*, 131.

22   For an excellent treatment of the features and significance of the carnival and the carnivalesque, see Peter Stallybrass and Allon White, *The Politics and Poetics of Transgression* (Ithaca: Cornell University Press, 1986).

23   Karl Marx, *Capital*, vol. I: 152.

24   J. G. A. Pocock, *Virtue, Commerce, and History*, 112, 113.

25   See Georges Bataille, "The Notion of Expenditure," in *Visions of Excess*, trans. Allan Stoekl, Carl Lovitt, and Donald Leslie, Jr., ed. Allan Stoekl (Minneapolis: University of Minnesota Press, 1985), 116–129.

26   Jacques Derrida, *Writing and Difference*, trans. Alan Bass (Chicago: University of Chicago Press, 1978), 259.

27   See Samuel Taylor Coleridge, "Christabel," in *Coleridge: Poetical Works*, ed. Ernest Hartley Coleridge (New York: Oxford University Press, 1912), line 169.

28   James Kerr, "Scott's Fable of Regeneration: *The Heart of Midlothian*," *ELH* 53.4 (1986): 812.

29   This reminds us once again of the circulating-library novel and the
      authorial coining that Scott distances himself from.
30   It is worth noting that here, once again, superfluity is rendered benign
      and comic by means of a birth metaphor.
31   Quoted in Mary Poovey, "'Scenes of an Indelicate Character': The
      Medical 'Treatment' of Victorian Women," 145.
32   According to *The Oxford English Dictionary*, "euphemious" means "fair of
      speech, also well reputed" (*Oxford English Dictionary*, 2nd. edn, prep. J. A.
      Simpson and E. S. C. Weiner [Oxford: Clarendon Press, 1989], vol. v:
      436). Effie becomes, by the end of the novel, fair of speech in two ways:
      she is both well-spoken and well spoken of – profoundly euphemistic in
      the worst sense.
33   See Scott, *Midlothian*, 509–512.
34   Michel de Certeau, *Heterologies*, trans. Brian Massumi (Minneapolis:
      University of Minnesota Press, 1986), 145.
35   Kathryn Sutherland, "Fictional Economies: Adam Smith, Walter Scott
      and the Nineteenth-Century Novel," *ELH* 54.1 (1987): 99.
36   See, for instance, Scott's list of London purchases for Abbotsford (*LWS*,
      164).
37   See *LWS*, 40.
38   Gaston Bachelard, "The Dialectics of Outside and Inside," in *The Poetics
      of Space*, 213, 215.

EPILOGUE

1   Hannah More, *The Complete Works of Hannah More*, 2 vols., (New York:
      Harper and Brothers, 1835), vol. 1, pp. 33, 35.
2   William Blake, *The Marriage of Heaven and Hell*, ed. Geoffrey Keynes
      (Oxford: Oxford University Press, 1975), xvi.
3   Samuel Taylor Coleridge, *Poetical Works*, 487.
4   William Wordsworth, *The Borderers*, ed. Robert Osborn (Ithaca: Cornell
      University Press, 1982). All quotes are from the early version of the play
      (1797–1799).
5   Alfred, Lord Tennyson, "The Palace of Art," in *The Poems of Tennyson*, ed.
      Christopher Ricks (Essex: Longman, 1987), vol. 1, p. 453, line 223.
6   William Hazlitt, *The Complete Works of William Hazlitt*, vol. XVII, 274.

Bibliography

Abrams, M. H., *Natural Supernaturalism* (New York: W. W. Norton, 1973).

Ackerknecht, Erwin, *A Short History of Medicine* (Baltimore: Johns Hopkins University Press, 1982).

Agnew, Jean-Christophe, *Worlds Apart: the Market and the Theater in Anglo-American Thought, 1550–1750* (Cambridge: Cambridge University Press, 1986).

Altick, Richard D., *The English Common Reader* (Chicago: University of Chicago Press, 1957).

Althusser, Louis, "Ideology and Ideological State Apparatuses," in *Lenin and Philosophy*, trans. Ben Brewster (New York: Monthly Review Press, 1971), 127–186.

Aristotle, pseud., *Aristotle's Master-Piece Compleated* (Glasgow: Booksellers, 1784).

Arlbury, William Randall, "Experiment and Explanation in the Physiology of Bichat and Magendie," *Studies in History of Biology* 1 (1977): 47–131.

Arney, William Ray, *Power and the Profession of Obstetrics* (Chicago: University of Chicago Press, 1982).

Bachelard, Gaston, *The Poetics of Space*, trans. Maria Jolas (Boston, Mass.: Beacon Press, 1969).

Barbauld, Anna Laetitia, *Works*, ed. Lucy Aikin, 2 vols. (London: Longman, 1825).

Bataille, Georges, *Visions of Excess*, trans. Allan Stoekl, Carl Lovitt, and Donald Leslie, Jr., ed. Allan Stoekl (Minneapolis: University of Minnesota Press, 1985).

Baudelocque, Jean-Louis, *An Abridgement of Mr. Heath's Translation of Baudelocque's Midwifery*, by William Dewees (Philadelphia: Thomas Dobson, 1811).

Baudrillard, Jean, *Selected Writings*, ed. Mark Poster (Stanford: Stanford University Press, 1988).

Bichat, Xavier, *Physiological Researches on Life and Death* (1827), trans. F. Gold (New York: Arno Press, 1977).

Recherches physiologiques sur la vie et la mort (Paris: Charpentier, 1859).

A Treatise on the Membranes in General, and on Different Membranes in Particular, trans. John Coffin (Cambridge: Hilliard and Metcalf, 1813).

Blake, William, *The Marriage of Heaven and Hell*, ed. Geoffrey Keynes (Oxford: Oxford University Press, 1975).

Bloom, Harold, *The Ringers in the Tower* (Chicago: University of Chicago Press, 1971).

Bridges, Thomas, *Adventures of a Bank-Note* (London: T. Davies, 1770).

Broussais, F. J. V., *Principles of Physiological Medicine*, trans. Isaac Hays, MD and Eglesfeld Griffith (Philadelphia: Carey and Lea, 1982).

 A Treatise on Physiology Applied to Pathology, trans. John Bell, MD and R. La Roche, MD (Philadelphia: H. C. Carey and I. Lea, 1826).

Burke, Edmund, *Reflections on the Revolution in France* (Garden City: Anchor Books, 1973).

Burton, John, *A Letter to William Smellie, M. D.* (n.p., 1753).

Butler, Judith, *Gender Trouble: Feminism and the Subversion of Identity* (New York: Routledge, 1990).

Bynum, W., and Roy Porter, eds., *William Hunter and the Eighteenth-Century Medical World* (New York: Cambridge University Press, 1985).

Byron, George Gordon, *Lord Byron: The Complete Poetical Works*, ed. Jerome McGann, 7 vols. (New York: Oxford University Press, 1986).

 The Oxford Authors: Byron, ed. Jerome J. McGann (Oxford: Oxford University Press, 1986).

Carter, Angela, *The Sadeian Woman and the Ideology of Pornography* (New York: Pantheon Books, 1978).

Cash, Arthur H., "The Birth of Tristram Shandy: Sterne and Dr. Burton," in *Sexuality in Eighteenth-Century Britain*, ed. Paul-Gabriel Boucé (Manchester: Manchester University Press, 1982), 198–224.

Castle, Terry, "Phantasmagoria: Spectral Technology and the Metaphorics of Modern Reverie," *Critical Inquiry* 15.1 (1988): 26–61.

 "The Spectralization of the Other in *The Mysteries of Udolpho*," in *The New Eighteenth Century*, eds. Felicity Nussbaum and Laura Brown (New York: Methuen, 1987), 231–253.

Chaber, Lois, "Matriarchal Mirror: Women and Capital in *Moll Flanders*," *PMLA* 97.2 (March 1982): 212–226.

Christensen, Jerome, *Practicing Enlightenment: Hume and the Formation of a Literary Career* (Madison: University of Wisconsin Press, 1987).

Coleridge, Samuel Taylor, *Coleridge: Poetical Works*, ed. Ernest Hartley Coleridge (New York: Oxford University Press, 1912).

Copley, Stephen and John Whale, eds., *Beyond Romanticism* (New York: Routledge, 1992).

Cowper, William, *Selections from the Poetical Works of William Cowper*, ed. James Murray (Boston: Ginn and Company, 1898).

Cox, Jeffrey, *In the Shadows of Romance: Romantic Tragic Drama in Germany, England, and France* (Athens: Ohio University Press, 1987).

Cross, Stephen, "John Hunter, the Animal Oeconomy, and Late Eighteenth-Century Physiological Discourse," *Studies in History of Biology* 5 (1981): 1–110.

Cunningham, Andrew, and Nicholas Jardine, eds., *Romanticism and the Sciences* (Cambridge: Cambridge University Press, 1990).

Curran, Stuart, *Poetic Form and British Romanticism* (New York: Oxford University Press, 1986).

    Shelley's Cenci*: Scorpions Ringed with Fire* (Princeton: Princeton University Press, 1970).

Day, William Patrick, *In the Circles of Fear and Desire: a Study of Gothic Fantasy* (Chicago: University of Chicago Press, 1985).

De Certeau, Michel, *Heterologies*, trans. Brian Massumi (Minneapolis: University of Minnesota Press, 1986).

Defoe, Daniel, *The Fortunes and Misfortunes of the Famous Moll Flanders*, ed. Juliet Mitchell (New York: Penguin, 1978).

    Robinson Crusoe, ed. Angus Ross (New York: Penguin, 1965).

Deleuze, Gilles, and Félix Guattari, *Anti-Oedipus*, trans. Robert Hurley, Mark Seem, and Helen Lane (Minneapolis: University of Minnesota Press, 1983).

Derrida, Jacques, *Of Grammatology*, trans. Gayatri Chakravorty Spivak (Baltimore: Johns Hopkins University Press, 1976).

    Writing and Difference, trans. Alan Bass (Chicago: University of Chicago Press, 1978).

Donohue, Joseph, *Dramatic Character in the English Romantic Age* (Princeton: Princeton University Press, 1970).

Elder, Thomas Balfour, "Godwin and 'The Great Springs of Human Passion,'" *Ariel: a Review of International English Literature* 14.1 (1983): 15–31.

Elias, Norbert, *The Court Society*, trans. Edmund Jephcott (Oxford: Basil Blackwell, 1969).

Erickson, Robert, *Mother Midnight: Birth, Sex, and Fate in Eighteenth-Century Fiction* (New York: AMS Press, 1986).

Fetter, Frank Whitson, *Development of British Monetary Orthodoxy 1797–1875* (Cambridge, Mass.: Harvard University Press, 1965).

Forbes, Duncan, *Hume's Philosophical Politics* (Cambridge: Cambridge University Press, 1975).

Foucault, Michel, *The Birth of the Clinic*, trans. A. M. Sheridan Smith (New York: Vintage, 1975).

Freud, Sigmund, *The Standard Edition of the Complete Psychological Works*, trans. and ed. James Strachey, 23 vols. (London: The Hogarth Press, 1974).

Fuss, Diana, *Essentially Speaking* (New York: Routledge, 1989).

Gallagher, Catherine, and Thomas Laqueur, eds., *The Making of the Modern Body* (Berkeley: University of California Press, 1987).

Garrison, Fielding, *An Introduction to the History of Medicine*, 4th edn. (Philadelphia: W. B. Saunders Company, 1929).

Gasking, Elizabeth, *Investigations into Generation 1651–1828* (Baltimore: Johns Hopkins University Press, 1967).

Gélis, Jacques, *La sage-femme ou le médecin* (Paris: A. Fayard, 1988).

Gelpi, Barbara Charlesworth, *Shelley's Goddess: Maternity, Language, Subjectivity* (New York: Oxford University Press, 1992).

Gleckner, Robert, *Byron and the Ruins of Paradise* (Baltimore: Johns Hopkins University Press, 1967).

Godwin, William, *Enquiry Concerning Political Justice* (1798) (New York: Penguin Books, 1985).

Graham, Harvey, *Eternal Eve: the History of Gynaecology and Obstetrics* (Garden City: Doubleday and Company, 1951).

Grant, William, and David Murison, eds., *The Scottish National Dictionary* (Edinburgh: Scottish National Dictionary Association, 1974).

Grierson, H. J. C., ed., *The Letters of Sir Walter Scott*, 12 vols. (London: Constable and Co., 1933; rpt. New York: AMS Press, 1971).

Haigh, Elizabeth, *Xavier Bichat and the Medical Theory of the Eighteenth Century* (London: Wellcome Institute for the History of Medicine, 1984).

Harvey, William, "Anatomical Exercises on the Generation of Animals," in *The Works of William Harvey*, trans. Robert Willis (Philadelphia: University of Pennsylvania Press, 1989), 145–586.

Hazlitt, William, *Complete Works of William Hazlitt*, ed. P. P. Howe, 21 vols. (London: J. M. Dent and Sons, 1930–1934).

Herrnstein Smith, Barbara, *Contingencies of Value* (Cambridge, Mass.: Harvard University Press, 1988).

Hill, James, "Experiments in the Narrative of Consciousness: Byron, Wordsworth, and *Childe Harold*, Cantos 3 and 4" *ELH* 53.1 (Spring 1986): 121–140.

Hogle, Jerrold, *Shelley's Process: Radical Transference and the Development of His Major Works* (New York: Oxford University Press, 1988).

Hume, David, *An Inquiry Concerning the Principles of Morals* (New York: Macmillan, 1957).
   "Of Money," in *David Hume: Writings on Economics*, ed. Eugene Rotwein (Madison: University of Wisconsin Press, 1970).

Hunt, Lynn, *Politics, Culture, and Class in the French Revolution* (Berkeley: University of California Press, 1984).

Hunter, William, *The Anatomy of the Human Gravid Uterus* (London: Sydenham Society Reprint, 1851).

Irigaray, Luce, *This Sex Which Is Not One*, trans. Catherine Porter (Ithaca: Cornell University Press, 1985).

Jacyna, L. S., "Romantic Thought and the Origins of Cell Theory," in *Romanticism and the Sciences*, eds. Andrew Cunningham and Nicholas Jardine (Cambridge: Cambridge University Press, 1990), 161–168.

Jordanova, Ludmilla J., "Gender, Generation, and Science," in *William Hunter and the Eighteenth-Century Medical World*, eds. W. Bynum and Roy Porter (New York: Cambridge University Press, 1985), 385–412.

Kant, Immanuel, *The Critique of Judgement*, trans. James Creed Meredith (Oxford: Clarendon Press, 1928).

Keach, William, *Shelley's Style* (New York: Methuen, 1984).

Kerr, James, "Scott's Fable of Regeneration: *The Heart of Midlothian*," *ELH* 53.4 (1986): 801–820.

Kiely, Robert, *The Romantic Novel in England* (Cambridge, Mass.: Harvard University Press, 1972).

Klancher, Jon, *The Making of English Reading Audiences, 1790–1832* (Madison: University of Wisconsin Press, 1987).

Kristeva, Julia, *Powers of Horror*, trans. Leon Roudiez (New York: Columbia University Press, 1982).

Lacan, Jacques, *Ecrits: a Selection*, trans. Alan Sheridan (New York: Norton, 1977).

Leask, Nigel, "Shelley's 'Magnetic Ladies': Romantic Mesmerism and the Politics of the Body," in *Beyond Romanticism*, eds. Stephen Copley and John Whale (New York: Routledge, 1992), 53–78.

Leavitt, Judith Walzer, *Brought to Bed: Childbearing in America, 1750 to 1950* (Oxford: Oxford University Press, 1986).

Levinson, Marjorie, *Wordsworth's Great Period Poems* (Cambridge: Cambridge University Press, 1986).

Lewis, Matthew, *The Monk*, ed. Howard Anderson (Oxford: Oxford University Press, 1973).

Liu, Alan, "Local Transcendence: Cultural Criticism, Postmodernism, and the Romanticism of Detail" *Representations* 32 (Fall 1990): 75–113.

Lonsdale, Roger, ed., *Eighteenth-Century Women Poets: an Oxford Anthology* (Oxford: Oxford University Press, 1982).

Lovelace, Richard, "To Althea. From Prison." in *Seventeenth-Century Prose and Poetry*, 2nd edn., eds. Alexander Witherspoon and Frank Warnke (New York: Harcourt Brace Jovanovich, 1982).

Lukács, Georg, *History and Class Consciousness*, trans. Rodney Livingstone (Great Britain: The Merlin Press, 1971).

Mackenzie, Henry, *The Man of Feeling*, ed. Kenneth Slagle (New York: W. W. Norton, 1958).

Martin, Emily, *The Woman in the Body: a Cultural Analysis of Reproduction* (Boston: Beacon Press, 1987).

Martin, Philip, *Byron: a Poet Before his Public* (Cambridge: Cambridge University Press, 1982).

Marx, Karl, *Capital*, ed. Frederick Engels, trans. Samuel Moore and Edward Aveling, 3 vols. (New York: International Publishers, 1967).

Grundrisse: Foundations of the Critique of Political Economy (Harmondsworth: Penguin, 1973).

Maturin, Charles, *Melmoth the Wanderer*, ed. Alethea Hayter (New York: Penguin, 1977).

McGann, Jerome, *Fiery Dust: Byron's Poetic Development* (Chicago: University of Chicago Press, 1968)

The Romantic Ideology (Chicago: University of Chicago Press, 1983).

Mellor, Anne, *Mary Shelley: Her Life, Her Fiction, Her Monsters* (New York: Methuen, 1988).

Michaels, Walter Benn, *The Gold Standard and the Logic of Naturalism* (Berkeley: University of California Press, 1987).

Michasiw, Kim Ian, "The Social Other: *Don Juan* and the Genesis of the Self" *Mosaic* 22.2 (1989): 29–48.

Mitchell, Juliet, *Women, the Longest Revolution* (*New Left Review*, November-December 1966; rpt. Boston: New England Free Press, 1967).

More, Hannah, *The Complete Works of Hannah More*, 2 vols. (New York: Harper and Brothers, 1835).

Moscucci, Ornella, *The Science of Woman: Gynaecology and Gender in England, 1800–1929* (Cambridge: Cambridge University Press, 1990).

Needham, Joseph, *Chemical Embryology* (Cambridge: Cambridge University Press, 1931).

   A History of Embryology (New York: Abelard-Schuman, 1959).

Negri, Antonio, *Marx Beyond Marx*, trans. Harry Cleaver, Michael Ryan, and Maurizio Viano, ed. Jim Fleming (New York: Autonomedia, 1991).

Nihell, Elizabeth, *A Treatise on the Art of Midwifery. Setting Forth various Abuses therein, especially as to the Practice with Instruments . . .* (London: A. Morley, 1760).

Nussbaum, Felicity, and Laura Brown, *The New Eighteenth Century* (New York: Methuen, 1987).

Oppenheimer, Jane M., *Essays in the History of Embryology and Biology* (Cambridge, Mass.: MIT Press, 1967).

Perkin, Harold, *Origins of Modern English Society* (New York: Ark, 1985).

Pickstone, John, "Bureaucracy, Liberalism and the Body in Post-Revolutionary France: Bichat's Physiology and the Paris School of Medicine," *History of Science* 19 (1981): 115–142.

Pinch, Adela, *Strange Fits of Passion: Epistemologies of Emotion, Hume to Austen* (Stanford: Stanford University Press, forthcoming).

Pocock, J. G. A., *Virtue, Commerce, and History* (Cambridge: Cambridge University Press, 1985).

Poovey, Mary, " 'Scenes of an Indelicate Character': the Medical 'Treatment' of Victorian Women," in *The Making of the Modern Body*, eds. Catherine Gallagher and Thomas Laqueur (Berkeley: University of California Press, 1987), 137–168.

Pope, Alexander, *Poetical Works*, ed. Herbert Davis (Oxford: Oxford University Press, 1978).

Porter, Roy, *English Society in the Eighteenth Century* (New York: Penguin, 1982).

Radcliffe, Ann, *The Italian*, ed. Frederick Garber (Oxford: Oxford University Press, 1968).

   The Mysteries of Udolpho, ed. Bonamy Dobrée (Oxford: Oxford University Press, 1966).

   The Romance of the Forest, ed. Chloe Chard (Oxford: Oxford University Press, 1986).

Rehbock, Philip, "Transcendental Anatomy," in *Romanticism and the Sciences*, eds. Andrew Cunningham and Nicholas Jardine (Cambridge: Cambridge University Press, 1990), 144–160.

Reddy, William, *Money and Liberty in Modern Europe* (Cambridge: Cambridge University Press, 1987).

Richardson, Alan, *A Mental Theater* (University Park: Pennsylvania State University Press, 1988).

Roe, Shirley A., *Matter, Life, and Generation: Eighteenth-Century Embryology and the Haller-Wolff Debate* (Cambridge: Cambridge University Press, 1981).

Rolfe, W. D. Ian, "William and John Hunter: Breaking the Great Chain of Being," in *William Hunter and the Eighteenth-Century Medical World*, eds. W. F. Bynum and Roy Porter (Cambridge: Cambridge University Press, 1985), 297–319.

Rubin, Gayle, "The Traffic in Women: Notes on the 'Political Economy' of Sex," in *Toward an Anthropology of Women*, ed. Rayna Reiter (New York: Monthly Review Press, 1975), 157–210.

Rzepka, Charles, *The Self as Mind: Vision and Identity in Wordsworth, Coleridge, and Keats* (Cambridge, Mass.: Harvard University Press, 1986).

Sade, Marquis de, "Philosophy in the Bedroom" ("La philosophie dans le boudoir"), in *The Marquis de Sade*, trans. Richard Seaver and Austryn Wainhouse (New York: Grove Press, 1965), 177–367.

Scarry, Elaine, *The Body in Pain* (Oxford: Oxford University Press, 1985).

Schapiro, Barbara, *The Romantic Mother* (Baltimore: Johns Hopkins University Press, 1983).

Schor, Naomi, *Reading in Detail: Aesthetics and the Feminine* (New York: Methuen, 1987).

Scott, Walter, *The Heart of Midlothian*, ed. Claire Lamont (Oxford: Oxford University Press, 1982).

Waverley, ed. Andrew Hook (New York: Penguin, 1972).

Sedgwick, Eve, "The Character in the Veil: Imagery of the Surface in the Gothic Novel," *PMLA* 96.2 (1981): 255–270.

Epistemology of the Closet (Berkeley: University of California Press, 1990).

Shakespeare, William, *The Complete Works of Shakespeare*, ed. David Bevington (Glenview, Illinois: Scott, Foresman and Company, 1980).

Shelley, Mary, *The Fields of Fancy*, in *Mathilda*, ed. Elizabeth Nitchie (Chapel Hill: University of North Carolina Press, 1959).

Frankenstein, ed. Maurice Hindle (New York: Penguin, 1985).

Mary Shelley's Journal, ed. Frederick L. Jones (Norman: University of Oklahoma Press, 1947).

Mathilda, in *The Mary Shelley Reader*, eds. Betty Bennett and Charles E. Robinson (New York: Oxford University Press, 1990).

Shelley, Percy, *The Complete Poems of Keats and Shelley*, eds. Bennett Cerf and Donald Klopper (New York: Modern Library, n.d.).

Shelley's Poetry and Prose, eds. Donald Reiman and Sharon Powers (New York: W. W. Norton, 1977).

Siskin, Clifford, *The Historicity of Romantic Discourse* (Oxford: Oxford University Press, 1988).

Smellie, William, *A Collection of Cases and Observations*, 2nd edn., 2 vols. (London: Printed for D. Wilson and T. Durham, 1758).

Set of Anatomical Tables, 2nd edn. (London: n.p., 1761).

A Treatise on the Theory and Practice of Midwifery, 2nd edn. (1752).

Smith, Adam, *The Theory of Moral Sentiments*, eds. A. L. Macfie and D. D. Raphael (Oxford: Oxford University Press, 1976).

An Inquiry into the Nature and Causes of the Wealth of Nations, ed. Edwin Cannan (New York: The Modern Library, 1937).

Stallybrass, Peter, and Allon White, *The Politics and Poetics of Transgression* (Ithaca: Cornell University Press, 1986).

St Clair, William, *The Godwins and the Shelleys* (Baltimore: Johns Hopkins University Press, 1989).

Sterne, Laurence, *The Life and Opinions of Tristram Shandy*, ed. Graham Petrie (New York: Penguin, 1967).

A Sentimental Journey, ed. Ian Jack (Oxford: Oxford University Press, 1984).

Stone, Lawrence, *The Family, Sex and Marriage in England 1500–1800*, abridged edn. (New York: Harper and Row, 1979).

Sunstein, Emily, *Mary Shelley: Romance and Reality* (Baltimore: Johns Hopkins University Press, 1989).

Sutherland, Kathryn, "Fictional Economies: Adam Smith, Walter Scott and the Nineteenth-Century Novel," *ELH* 54.1 (1987): 97–127.

Swift, Jonathan, "A Modest Proposal," in *The Writings of Jonathan Swift*, eds. Robert Greenberg and William Piper (New York: Norton, 1973), 502–509.

Taussig, Michael, *The Nervous System* (London: Routledge, 1992).

Tennyson, Alfred, *The Poems of Tennyson*, ed. Christopher Ricks (Essex: Longman, 1987).

Thornton, John L., and Patricia Want, "William Hunter and His Contributions to Obstetrics," *British Journal of Obstetrics and Gynaecology* 90.9 (1983): 787–794.

Tsouyopoulos, Nelly, "Doctors *contra* Clysters and Feudalism: the Consequences of a Romantic Revolution," in *Romanticism and the Sciences*, eds. Andrew Cunningham and Nicholas Jardine (Cambridge: Cambridge University Press, 1990), 101–118.

Ulmer, William. *Shelleyan Eros: the Rhetoric of Romantic Love* (Princeton: Princeton University Press, 1990).

"The Dantean Politics of *The Prisoner of Chillon*," *Keats-Shelley Journal* 35 (1986): 23–29.

Walpole, Horace, *The Castle of Otranto*, ed. W. S. Lewis (Oxford: Oxford University Press, 1964).

"The Mysterious Mother," in *The Works of Horatio Walpole*, 7 vols., vol. 1 (London: G. G. and J. Robinson, 1798).

Wasserman, Earl R., *Shelley: a Critical Reading* (Baltimore: Johns Hopkins University Press, 1971).

Webb, Timothy, *Shelley: a Voice Not Understood* (Manchester: Manchester University Press, 1977).

Webster, John, *Three Plays*, ed. D. C. Gunby (New York: Penguin Books, 1972).

Wordsworth, William, *The Borderers*, ed. Robert Osborn (Ithaca: Cornell University Press, 1982).

The Poems, ed. John Hayden, 2 vols. (New Haven: Yale University Press, 1981).

The Prelude, eds. Jonathan Wordsworth, M. H. Abrams, and Stephen Gill (New York: W. W. Norton, 1979).

Žižek, Slavoj, *The Sublime Object of Ideology* (New York: Verso, 1989).

Index

abjection, 6, 30, 38
Abrams, M. H., 1
Ackerknecht, Erwin, 64
actor, as model for the self, 38; in Shelley's *The Cenci*, 100–101, 104–105, 110; in Shelley's *Mathilda*, 121-124, 127; in Scott's *Heart of Mid-Lothian*, 142–144; *see also* theatricality; drama
Agnew, Jean-Christophe, 39, 57, 142–143
Altick, Richard, 137
Althusser, Louis, 3
aristocracy, 26, 27, 39, 41–44, 62, 76–81, 87–89
Aristotle, pseud.: *Aristotle's Master-Piece Compleated*, 35
Arlbury, William Randall, 178 n28

Bachelard, Gaston, 10, 93–94, 162
Baer, Karl Ernst von, 33
Bagehot, Walter, 110
Baillie, Joanna, 133, 137, 157, 170 n22
Baillie, Matthew, 170 n22
Ballantyne, John, 137
Barbauld, Anna Laetitia: "To a Little Invisible Being Who Is Expected Soon to Become Visible," 36–37, 62
Bataille, Georges, 5, 145, 151
Baudelocque, Jean-Louis: *A System of Midwifery*, 16–17
Baudrillard, Jean, 50
Bichat, Xavier, 81, 162, 177 n26, 178 n28; *Anatomie générale*, 65; *Discourse on the Study of Physiology*, 66; *Physiological Researches on Life and Death* (*Recherches physiologiques sur la vie et la mort*), 66–74
binary opposition, 3, 54
Blake, William: *The Marriage of Heaven and Hell*, 163
Bloom, Harold, 1
Blumenbach, Johann Friedrich, 31
body: as locus of identity, 8, 53–54, 63–74, 94–95, 96–102, 111–120; maternal, 11, 14, 18–23, 27–30, 33–37, *see also* maternity

Bonivard, François, 75–76, 78, 81
Bonnet, Charles, 171 n42
Bridges, Thomas: *Adventures of a Bank-Note*, 44
Broussais, F. J. V., 75, 81; *Principles of Physiological Medicine*, 70–74; *A Treatise on Physiology Applied to Pathology*, 70–74
Brown, John, 177 n26
Bunyan, John: *The Pilgrim's Progress*, 146
Burke, Edmund: *Reflections on the Revolution in France*, 45–47, 88
Burns, Robert, 170 n22
Burton, John: *A Letter to William Smellie, MD*, 16
Butler, Judith, 175 n43
Byron, George Gordon, 163; *Manfred*, 146; "The Prisoner of Chillon," 8, 60, 75–86; "Sonnet on Chillon," 8, 60, 75, 87–89, 92, 94; *Childe Harold's Pilgrimage*, 78, 87, 89–94

Cabanis, Pierre-Jean-Georges, 65–66
Camper, Petrus, 169 n20
capitalism, 57, 160; and circulation, 130–138; and production, 6, 11, 12–13, 37; and social mobility, 142–144; and value, 7, 12–13, 38–45, 49–56
capitalist class, 27, 39–40, 44–45, 49, 56–57, 87
Carter, Angela, 27–28
Castle, Terry, 51, 174 n32, 182 n40
Certeau, Michel de, 155
Chaber, Lois, 12–13, 168 n6
childbirth: metaphors of, 131, 134–135, 150–153, 184 n30; models of, 11–12, 14, 18, 23, 26–31, 34–37, 168 n6; *see also* parturition; maternity
Christ, 111, 115, 119–120
Christensen, Jerome, 172 n9
circulating library, 136–138
circulation, 5, 9–10, 44, 68–69, 130–145, 150, 151–152, 155–162
classification, 7–8, 59–60, 63–65, 70–74
clothing, as metaphor for the body, 67, 96, 100–102, 168 n6
Coleridge, Ernest Hartley, 79

194

CAMBRIDGE STUDIES IN ROMANTICISM

GENERAL EDITORS

MARILYN BUTLER, *University of Oxford*
JAMES CHANDLER, *University of Chicago*